After the Eclipse

After the
ECLIPSE

A MOTHER'S MURDER,
A DAUGHTER'S SEARCH

Sarah Perry

Houghton Mifflin Harcourt

BOSTON   NEW YORK

2017

ISBN 9780544302655

Book design by Jackie Shepherd

Printed in the United States of America

For her

To the living we owe respect,
but to the dead we owe the truth.

— VOLTAIRE

PREFACE

One cold March, just a few years ago, I rented a flawlessly clean silver car and drove up to Maine from my home in Brooklyn. I'd made it just north of Boston when the trees started to press in close, and as the network of pavement thinned down to I-95, I began hours of sitting in the dark, following that one road ever north. I held my left hand steady on the wheel at six o'clock, sifted through pop songs and ad spots with my right. I missed my early twenties, when I still had my own car and still smoked, moodily exhaling into the night on my semiannual trips up and down the East Coast, from college to home and back again. Once I entered Maine, I tuned in to WBLM, the classic rock station, one of the few clear signals that holds on through the mountains. 'BLM had been our station, the one Mom and I listened to on countless Sunday drives through tunnels of sunlit trees. I listened to David Bowie and Aerosmith and Fleetwood Mac and Heart, and Mom was alive again, then newly dead again, then long gone and faded away. I still knew all the words.

About an hour into Maine, I finally turned off the highway, winding farther north until I reached my aunt Carol's house. It was midnight, and I shivered as I got out of the car, unprepared for the crystalline cold that had been waiting for me. Carol and her husband had been asleep for hours, but through a front window I could see they had left the yellow light on over the stairway to my old bedroom. The car door made a sharp sound when I pushed it shut, the trees replying with a softened echo. I stood outside for a minute, head swiveled up to the crowded stars, until something rustled in the ditch along the road, and I remembered where I was, and the fear moved back into me, running along my veins, racing up and down my limbs, warming me and settling in.

The fear waits for me still, always worse when it is dark or cold. But it's the half hour of transition from day to night that's hardest, watching the light seep from the landscape, taking with it its illusion of safety. On the rare days when I'm here in winter, when dusk starts sliding over this valley at four o'clock or even earlier, I have to fight against panic. I turn away from the windows, stir my aunt's soup, sit with my silent uncle watching race cars hypnotically circle an endless oval track. Once it is truly dark out, I feel a bit better: there may be hours of nervousness to get through, but now I'm in them. I've been here before, and no matter how bad things get, some part of me always remembers that I'll come out the other side.

So it's good that I drove as the darkness came down, listening to the old soundtrack. It all makes sense. It's more important that this trip be true than easy.

—

I get up early the next morning and have coffee and cereal with Carol. She is cheerful and I am cheerful and we do not mention why I am visiting. I don't visit often.

I get into the car and make my way to the Maine State Police barracks in the town of Gray. It's a two-hour drive, and I retrace much of last night's ground, this time in cheerful daylight. I stop at Dunkin' Donuts and everything tastes like high school.

Twenty minutes later, I turn into the barracks parking lot, sand and salt crunching under my tires, and park in front of a long, low building covered in sky-blue clapboard. This is not the imposing cement-and-glass fortress I'd imagined. There's a little portico above the entrance, held up by thin blue columns. The windows are small. It looks like a nursing home, or a motel in a deserted oceanside town. There are about ten spots in the parking lot, only two of them filled by cruisers.

A flagpole rises from a closely shorn strip of dull winter grass, and a police officer is raising the flag. He's the only person in sight: dark gray buzz-cut hair, torso bulky with muscle beneath his neat blue uniform, pulling a flimsy chain, hand over hand. He turns toward me and I pause before getting out. It's Walt, the detective I know best. I know it's him, but at the same time I'm unsure; at this distance, cops all look the same. He gives me a broad smile as I step out of the car and walk closer.

Walt greets me with fatherly effusiveness, and I feel guilty for my hesitation. He's a kind man who has seen the worst of human behavior, with a carefully restrained sense of humor and a broad accent; a north woods version of the classic gumshoe. He's now commander of the Maine State Police field troop unit in southern Maine, but he spent many of his years in the division devoted to major crimes. A few detectives led Mom's case over the years, but Walt was the one in charge the longest; he knows so much about my early life, more than anyone. More than my aunts and uncles. More, in fact, than me.

Walt ushers me to a conference room that's been reserved for the next few days. Susie, a witness advocate from the attorney general's office, is waiting; she greets me with a warm hug. I haven't seen her or Walt since the trial four years ago, and this reunion gives me comfort: there is so much I don't need to explain to them.

Susie is chatty as I settle in and scan the room. This is more like what I had expected: laminated wood conference table, big projector screen, American flag hanging limp in the corner. Susie asks about my apartment, my work, what it's like in the city. I answer her questions while trying to remember what I know about her. I ask about her fiancé, her teenage niece.

Soon Walt excuses himself to go down the hall to his office, says he'll be around all day if I need him. Susie and I turn to the boxes and binders on the conference table. There are about ten four-inch binders, each crammed with paper, plus three cardboard file boxes. Susie lifts the tops off them one by one — they, too, are full of paper.

"So . . . there's a lot here," she says. "I'm not sure what you're lookin' for, but you can have anything you want."

We agree that I'll sit down and sort through everything, and that as I identify things I'd like to take with me, I'll hand them to her and she'll make copies. I am embarrassed by her generosity; I had expected to do all the work myself, but she assures me she's happy to help. She's set aside three whole days. As I start sifting through handwritten police notes, transcripts of interviews, and forensic documents, it becomes clear that I want nearly everything. I don't know yet what will be helpful; I need to get it all home with me so I can really look at it. Hold it close. Think. So many other people have seen this material, and now I want it for myself. The prosecution kept the story necessarily simple: here's the man who killed her; this is how he did it. But a violent act is an epicenter; it shakes everyone within reach and creates other stories, cracks open the earth and reveals buried secrets. I want those stories, those secrets.

My mother's killer had twelve years of freedom before he was identified. In all those years, the state police and the cops in my hometown kept searching, kept interviewing, adding to this huge file. When asked why he and his colleagues remained so actively involved in this particular case, Walt said there were two reasons. The most obvious was that they had a huge amount of evidence; the case was tantalizingly solvable. But there was a more personal reason, too. They were angered and saddened by the fallout: the only child of a single mother, left alone.

Susie warns me, right away, about photos. She thinks she pulled them all out, but the files are disorganized, having passed through so many hands over the years. I agree to give her any photos I find without looking at them, if possible. I saw them at the trial four years ago; I don't need to see them again.

About an hour later, I pull a sheet of paper off a pile and beneath it is a photo, facedown, thick smooth paper with the brand name printed diagonally in ghostly blue. Susie's down the hall, and because she's not standing right here, my hand turns it over before I can stop. I watch this hand move of its own accord, and as the photo flips, I think, *I can take it. It'll be fine.* But it's the worst one, a horrifying picture of my mother's body. A close-up. And I am instantly angry with myself. I am tired of this impulse to wound myself so that I can prove that I'll heal.

When Susie comes back, I say only, "I found a photo," and hand it to her. She sighs, makes a clucking noise with her tongue, apologizes. I hold my face perfectly still. If I worry her, she might put a stop to this. And if there are more file boxes somewhere, I don't want her holding them back.

For four hours, I do my best to flip through documents quickly, taking stock of them, adding each item to the "yes" or "no" pile. But it's hard not to get sucked in, and some of the interviews are magnetic. When Susie's in the room, I try to keep a neutral face, but when I smile, I can feel my mouth twisting weirdly. My movements feel sharp and fast and unnatural. Each time I find a particularly bizarre detail, I share it out loud, and my laughter is edged with hysteria. Susie easily joins in, makes me feel more human. She'll say, "Oh, yeah. I remember that guy. He's a total friggin' nutcase." She is professional without being impartial, which feels like a gift.

I'm laughing with Susie when Chris Harriman comes into the room, having just returned from the field. I don't know Chris very well. He began working on the case after I'd left Maine for college. He's younger than Walt, and smaller, with a round, affable face. He tells me he went to high school with Mom, although they weren't close friends. He was an athlete, so they ran in different crowds. But he remembers her bright red hair.

He surveys the conference table and then says, "Do you want evidence?"

Susie jumps in. "Evidence?" she says, suddenly serious. "Like what?"

"Y'know, like stuff from the house. We've got it all downstairs in the basement. By law, you have to keep everything for fifty years."

I'm curious about this evidence. I've always felt like I was missing some childhood photo albums; maybe those will turn up. I tell Chris, "Yeah, sure, that'd be great," like someone just asked if I want a cup of coffee. But then I picture a vast basement beneath us, cement walls lined with hundreds of these cardboard storage boxes. In my mind, the place is dark, moisture leaking in from cracks in the walls. A subterranean maze holding fifty years of family time capsules, with all the worst memories preserved.

Chris comes up with a box about twenty minutes later. He sets it on the table next to the others, then goes back to his office. Susie goes down the hall with another binder to copy. It's a big one; I know she'll be there awhile.

I walk over to the new box and lift the lid. Inside is a folded sheet of plastic, wrinkled, vacuum-sealed around something. I take it out and unfold it; it's about the size of a newspaper. I look at it and my thoughts grind against one another, the gears slipping and slipping, until finally they catch and I understand what I'm seeing. Between the layers of plastic is a pair of underwear, white cotton with small flowers. A urine stain. The underwear seems too big, until I remember that Mom always bought bigger sizes than she needed to. A funny sort of modesty. And I remember the detail about the stain, from the autopsy report I skimmed through an hour ago.

I fold the plastic again and lay it down next to the box. My forehead feels prickly, and the air in the room is suddenly too thin. I put both hands flat on the table for a moment, and its surface is cool and solid beneath my palms.

The next item in the box is a framed photograph of Mom and her fiancé, Dennis, a man ten years her junior. The Sears photographer had posed them like mother and son, and we'd all been too embarrassed to correct him. Beneath that is the calendar that hung on our kitchen wall. The calendar feels tainted, having hung in the room where she died. But I'm so happy to see Mom's neat, looped handwriting, the same half-cursive script I remember from lunchbox notes and birthday cards. On the fifteenth of January, she's written the amount of her house payment: $271. I think about how much I could help her now, how easy it would be to come up with that money. I flip through the months, smiling sadly over fun things we did, dates of movies and hikes along nearby mountain trails. The notes are plentiful, four or five per week, and it's thrilling to read them. I'm grateful to have these memories back, to remember again how full our life was. I get so drawn in that when I turn to June and find it suddenly blank, it takes me the longest time to remember why.

—

That night when I get into bed, I am nervous and jumpy. I need to clear my brain so I can relax enough to sleep, but behind my closed eyes all I can see is that underwear. I see the little flowers and the yellow stain and the wrinkles under the thick plastic. The moment keeps playing on a loop in my short-circuited brain. "Do you want evidence?" I think I do.

I'm just not sure of what.

PART ONE

SPLIT

before

I want to tell you about my mother.

I am trying to detail her precisely. Primary fact: she did all the motherly things. She was mostly gentle and affectionate, and I always knew I was loved. Her friends and family tell me that I was the most important thing in her life, that she said it often and showed it clearly.

She tucked me in almost every night of our life together, those twelve years. She sang to me while sitting on the edge of my covers, smoothing my hair with a gentle hand.

When I was sick or crying, she came to me with a cool washcloth for my head. She called me Cutie Pie longer than I would have wanted my friends to know. She made me pancakes and bacon most Saturday mornings, and let me drown them in lakes of syrup while I watched *Garfield,* my favorite cartoon, and she watched with me. She made sure my homework was done, my lunch was packed, and my sweater matched my shoes.

But this is all familiar stuff, and adds up to so many other women who love their children.

Let me try again.

My mother was full of energy and passion. She believed in the souls of housecats and in the melancholy of rainy days. She believed in hard work, and the energy she poured into her job — hand-sewing shoes at a factory — seemed boundless. She believed in spontaneity, and once urged me to sing into her boyfriend's CB radio on a common frequency, the two of us calling out that we were "b-b-b-b-bad to the bone!" until he emerged from the House of Pizza, hands full, shaking his head while we giggled.

She was graced with bright red hair, a golden tone of red I've seen only a handful of times. As a child, I never tugged on the wrong coat sleeve in the grocery store, I never wandered away and got lost; I just kept that bright hair in sight. Now, on those rare occasions when I see a woman with that hair, my mouth goes dry. I stare and keep on staring, and my hands feel empty, and I hope she doesn't notice.

In the short Maine summer, she sunbathed for hours, lounging on a narrow strip of lakeside sand, reading a novel behind oversize white plastic sunglasses. She was very thin, with finely turned collarbones and a constellation of freckles all over her body, which would deepen and multiply as the day passed. I baked along with her, my blond hair glowing blonder as the summer rushed toward bittersweet fall, when the trees turned red and yellow and orange, like a fire burning up all those languid weekend afternoons.

A couple times a year we would drive to the ocean just south of Portland. Her favorite thing to collect from the beach was sand dollars, and I loved walking up and down the yellow sand and finding them for her. They were plentiful when I was little, but something changed as the years went on. The water got colder, or warmer, or there were more predators than before.

She felt decidedly, unabashedly superior to women who dyed their hair red. She pointed them out to me — how the color was too even, their eyebrows too dark, their skin not pink enough. Now I'm one of these women, but her genes help me fake it. My driver's license even has a little "R" next to "Hair."

Real redheads, on the other hand, were part of a secret sisterhood. She loved the royal Fergie, Wynonna Judd, Bonnie Raitt, even Pippi Longstocking.

When I was about eight, we went to the salon and got our first spiral perms together. I loved the attention, the hours of sitting in the chair and being fussed over, but I hated the choking chemical smell, the tight pull on my scalp. This was when I first learned that pain could yield beauty.

She was terrified of birds, at close range, and moths, at any distance, their blurred wings beating the air, their flight paths unpredictable. She had seen Hitchcock's *The Birds* when she was four. Still, she continued to watch horror movies and let me see plenty I shouldn't have, including *Single White Female* when I was eleven. *The People Under the Stairs* that same year. And *The Stepfather*.

She wore denim-blue eyeliner nearly every day I ever saw her, focusing her soft blue gaze. From small-town stores and crumbling rural malls she assembled a strange and glorious wardrobe. When she went out — once a month or so — she dressed up as though headed somewhere much more glamorous than a dark bar or a town hall dance. She favored white, gauzy shirts with big collars and French cuffs, fitted sundresses with big, cheerful floral patterns, black satin skirts with tiers rustling down to her knees. Her jewelry box was filled with costume pieces — faux gold earrings in the shape of cats, faceted glass hearts on silver hooks, tiny shells strung together on fishing line, which we bought together at the beach. She had a small collection of thin gold rings with semiprecious stones — amethyst was her favorite — bought from Kmart and Ames. On her dresser stood a city skyline of perfumes — Exclamation, Baby Soft, Xia Xlang, Tabu. Gentle, crisp scents she found at the pharmacy, next to the holiday cards.

The clicking of her high heels on our kitchen floor meant happiness to me, vicarious excitement; she put them on only at the last minute, at the very end of getting ready. We'd drive to her best friend Linda's house, just a couple of miles toward town, and climb the wooden porch to her screen door. Mom would call out, "Hey!" and Linda would tell us to let ourselves in, her voice rising above the radio as she bustled from bathroom to bedroom to kitchen, sipping coffee in between wardrobe changes and applications of lipstick and mascara, her bangle bracelets ringing like bells. I loved Linda, with her year-round tan and big smile. She was a small woman, but she gave good, solid hugs, her blond-highlighted curls brushing my face, stiff with gel and smelling of perfume. She was always running just a little late, and I was always glad; this was the part of the evening I got to share, before the three of us got back into the car and drove across town to drop me off at my grandmother's, where I'd spend the night while they went out dancing.

Dancing was one of Mom's greatest joys, and she could fall into the rhythm of any song, her limbs moving with the graceful ease of a trusting swimmer. Her friends still talk about it to this day: how she just lost herself on the dance floor, and carried them along with her.

Even in the car, she liked to move, wiggling her torso in something she called "car dancing" while she sang along. She often quizzed me, challenging me to identify a band or song title before the chorus came in. She'd belt out the words, loud and a bit out of tune, while I mumbled, self-conscious and shy. She'd elbow me gently: "Cutie, sing!"

Once, in a moment of childish, ten-year-old bald honesty, I looked at her thighs, smushing over the driver's seat, half-covered in shorts, and pointed out how big they were compared with the rest of her. She got very serious and, in an edgy, no-nonsense tone I'd never heard before, said: "I'll have you know that these thighs are what many men love best."

Which led to a similar moment: one day in fifth grade, I wore hot pink high heels to school. I remember her mischievous smile when we got them — they were steeply on sale, a fun, weird splurge. I wore them with leggings and a long, hot pink crocheted sweater, and even though I was in my fat phase, I felt fantastic. While I was standing out in front of the school on the ice, waiting for the doors to open that morning, an older girl ridiculed my shoes and for once, for just once, the teasing didn't bother me. I told her she was jealous. I told her I looked fabulous. And I believed it, staring down this boring little bitch in her snow boots.

Once, a boyfriend left Mom suddenly, on the Fourth of July. He woke up at our place, went home to pick up some things before meeting her at a friend's barbecue, and never showed up. A couple of weeks later, we drove to his house. I sat in the car while she went inside. After about half an hour, she returned, throwing herself into the seat, her right hand wrapped in a paper towel. It had little flowers printed on it and blood was soaking through, a dark, fast-spreading bloom. Many years later, I learned that she had slammed her fist into a window in a rage and broken through. But if I saw her explode that day, I don't remember. Instead I remember her mouth in a taut line, and her left hand palm-flat on the steering wheel, carving a smooth arc as she backed us up the steep driveway and onto the road in one perfect, sweeping motion.

When she made the bed with newly clean sheets, she sprinkled baby powder between them. Under the covers, it was soft and crisp and dry and cool. She tucked the comforter an inch or two under the pillows before smoothing it up over them. She believed in bedskirts.

She had the beginnings of carpal tunnel. She had terrible migraines. Because of these, she eventually had to give up chewing gum. And then caffeine.

I've had one migraine in my life, when I was eleven, and even though she darkened the house and turned down the stereo, I'm convinced she didn't believe me, that she thought I was faking, replicating her symptoms for attention. I wasn't; I remember the pain vividly and terribly — and, worse, that it had started with fear. I'd been reading and suddenly the words didn't make sense to me, became nothing more than black marks I couldn't decipher. I was afraid they would stay that way forever.

In a town where no one did, she locked every single door at night. She checked and double-checked, flipping the brass bolts in and out. If it was hot out, she would leave a few windows cracked open. But it made her a little nervous.

She ate pickled green pepperoncini by the jar, sitting on the couch and pulling them out by their shriveled stems. She loved ice cream, could eat a pint in one sitting.

When kids at school called me Heifer, she told me to ignore them, as though this were possible.

Once, in sixth grade, two friends and I — all of us studious, generally well-behaved kids — got caught writing mean notes about our pregnant teacher, Ms. Shane, scribbling back and forth on a big, unlined sheet of paper. We were forced to take a photocopy of the note home and have it signed by our parents so they could see what we'd done. This was the most perfect, most terrifying punishment: I couldn't stand it when my mother was disappointed in me.

When I showed her the note, crying already as I handed it over, she took a few moments to read it, and then said, simply, "Don't get caught next time." This was completely out of character, a gracious, one-off reprieve.

When some punk teenagers smashed the huge pumpkin we carved one Halloween, she wrote a letter to the editor of our local paper to shame them. Another time, she and her boyfriend passed a struck deer on the side of the road, still alive. She insisted they circle back, haul it into the bed of his pickup, and take it to a wildlife rescue farm. She appeared in the paper again for this kindness.

In her romantic selections, she could have done better, and she could have done worse. She was often imperfect in her own love, but that didn't lead to her death.

Because of her, I used to try to save the tiny moles our cat chased in the yard.

Because of her, I sing along to the radio, in my terrible voice, and I drive with the windows down, the air whipping across my arms.

Because of her, I will always believe love is possible.

Her name was Crystal. She cast light.

—

Two days before my mother died, the sun hid behind the moon. For years, I would remember the eclipse as having occurred weeks before, a beautiful event that I — a precocious, nerdy twelve-year-old — had anticipated with great happiness. My memory wrapped it in weeks of empty time that had not existed, trying to keep it untainted, pristine.

It was a Tuesday of bright sunshine. I remember standing on the school lawn with my classmates, cardboard pinhole viewers held up to a greeting-card sky — solid blue, accents of puffy cloud. Everyone was giggling and jostling; we couldn't see the moon approaching. But when the songbirds went silent and the disk of the moon appeared, not like a hole but like a solid piece of construction paper sliding across the surface of our viewers, everyone quieted down. As the edge of the thing bit into the sun, we gasped. I stood transfixed as it slid into place, much faster than I'd expected, and willed it to stop. If it had, we could have stayed right there in that perfect moment indefinitely, safe on the border of night and day, childhood and adolescence, school and home.

It was an annular eclipse, the moon not quite obscuring the entire sun, instead forming a glowing band of light along its edge. I snuck a glance directly at the sky and found a ring that was more beautiful and more piercing than a full sun could ever be. A glowing yellow ring. I could slip my finger through it, hold it on my hand, bring it back to my mother and replace the one she wore, the one she pulled off and pushed on as she fought and loved and made up with her volatile young fiancé. I could replace that ring that came and went like the tides with something eternal; I wanted to give her a beauty that would burn forever. But the ring in the sky lasted for only a moment.

The eclipse proved something to me. I had been waiting for years to see one and it had finally come, as though my wishes had made it manifest. At the time, the eclipse seemed a culmination of so many good things that were happening in my life — I had begun to write something I thought of as a novel, I was making more friends, my chubbiness was melting away. And most important, my mother seemed happy; that gold band and its small diamond had been sitting on her finger more often than not. That slice of night in the day seemed like a miracle, a singular event that showed, just by its existence, that regularity and constant motion ruled the universe.

But historically, eclipses are not good signs. Eclipses are threats to safety and order. Angry gods flaunting their power — frogs, dragons, and demons eating the sun. Eclipses portend war, famine, and death. After the eclipse come chaos and disorder, raping and pillaging. When I looked up at the sky, I saw none of this. I saw only beauty in that fire-ringed darkness. I didn't know that one small moment of darkness foreshadowed a much greater one. One that would block out the light entirely, and hover there for a very long time.

the night

The horror begins quietly, in the midnight hours between May 11 and May 12, 1994, after one day has faded and before the next has begun. I've been sleeping for hours, curled on my side and wedged among my many stuffed animals, surrounded by the white, filigreed metal of my daybed, one palm pressed flat under my pillow. Then, through the fog of sleep, muffled voices push their way into my brain. An argument. A high voice, a low one. They come to me as if through deep water. I've heard this angry duet before, and it awakens me no further. I remain submerged, and moments later I slip back into unconsciousness. Uncountable dreamless minutes pass.

The stillness is shattered by my mother screaming "No! No! No!" Over and over and over. My body lurches into a sitting position as quickly as my eyes open, and suddenly all the lights are on inside me, my blood is slamming through my veins, a high humming is beginning in my head, and I can feel my eyes continuing to open, stretching wider and wider, as though alertness alone could serve as a defense. I'm frozen bolt upright, palms flat beside my thighs, fingers clenching the sheets tighter and tighter as my mother continues to scream. She's so loud it's inside my every cell, so loud her screams turn the wall beside my bed to paper. That wall is all that separates my room from the living room, which opens up into the kitchen. I think she's right in the middle, in the broad opening between those two rooms. I can hear her voice ring off the linoleum, the sturdy cabinets and drawers. We are maybe fifteen feet away from each other. We live alone. Just the two of us.

Panic spills out of me in one word: "Mom?!" Then I try to recall that word, to pull that air back in, gasping sharply because I realize, suddenly, that she can't answer me without giving me away. I ball my hands into fists and my spine bends down sharply, as though expecting a blow to the head. I shut my eyes for just a second and will myself to disappear. Then I open them wide and listen for any sign that whoever's out there with her has heard me. I hope that her terror has drowned me out. This hope feels selfish, even in this moment. The screaming continues, and I hear no footsteps approach my room, so I assume I'm safe. Something terrible is happening, and I can still try to get help, try to get us through it. Mom is still screaming "No!"

I swing my legs over the side of my bed and take two steps to my bedroom door. My electrified body registers my footprints in the short, bristly carpet. I lift my bathrobe off the hook and wrap it around myself, holding my breath as the slightly rough terry drags across my bare skin. My partially open door lets in a faint orange light from the kitchen; the dimmer switch must be on low. But the hinges are on the far side, so I can only see down the hall, away from the screaming. I cannot risk opening the door farther and peering around to see what is happening. I don't need to see. I need to survive. Mom is still screaming "No!"

I grip the door handle tightly in my sweating palm, turn it slowly. I hold the latch in while I push the door shut, as silently as possible. There is no quiet way to push the button to lock the door, and it sounds like a gunshot announcing my presence. I flinch and wait, but nothing changes. I sit back down on the bed. My feet hover parallel to the floor. My posture is perfect, and my eyes are still wide-open; even my ears feel wide-open. Mom is still screaming "No!" I can think of nothing to do but wait, silently, and strain to piece sound into meaning.

Then. Boots thundering across the linoleum. A drawer pulled to the end of its runners, slamming at the end. Metal on metal, a knife pulled out, surely. Impossibly, her screaming gets louder. In that scream I hear absolute terror, terror I didn't even know existed. But there's fury, too. In my bedroom, I'm still, so still my locked joints ache. I hardly blink or breathe. And then.

A heavy, wet thudding, fast-paced. My hectic mind brings me the image of a gigantic fish, a five-hundred-pound deepwater sturgeon, wet and thrashing for air and life on the hollow kitchen floor. A hopeless seizure. I know there is no fish. The fish is insanity.

The no's continue, now quieter and quieter, automatic animal moans, drained of anger. A sound of defeated sorrow. In tandem with one of these last moans, I hear a deep grunt, the sound of pure hatred, disgust. A finishing. Then, the staccato, robotic pulse of a phone left off the hook, beep-beep-beeping into the new silence.

Finally, the phone stops screaming, the prerecorded alarm reaching its limit. The house is utterly still, and the silence presses into my ears as though I've gone deaf. I do not hear a door open, do not hear anyone leave. I know I'm not safe but it's quiet now and this is what I've been waiting for and if I don't move now I never will. The gray morning light will creep into my window and I'll still be sitting here, wide-eyed on the edge of my bed. I'll have to go out there and see everything in the light, and no ambulance will have come. I have to get someone to come.

I stand up. I take two steps. I slowly start to open my door. Quiet still: grip doorknob, turn it to retract latch, pull door smoothly open. The button of the lock pops softly against my palm. The orange kitchen light has been switched off, but the night-light still shines dimly from the bathroom across the hall. There's a clock there in the bathroom, and I stare at it as I step into the hallway. It is exactly one o'clock, and the second hand is nestled in with the hour and minute hands. The trio makes a black mark on the night, and the black mark is, for a brief, horrifying moment, a large, segmented insect. A quivering insect, made of time. My eyes widen further, and then the funhouse mirror warps again and it is just a clock on the wall, ticking in the silence. I turn away, toward the living room, toward the kitchen.

Blood on the floor, on the part of the floor I can see past the couch, blood on the chair by that entryway, on the wall above the back of the chair. There are more pools and spatters, too many for me to take in;

they are black, darkness within darkness. A little hope blooms in me, a desperate, fervent vision: my mother standing over a body, holding a bloody knife and staring at me, wide-eyed, terrified, ashamed. Self-defense, like on TV.

I step slowly past the couch, avoiding my reflection in the wide mirror above it. I can see myself peripherally there, my slow-moving shadow, and I know that if I turn and see my own face, see myself in this horror, something in me will break and stay broken.

I approach the body, a crumpled shape wrapped in a familiar blue bathrobe. It's her, as I knew it would be. I shriek, "Mommy!" High-pitched but quiet, my throat compressed with fear. I hear myself do this, and I fear for myself, because I haven't called her that since I was very small. I can't slip now, I have to get help. Now is not a time to be small. A new part of me is born right here in the kitchen. This one doesn't waste time on terror or sadness; her only goal is to find a phone and make a call and get herself and me and Mom out of this alive. This second self begins acting without hesitation, propelling my body along, forward, forward, forward.

When the weak one screams out, the other one hushes her, hurries her along. *We can't stay here,* she says. *We have to get out of here,* she says. *You want to help her, right?*

And so I say nothing else, but open my eyes wider in the darkness. I perform one small test: I pinch my arm, clamping the flesh tightly for several seconds. I've had lucid nightmares before, and this is how I always escape. I wait for the moment when I pivot upright again in my bed, sweating, gasping, shaking off the residue of this vivid dream. Pain spreads from that point of contact, but I remain in the dark.

Reality confirmed, now comes the time for action. Her body is lying in front of the door. This helps the second self prevent the weaker one from running away. Another test: We reach a cautious foot out, touch the back of her pale, exposed calf. This is further proof that we aren't hallucinating. She is still, and we recoil at the solid fact of her. Her head is in the corner, near the hinges of the side door that is closed to the night outside. A glass panel in the door admits weak gray light from a far-off streetlamp. The longer we stand here, the more we can see. The corner is dark, her hair is too dark. We can see the red now, closer to the light, but there is too much; we can't understand what we're looking at. There is a thick, fluid shadow covering her head, and it's impossible to figure out what is casting it. We quickly look away, to the safer territory of the leg.

˷ The phone receiver lies on the floor, at the very end of its curly cord, near but not quite touching her hand. The very tip of it rests lightly on the linoleum. When we heard the droning of the open line, the tension of the cord must have drawn the receiver back across the floor, away from her.

We step over the legs and pick up the receiver. We must complete her last action. We would like to make a call. But nothing happens. We punch 911 repeatedly, and with some speed. Listen. Nothing, no sound at all from the plastic receiver. We punch 911 repeatedly. Silence. We return the phone to its cradle on the wall, turn away.

Now a journey begins. The house is very small, but the other phone is on the opposite end of it. We turn back toward the hallway from which we came. Step over the legs again. Do not give a final look to the mother. Either she is not the mother anymore, or we will succeed tonight, save her, and see her again, whole.

The hallway is short, but there is time for one distinct thought before we reach the end of it. It comes suddenly and fully formed like a voice, the voice of the second self, reverberating in my head: "There is no God." She's casting off comforting fantasies, stripping existence down to this carpet, these close walls, this hallway, the phone at the end. The short, swift feeling of desolation that follows is a surprise, because I had never believed in God before.

Her bedroom presents a challenge: it's dark, and the light must be turned on. A bit of terror leaks through the numb, autopilot feeling, a lightning flash of fear between darkness and exposure: what will the light reveal? Flip the switch: Nothing out of the ordinary. Empty room.

The bedroom smells like her, and the covers are neatly folded back. We note these details, to carry to the police later — we are already thinking about interviews in the safe fortress of the station downtown.

But the phone under the bed doesn't work, either. We dial over and over. Silence. We are huddled here in a blind corner. We did not hear anyone leave.

We must leave the house.

We go back to the living room, careful not to look back into the kitchen. We leave by the front door, which is very rarely used. We step out into a prickly, light rain, feel the sharpness of the cement porch under bare feet. Any working phone is our polestar, and now we will navigate through the dark, nausea gripping us as if from an ocean swell.

—

We come out onto a two-lane road that cuts through thick forest. A halogen lamp propped on a wooden pole casts a cloud of white-blue light near the tops of the trees. We can see the mist cutting across the light, sharp sparkles materializing in its periphery, then driving back down into the black. It is the only light for a mile or two, except for the dim porch lamps of the few neighbors along this road, a ragged constellation.

The Demeritts live next door; they are kind people. They brought brownies when we first moved in, about two years ago. Like us, they have two doors: one often-used, one hardly ever used. To reach the often-used one, we will have to descend a very dark dirt path into the dripping trees. We contemplate this. The door hardly ever used stands in a clearing, broadly lit by that one shining beacon on the pole. We can see the whole way there.

We approach the door hardly ever used. We knock. We punch it with our fists. We yell, we scream. We say things like *My mother's been stabbed.* Things like *There's someone in my house.* Things like *Help me.* But we are met by silence. We can hear how the rain is stealing our sound. We throw our body against the door, forearms braced for maximum impact, a knee slipping out of the flapping robe and hitting the unyielding metal. We are at war with the solidity of this house, with this door that will not rattle. We yell. We wait. We wait. More silence.

There is another house across the street. A large, white house, beautifully kept, with a nicely clipped lawn. We have never met the people who live there. It sits under the cast of that one streetlamp, shining like a lighthouse in the night. We turn from the Demeritts' and run to that place, feel the soft, even grass under bare feet. The bathrobe flaps open a little, lets in rain.

There is a screened porch connected to the house, and we knock on the outer door first. Ring the little electric doorbell, another dim orange light. We yell. We wait. Try the screen door, find it unlocked. We hesitate, don't want to enter without permission. Then plunge forward to the more substantial inner door, a hollow one that accepts our banging and rings out sound. We can hear how it fills the hallway just beyond this door. We repeat our pleas.

Somebody stabbed my mother.

Please, you have to help me.

There's somebody in my house.

We wait. We wait. Silence. We conclude that everyone is dead.

We resolve to try every house on the sparsely populated road. We imagine doing this until we reach the center of town, where there are more houses, pushed together into the communal safety of neighborhoods. We will try each one until we find the living. Linda is closer to town. We imagine her sleeping, alive, unaware.

We turn around, passing our house on the way toward town. It takes maybe five minutes to get to the next house. We are running as best we can.

Somewhere in those five minutes, there is a moment of grace in which the second self, the strong one, gets distracted and allows another clear thought to cut through the darkness. I feel the precise moment in which my mother's soul departs the earth. I feel this so strongly that I stop in my quick march along the double lines of the road. I stand there, one foot on a smooth, dull yellow line, one on the rough pavement. I feel no danger. I think of her leaving, of her sadly giving up on this night, on all the years to come. I mouth, "Goodbye." But then the actual organ of my heart contracts suddenly and painfully, trying to draw itself inside its own chambers. It is a thick, collapsing feeling. So the second self reaches into that heart, sets emotion aside again, and walks the body on.

We come to the third house. This one is tough; sitting in deep darkness, down a steeply sloping driveway. It might be hard to get back up out of there. But we sort of know these people, have at least seen them outside: a family of four, plus a bounding yellow dog. We descend. Stand exposed in their porch light. We repeat the knocking, the yelling, the waiting. We try to yell things that are less scary, just in case. Remember to say "Please."

Still, no one comes. No way to tell if they are dead or sleeping.

We turn back toward the road, see the lights of an approaching car. Hustle a few steps up the steep driveway, then stop short. It could be anyone. We are a live witness, and wish to remain so. We stay down in the darkness and come back up only when the lights have passed.

Next we are faced with a long stretch of woods and road, perhaps ten minutes' worth, before we will reach the house of the Wilson family. We walk along the center of the road, the smoothness of the stripes a relief. The skipping lines of the passing lane are so much longer than they usually look. About halfway through, something makes us look back and we see, shining through the trees, the unmistakable gleam of a flashlight.

We must walk faster. But of course we have to stop at the Wilson house. This time, we barrel right through the screen door to the inner door of the porch, yelling and banging and trying not to think of that flashlight advancing.

But the Wilsons don't come, either.

There is one more building before we reach the intersection with the larger two-lane state road, Route 302, where the town truly begins. This walk takes another five or ten minutes. It is impossible to tell exactly how long. We are thankful for the rain, which must be keeping the pavement from cutting our feet. We are concerned about that flashlight, which looks closer now.

Time bends and stretches and we are becoming convinced that the rest of our life will be spent walking along this road in the rain. We start thinking ahead. The tough one steps aside, trusting me to keep walking, propelled by fear of that bobbing flashlight. I wonder where I might live next. Maybe my friend Marie's mom will take me in. Their house always smells like oil paints and cheesecake.

At the very end of the road lies the Venezia, an Italian restaurant. I've never been inside; it's fancy. There's a porch light and screen door at the back, next to a glowing square of yellow window. I step from the pavement. My footsteps are cool in the sandy ruts of tire treads, threaded through with uncut grass. I hold my breath tightly as I bang on the frame of the screen door. In the rain, the door makes a rhythmic, wet drumming sound, warping and thwapping against the threshold, wood hammering on wood. I call out, yelling over the sound of my own fists.

And a dark-haired man comes to the door. He squints at me. His hair is thick, his features small, and for a moment he reminds me of my father. I take a step back. Put my fist down at my side. I become more sharply aware of the rain, which is coming down harder now. An older woman, with the same cap of thick, dark hair, comes up behind the man.

The woman pushes him aside, unlatches the door. For a few moments they both stand in the doorway, looking down at me.

I tell them someone has stabbed my mother. I say, "I've never been so happy to see people!" Still, their faces look strange to me, seem miles away somehow, separated from me by a naked incredulity.

But they let me in to use the phone. I find myself sitting on a floral couch in a small apartment at the back of the restaurant. The woman gives me slippers while the man dials. Receiver in hand, he looks at me sideways, says, "I need the police up here right away."

These words are so beautiful.

Then he says, "I have a girl here, claimed someone killed her mother. She's a little girl running down the road from somewhere."

I don't like that word, "claimed" — and "little girl" is so inaccurate now. In a moment, the phone is in my hand, and I'm doing my best to explain to a soft-voiced woman what has happened. I try to be specific and precise, not like a little girl at all. Years later, I will hear that 911 tape. I sound so calm, so incredibly calm.

After the call there is a period of waiting and quiet. I try not to think about the flashlight. I don't tell anyone about it. I go to the bathroom, and there is blood on the right side of my face. Not mine. Somewhere deep within me I feel horror, but the feeling stays there, far below the surface. I do not cry or cringe; I reach for a washcloth, run warm water over it, and wipe mechanically at my faraway reflection. I think, *This is a thing I must do.*

3

before

In the last two years of her life, my mother and I lived in a neat little black-and-white house on a quiet road, in an inland Maine town of five thousand people: white Congregational church spire, an unusual abundance of calm cool water, thick snow sifting out of a gray sky in winter. The town's waters collected in two big lakes, called Highland and Long, and its snow powdered a tiny ski resort whose trails spelled out LOVE when lit up in the night. The word was an accident of topography, the treeless spaces carving out clear letters. Route 302, a two-lane state road, ran in front of the mountain and southeast into town, becoming High Street until it became Main Street at the War Memorial, an armed Union soldier atop a granite pillar. From there, Main coasted down a steep hill, bent away from the Highland lakeshore, and edged past steady storefronts — the Magic Lantern theater, Renys discount store, the Flower Pot, Food City, the Black Horse Tavern — before diving back into the forest and becoming Route 302 again, threading through two smaller, satellite towns and then running an hour south to Portland. At the town's one traffic light, another state road wound north to smaller, more isolated towns. Inundated with city tourists in the summer, closed and private in the winter, we were a border place, a portal between inside and outside, in a state with a keen, often claustrophobic sense of insularity.

Our town was called Bridgton, and its people knew Crystal Perry, the pretty young redhead who had lived there nearly all her life. Her path to that little black-and-white house was a long one. She was a good mother, and a homeowner. The little money she earned, she managed well: I still remember shopping with her in the grocery store over the New Hampshire state line — there's no sales tax there. She'd push the cart along with her forearms, clutching a memo pad, a Bic pen, and a tiny pink calculator in her hands. Luxuries — new clothes, car stereo — were earned with patience, over long layaway periods, and everything was funded by the days she spent locked in a factory, her hands expertly whipping thread through fine leather shoes. The work was hard, but it was stable. She had good friendships with at least two of her six sisters, and a better one with her friend Linda, whom she had known since she was eight years old. We'd visit her on weekend afternoons and stay for hours, Linda's charm and silliness unraveling the anxiety that Mom almost always held just below the surface.

Mom spent much of her life trying to find and keep good love — for her own sake and, she thought, for mine. She dealt with alcoholics, welfare cheats, hot tempers. She extracted promises of undying devotion that brought with them efforts at control and verbal abuse. After wisely divorcing my father, Tom, when I was still very young, she found Dale, a man who was unfailingly good to me, like a father should be, and good to her, too, but she lost him a few years later. Her next love was Tim, whom she longed for desperately but could not hold, like a comet that would swing close and then recede. And her last was Dennis, her fiancé at the time of her death, the most complicated of them all, the one that I will forever turn over and over in my mind. There were others, of course. She was a beautiful young woman who'd been taught that she needed a man. And they found her, for a night or a week or a few years. But she never found the one that she needed.

—

My mother was a very private person; exposure was the final indignity of her murder. Her violent end was illuminated in full detail for a hungry public. The curtains were stripped from her home; anyone could press their nose to the glass. But the beauty of her existence was not reported or filed, was not documented or reenacted on cable television; her light was blocked out by terror. I want to push away that darkness, to travel back through fear and reunite with her as she was before.

My mother gave birth to me when she was eighteen years old, and she was killed when she was just thirty. I began this story eighteen years after her death — when I myself was thirty. In that moment, we had lived without each other for an equal amount of time. A deep part of me had always suspected that I would never live longer than she had, that something would happen to ensure that I would never become older than her. But the months passed and I found myself living years she never had, years that had been impossible to imagine. I have worked to bring her forward into them, with me.

after

On the first morning after the murder, I awoke heavy and still, in my grandmother's house. It felt as though only seconds had passed since I'd knocked on the door of the Venezia, and so I was spared the moment that so many talk about, when the brain forgets the tragedy in the first moments of waking and then the heart is crushed again by the realization of what has happened. I lay flat on my back under a staticky velour comforter in a room I'd once shared with my mother, before we bought our house. The bed that had been hers was now mine. I stared up at the ceiling and thought about how much energy it would take to move my body, and how I would have to keep moving, day after day after day.

I am forever grateful for the blank sleep of that first night, that perfectly dreamless stretch of mental silence. For if nightmares had come, I would have spent every night after fearing their return, and that fear would have been an open door, beckoning the shapes of darkness. As it was, there would be plenty of fear without the aid of dreams.

The rain had stopped and sunshine blared through the slatted blinds, obscenely bright—the blazing lurid sunshine that suffocates with humidity, unwelcome after a storm. I was alone in the room, and I could hear people in the kitchen, recognize the voices of a few of my aunts. We had left the hospital at six thirty, in the gray light of a rainy dawn. It was still not yet noon.

I had spent three timeless hours in the hospital, moving through a thick, underwater terror, everything slow and unreal. I remember a pediatric examination room. I sat on a cushioned, paper-covered table while a nurse took my blood pressure, shone a light for my eyes to follow. The other lights were dim; no fluorescent to blare down on me. The nurse made some notes, told me to lie back on the reclined table and just breathe quietly for a few minutes. As I did, I pictured Mom, or Mom's body—I wasn't sure which—lying on another table somewhere in the building, doctors and nurses and beeping machines working frantically over it. Over her.

Then I let my mind empty out. I sat motionless and stared past the colorful mural painted on the cinder-block wall of the room. I do remember the mural, though: a cheerful tiger peering through wavy blades of jungle grass. I might have seen it before, that Christmas when I got the flu.

Moments later, Officer Kate Leonard, who had ridden with me in the ambulance, came into the room. She took my hand, and I knew that was bad. She had tears in her eyes, but she said, simply:

"She's gone."

I nodded once, and then I began to cry for the first time that night. Finally, there would be no more forward motion, and pain came out and over me like a wave. All the muscles in my body contracted, starting with the hand that Kate held, then my arms, chest, neck, torso. Legs. Feet. Face. My body writhed on the crinkly paper as pain rippled through me: hope I didn't realize I had, flushed out by those two words.

What Kate didn't mention was that Mom's body had never reached the hospital. The ambulance that went to our house had been sent away immediately. Lights off. Empty. No use.

If I'd saved anyone, it was only myself.

Memory recedes here, falling into a hospital-white mist, an inconsistent curtain that rolls over the hours, obscuring some moments, parting to let others through. In the next clear shot, a woman—the nurse?—is leading me down a hallway, gently guiding me by the arm. We're headed to the chaplain's office, and I'm vaguely bothered by this, because Mom and I aren't religious. No one seems to understand that this isn't where we go in times of tragedy, but I don't know where we do go, so I let them lead me.

The ceiling of the hallway is low, the floors thick with wax that pulls slightly at each step. I feel the nurse stiffen as we approach a couple of cops talking to a young man who stops talking, looks at me. It's my mother's fiancé, although the nurse doesn't know that, or what that means. But she walks me past him and the cops urge him to walk in the other direction. As we pass each other, Dennis and I lock eyes; I can see how bloodshot and pink his are, how anguished he looks. He seems to tower over the cop holding his arm, and he shifts his weight from one foot to the other and back again, lifts a strong hand and runs it through his light brown hair, his long limbs in constant motion, full of that same agitated energy with which I'm all too familiar. The proximity of our bodies rings out at me, takes my breath away, strikes up a vibration that I try to read: Was he in my house a couple of hours ago? Or was he home sleeping?

His clothes and bare forearms are clean, but there would have been time to go home and shower. Just barely. I'm certain I see heartbreak on his face, but I don't have time to look for anything else.

For years, I will think how strange it was, how inept the police were to let us get that close to each other when they already suspected him, when I wasn't sure whether or not to. How in that moment, no one seemed to understand, yet, quite what had happened. What the possible stories were.

The nurse and I pass Dennis, and he fades from my mind; each new sensation overwrites what came before as I try to remain alert to my surroundings, deal with each moment as it comes. The chaplain's room is tiny and bare, and there's no chaplain. There's a hard little couch. Simple chairs. Wood-laminate desk, gray metal filing cabinet. I'm left alone there for a few moments, moments I try to maintain in quiet emptiness. And then someone brings in my grandmother, sits her in a chair, goes back out the door. Leaves her there with me, just the two of us.

Grammy's eyes are round, and I can hear the whispering shush of her dry skin as she works her hands over and around each other, her wedding ring on one clicking quietly against her mother's ring on the other. Her purse sits like a comforting pet in her lap. She is seventy-five years old.

"Something happened to Crystal. Something happened, I don't know, they won't tell me anything. She's been hurt and, oh, we don't know what happened! The police came and got me, they didn't tell me anything. There's been an accident! Did somebody hurt her?"

She keeps talking and talking, and tremors are running through me. Grammy's hysterical, talking and talking, and I'm the one who has to say:

"I don't know, Grammy . . . Yes, I do think they should tell us something. Something happened, I'm — I'm not sure . . ."

She interrupts me with more questions, but I sense that since the cops and the nurses haven't given her any answers, I'm not supposed to, either. They brought her here in an ambulance. They are being very careful with her.

The minutes stretch out while I'm alone in this tiny room with the swirling storm of Grammy's confusion and fear. I am furious that I'm left to do this, that no one else is here, but I'm also ashamed, because the soothing words I offer her, my faltering half answers, are mostly attempts to maintain my own sanity. I must calm her down.

I must not scream at her: "She was stabbed to death! She was stabbed to death and I was there and no one is helping me and you have to *shut up* right now!"

And I don't want to do this to my grandmother, not really. I don't want to see Grammy's face as I tell her this terrible thing, I don't want to strike this blow. So the rage does come back around again, to love.

Then, finally, I'm rescued as aunts and uncles start to flow in: Gwen arrives from New Hampshire; Wendall and Carol from Oxford County, in the north. Glenice from Boston. She must have driven very, very fast.

I can't remember my aunts' and uncles' faces; the remaining hours at the hospital recede behind that misty curtain. For the rest of my life, people will assume that my youth somehow wiped out the memory of the murder. It's a thought they use to console themselves, not me. The thudding and the blood and the run along the road will always be sharp and clear. It's the shock and confusion of family, the soothing words and hugs and questioning eyes, that have barely ever existed as memory.

5

before

My grandmother passed away more than a decade ago. Still, she remains changeable, complicated, hard to pin down. It's easy to see how difficult her life was, but it's also easy to see how she could have done better, or at least pushed her girls to try for better. I have never known my uncle Webster to call her anything other than Gracie, a name that some of the older siblings use, too. But in the family, she is more commonly Mumma. Or Grace, when people are sharing unflattering information. Or sometimes Grammy, especially when they are talking to me, or feeling generous or nostalgic. Grammy is sweet. Mumma is exasperating. Grace is wild. Gracie is both a mother and a child.

—

It's 1954, and Gracie is running through a long-grassed field, cutting across its slope instead of down to the river, trying to reach her neighbor's house. She's in her mid-thirties, seven or eight months pregnant. She runs fast — she's had practice. But her husband, Howard, is close behind her, and her belly weighs her down. He grabs her arm, he grabs her red hair. She stumbles as he starts pulling her down the hill. He strikes her face, adding to the bruises already blooming from the fight that started in the house. She yells, digs her feet into the singing grass. Calls him a bastard. Begs him to stop. He hollers, *"I'll friggin' drown you! Then I'll stop."*

But when blood comes out on her dress, it halts them both. For all his meanness, Howard gets scared. Instead of the river, they go to the hospital. They have two boys already: Wendall and Wayne. This would have been Walter.

Miscarriage is a strange word. *Mis-carry*. It implies that the woman did something wrong, that she didn't hold on properly. Perhaps in this case it was the holding on itself that was the problem.

There are girls at home, too: Betty and Carol, and Gloria and Glenice. Another boy will come later, Webster, and another girl, Tootsie. Finally, the two smallest: Gwendolyn and, ten months later, Crystal.

Crystal was the third redhead, the tenth child of the household. The eleventh or twelfth or thirteenth born to Grace, depending on who's asking, and who's telling. At the age of eighteen — before Howard, long before Crystal's birth — Grace had married a man named Ray Bartlett, with whom she had her first child, Keith. Soon after, Ray went into the Navy, and while he was away, rumors spread that Grace was running around behind his back. She may have been; she didn't know how to live without a man. Ray's parents convinced him to divorce her, and they took Keith, raised him as their own. They had money.

After Keith came another lost child: Richard, Grace's second, his father forever a mystery. She had moved back home after her divorce from Ray, and her mother made her give him up to strangers who lived in the area. When Grace's other kids were little, Richard was the family's milkman. Some of them knew he was their half brother, some of them didn't. It didn't occur to those who knew to tell the others.

A few years after her divorce from Ray, Grace met Howard Farnum, the man who would chase her across the field and down the road and around the house, for years. He was a drinker like Ray, a fiery man with a handsome enough face. They soon married, and she stayed long enough to have most of those ten children with him. When he wasn't away with the Army he was often in jail: assault, petty thefts, house robberies. He and his friends Hoppy and Hornet took turns running jobs and serving sentences, but they weren't quite organized enough to be called a gang. They traded horses and conned whomever they could. They tried robbing the funeral home, even as Howard's uncle was lying in it. But a safe is a tough thing to breach or steal; they got caught.

Each time Howard was released, he would return home in a taxi, stepping out in the new suit the prison issued upon discharge in those days, a hundred-dollar bill in his pocket. One fresh start after another. But the house didn't match the suit. It was a camp, really, in a place called Milton Plantation, too small to this day to be called a town. One room downstairs, another upstairs, all the kids crowded into one bed, no matter how many there were. Grace and Howard's bed just feet away. Winter heat provided by a sheet-metal stove in the center of the room, its thin walls glowing red. Crescent moon outhouse. Water from a bucket thrown down to break the ice, until Howard installed a hand pump on the well. A big step up.

—

When I visit the Maine State Archives in Augusta, curious about Howard's criminal convictions, I find less and more than I expected. Just one record, just one crime: convicted of rape, October 1958. Sentence: ten to twenty years. The victim: one of his oldest daughters, age thirteen at the time.

The trial record contains only one piece of admitted evidence: a typewritten letter from the victim, retracting her original charge, saying that she'd lied to the neighbor woman she told. I suspect this was coerced. For Howard to have been convicted, in that era, especially considering this retraction, there must have been little doubt of his guilt. I later learn that she was sent away for a while, alone, to a school for wayward girls. When I ask another aunt why, she says, "I guess people wanted her out of there. People thought she'd done something wrong." She doesn't say quite who she means by "people." Of course that young girl hadn't done anything wrong. I'm sad that she was sent off alone, but I do hope that being away from that house, Howard or no, helped her.

It turns out that Grace visited the prison regularly, but never went to the school to see her daughter. And then Howard returned home after less than five years, in time to father my mother, Crystal. Grace was forty-four years old; Crystal was her last child. If Howard had served the maximum term of his sentence, or if Grace hadn't taken him back, my mother would not have been born.

—

Even when Howard was living at home, Grace tried to go out on the town. She'd wait until Friday night and then pick a fight with him so he'd run off, get too drunk to come back until morning. Sometimes, she got more than she bargained for. He'd rage at her, shake and hit her. She'd yell, "Howard! Oh, Howard!" He liked this. He liked her scared. And she knew it, too: she could amplify the sound of her own fear for his pleasure, her yells operatic and trembling, until finally his hands got more gentle. These were the nights he stayed home.

But most Fridays, Howard was out finding trouble or getting punished for it, and Grace didn't have to pick a fight. She would curl her hair and put on her best dress, enlisting Glenice's help. And her ex-husband, Ray, would appear in his teal Thunderbird, tailfins cutting the dust of the road, to take her out dancing and more. She didn't always come home on Saturday. Or Sunday, or Monday. She didn't always go out with Ray—sometimes there were others. Grace favored the Top Hat, a long, low dance hall in the woods at the base of a steep mountain. A dark place, for open secrets.

Whenever Grace didn't come home on Monday, Glenice, still only about twelve years old, had to miss school to take care of the five younger kids. Her older siblings had all moved out by then. Sometimes there wasn't any food in the house, but she knew that her mother had chocolate bars and new stockings hidden away, that she denied herself nothing. When Crystal and Gwen were just toddlers, mobile but too little to understand very much, the river was a problem, always cold and clear and running swiftly behind the field, as though waiting to take a younger one under. Glenice worried about it constantly. But she couldn't watch them every minute. There were Wayne and Webster, and then there was Tootsie and, even younger, Gwen and Crystal, but those two stayed together, could watch themselves, a little. Glenice got distracted; there was so much to do. And they disappeared so quickly.

One afternoon she was in the house, making sandwiches out of the little she could find, and suddenly it was too quiet. Suddenly she knew: the river.

She ran through the field, the sharp edges of deer grass pulling at her pant legs, long, dark blond hair streaming out behind her. She ran faster than ever, because she knew. The river, oh God.

She found Gwen facedown in the water, arms splayed out, alone. Gwen was about four, kept forgetting she couldn't swim. Loved the water. When Glenice turned her sister over, she was blue in the face. They were alone on a strip of sandy beach, no parents to help. Glenice was overcome with rage. The rage carried her running back through the field, carried her as she carried the inert weight of the wet child, her sister.

She got to the dusty road and, miraculously, improbably, there was a car. There was a car, and an adult, and help, and Gwen survived.

This wasn't the first time Glenice had pulled her little sister from the water, but it was the worst. For years to come, she would suddenly notice Gwen gone from the room, panic and call out for her. Gwen would sometimes hide on purpose, and the other kids would laugh —not at Glenice, really, but at fate. Luckily, Crystal was too little to wander that far, and once she was, she was a stronger swimmer, and tougher, less prone to mishaps. She was the baby of the family, but everyone knew she could take care of herself.

Eventually Glenice stopped helping her mother get ready to go out. The tender ritual, perhaps their only one, of helping Grace curl her hair and button up her dress, disappeared in Glenice's anger. "You need to stay here and take care of all these kids!" she'd yell, still just a kid herself. At the age of fourteen, she left for good, slapping her mother's face on the way out. She felt guilty for years — not about the slap but about leaving her brothers and sisters there. But she knew that if she didn't leave, she would miss too much school and eventually fail out, and then she wouldn't be able to help anybody, not really.

Gracie wasn't malicious; there were just a lot of things that she couldn't handle. One day, she was home with the kids when Gloria tripped on the stairs, landing on an exposed nail that ripped her thigh open. The other kids tended to the wound; Gracie was too scared. She locked herself in the bedroom and wouldn't come out.

—

It's unclear exactly when Grace decided to leave Howard, or even whether she was the one who did the leaving. But at some point, when my mother was four or five, the two divorced. Soon after, Grace married Ray — of the teal Thunderbird and the first child — for the second time. He had left the Navy with a decent pension and was able to move the family to a modern, three-bedroom house in the town of Bridgton, about an hour's drive south of Milton. It was a real town, with a post office and a police station and a stoplight town center.

Grace must have exerted a truly powerful, undeniable pull on Ray, because he hated children, and five of hers were still living at home. Ray demanded quiet in the house at all hours; even a whispered conversation in another room could send him into a fit. He was especially intolerant when he was drinking, which was often. The kids — Tootsie, Gwen, and Crystal, and Wayne and Webster — couldn't really play, couldn't have friends over. Glenice and Gloria picked them up for weekend visits whenever they could, driving them back north to the towns they'd escaped to from Milton, either to Glenice's house in Rumford or to Gloria's in Dixfield, a few towns downriver. They even tried to take Gwen and Crystal for good, but Grace wouldn't let them.

Ray wouldn't let the kids take showers; they could only take baths, and he allowed them just a shallow measure of water. He didn't want to waste it on them, he said. They weren't allowed to eat at the table; Grace cooked elaborate dinners for Ray alone and sent her children to their rooms with bowls of cereal.

Sometimes Ray hit Grace, but he generally didn't strike the children. Instead he growled at them from around corners, cursed at them and told them they were worthless. "I can't stand to look at you," he'd say to a braided, freckled, six-year-old girl. He ordered Grace around and she took it. She did whatever she could to make her children be quiet, to keep them from bothering him in any way. Grace was more passive with Ray than she had been with Howard, possibly because Ray was a little less extreme; there was less opportunity for open brawling. Ray also provided more material benefits. He agreed to tolerate the children — just barely — and she agreed to do what she could to shut them up. He got access to this woman who so compelled him, and she got a nice house to live in. The deal mostly worked for them. It just didn't work for anybody else.

There were some good days, when Grace was fun, singing old show tunes while dancing around the kitchen making homemade doughnuts, or playing with their brown toy poodle, Coco. She was full of colorful idioms: she wasn't usually vulgar, but often, when she had to use the restroom, she'd say, "I have to piss like a racehorse!" She'd come home from shopping, having talked someone into giving her a deal, and announce, "He gave me a rake-off!" Frequently, these sayings would come out confused, such as "That's water over the bridge," or "It's not rocket surgery."

Sometimes Grace would say something strange to someone and not realize it until later. She'd tell the kids about it, laughing at herself, and they'd laugh along with her. But then she would suddenly get mad and start crying, saying, "Oh, no! Are you laughing at me?" Her mood often turned swiftly, without warning. With her red hair, which she maintained with Clairol until the day she died, she looked like Lucille Ball. But Ray wouldn't tolerate any of her silliness, her singing and dancing, so she could play only when he was out of the house.

At some point, the boys became too much trouble and they were sent to live with their nomadic father, Howard, who had run away to Texas. Finally, only three children were left at home: Tootsie, Gwen, and Crystal. Tootsie clashed most fiercely with Ray, and she passed the cruelty on down to her younger sisters, beating them up whenever she got the chance. In her early teens, she more or less moved in with the Wards, a nearby family with so many children they hardly noticed one more. Her memories of Ray seem more detailed, her accounts free of the circumspection I sense from the others; she once said that he hit her with electrical cords when she misbehaved. When I mention this to my other aunts, they don't contradict her; they frown and tell me the problem was that Tootsie never learned to keep her mouth shut.

—

Gwen and Crystal, Grace's two youngest girls, continued to raise themselves, mostly. The two were a cutely mismatched set, so close in age that some playfully called them "Irish twins." Gwen was a soft-spoken brunette with small features and a halo of frizz, a cautious girl who liked to sew on her grandmother's old Kenmore. Crystal was lanky and wilder, with carrot-orange hair and a forceful mind of her own. If one sister got something, the other had to have it, too; when it was Gwen's birthday, Crystal also got a present. If the toys matched at first, they didn't for long; Crystal would take out her things and use them up, tattering their edges and smudging their clean parts, while Gwen liked to put her belongings on a shelf so she could look at them and keep them nice and new and pretty. But the girls did everything together — they built a tree fort in the woods behind the house, rode their bikes for miles into town to get penny candy, swam together down at the nearby shore of Long Lake. They fought constantly, like many sisters, but they also tried to keep each other cheerful under the pressure of Ray's control. Their mother always bought them matching outfits in slightly different colors, even though they insisted, "We're not twins!" Their biggest difference was how they responded to Ray's meanness, to their mother's inability to protect them. Gwen learned to hide, wait it out. Crystal learned to escape. Gwen was lucky: at nineteen, she would meet a man named Dave — her safe harbor from that moment through today, a man who didn't ask her to put up with the burdens that Howard and Ray had laid upon Grace. Crystal would have a harder time finding a good man to lean on, and would slowly, but too slowly, realize that she didn't need to.

6

after

I have always remembered how the sunshine streamed in upon my first waking moment at Grammy's in that little room I'd once shared with Mom, but now I find that history contradicts me. It was gray, still rainy, just as it was when we'd left the hospital. The sunshine must have been the world pressing in on me, all the sensation and noise and light that I wasn't sure I could handle.

Gwen soon came in and encouraged me to put on a bathrobe and come out and eat. The bathrobe was Grammy's — purple quilted polyester trimmed in scratchy lace. I had left the hospital in nurse's scrubs, my own robe having become evidence. I found Grammy in the kitchen, wiping counter edges with the flat of her hand, straightening the line of cookie jars, uncharacteristically quiet. Someone placed a plain doughnut in front of me, the kind that comes in a plastic wrapper. I had eaten these often at Grammy's, sometimes heated up in the microwave. She always let me eat as many as I wanted. I picked the doughnut up. I put it down. I couldn't stand the thought of chewing, of transforming an object into blood and muscle; the idea was grotesque. I looked down at my bare legs, the blue shadows of veins under pale skin, and felt revulsion ripple through me. I pushed the little plate aside.

Within the hour, a woman named Cheryl Peters, a social worker employed by the state, arrived. She had a laptop with her and said

I could play with it while she filled out some forms. The idea that I might want to play, that day or ever again, struck me as absurd. I could see that she meant to be kind, but I felt almost mocked: playing was for happy children. I didn't touch the machine, but sat quietly on the bed. She asked me to tell her what had happened, and I recited the events of the night for her, even though I didn't really understand what she was there to do. Later, she told a police officer that she had met my family and, according to his notes, said, "They were all losers."

Shortly after, two police officers came, filling the tiny bedroom with their dark blue, rustling polyester uniforms. Several Bridgton officers had come to the Venezia, but these were new cops, state cops. One was Detective Dick Pickett, by then appointed leader of the investigation, a small, weaselly man with wire-rimmed glasses and a condescending manner. The other, Pat Lehan, I remember only as a generic cop figure, nodding along with Pickett. Lehan was one of more than two dozen policemen who would work on the case over the next twelve years, many of whom I would not meet and still know little about. I never spoke with Lehan again, but Pickett would stay in my life for some time, until the case got reassigned to someone else. On that first day, though, neither he nor I had any idea just how long our tense relationship would last.

I told Pickett and Lehan what had happened, focusing on one detail and then the next and then the next. Then we went over it again more carefully, Pickett stopping me repeatedly to ask questions, trying to get me to be more specific. I did my best to be thorough. Because I was a minor, Cheryl sat next to me while I answered questions. My aunts were left outside the door.

I was surprised to hear that there had been nothing wrong with the phones that night, and we have never really figured out why they didn't work. Now, I have theories, and those must suffice. In the kitchen, I failed to put the phone back on the hook after it had fallen to the floor, after the beeping of the open line had turned to silence, and so there was no active line to call out on. *If you'd like to make a call,* you must *hang up and try again.* And then when I was about fifteen, I had a sudden, unbidden sense memory of having frantically dialed 991 from Mom's room, rather than 911. The police have always been gracious on this point, have never dwelled on my failure to call out.

The phones are a failure of logic in the story; there is also a failure of memory. Although I could tell Pickett and Lehan everything that had happened from the moment Mom screamed that night, could march through every second and every detail, I could not remember the earlier part of the evening, before Mom and I had gone to bed. There was an utter blankness there, the terror of what came later destroying the final hours of our life together. The police wanted to know if Mom had seemed upset, if she had received any phone calls, when exactly she had gone to bed. No matter what they asked about those hours before the murder, or how hard I thought about them, I could not retrieve those details. It must have been clear to them that I would never get those hours back, because they were surprisingly merciful about them.

On all the other details, though, the investigators were relentless from the start. I gave Pickett all I had, but he wanted more.

"I really, really get the sense that you know who was there," he said. His attitude was slightly sarcastic, as though I were playing games with him and should cut it out. He raised his eyebrows and tilted his head back, inviting me to go ahead and give up my information.

When I described the sound of the kitchen drawer opening, of a knife being taken out, Pickett wondered how I knew it was a knife; the weapon had not been, and would never be, found. After I'd described, several times, the sounds of the stabbing and the silence that followed, he said, "Let me ask you this. How do you think your mother was hurt?"

Pickett found it suspicious that while I claimed I hadn't seen the killing, I was sure that a knife had been taken out of our kitchen drawer. He kept asking me why I was so convinced that she had been killed with a knife, was unsatisfied when I said that just seemed the likeliest explanation. When he said, once more, "And what makes you think it was a knife?" I replied, "Because of the sound I heard, and, well, I don't see how you could use a spoon or anything." When I read the transcript of this interview years later, I found that response both obnoxious and wonderful. I was proud of my little-girl self for pushing back, even when she was most broken.

Pickett was interviewing me because I was the only witness, as well as the person who was closest to my mother, because the things I had to say were important. But still, he didn't seem to really listen. He seemed to have already made up his mind, that very first day, about what had happened and who was responsible. His attitude implied that any answers that didn't conform to his theory were mistaken, ridiculous. He asked me a long string of questions about Mom and Dennis's fights. I said that Dennis had a temper, that they yelled a lot, and Pickett replied, illogically, "It sounds like you really think a lot of Dennis."

Later in the interview, Pickett asked the question that most clearly told me that we would never understand each other. "Is it possible that the person that was there is somebody that you care a lot about and don't want to get into trouble?" he said. "Even though, even though you know what happened was wrong?"

"I don't know who it is," I said once again, my voice straining with frustration. My love for my mother didn't seem to matter much to Pickett; he was not going to assume that I cared more about her than about getting her killer "in trouble." I realized that to the police — these people who had so much power — I was not a person who could be counted on to behave ethically. I looked at him, still not entirely sure he was serious. But he kept looking back at me, waiting.

I knew that the police and my family thought it would be additionally tragic if the killer was someone known to me, that they thought I would feel betrayed, confused, hurt. But I didn't care if the killer was someone I knew, or someone I had previously cared about. Mom was dead. Nothing else had meaning. Whether it was a man I knew or a man I didn't mattered very little in comparison with the fact that I would never see her again. It was one of the many things that no longer mattered at all.

I looked at Pickett's impatient, self-assured face. "I don't know," I said again, slowly and clearly, while cursing my own ignorance. He and Lehan said they thought that maybe I had come out into the living room and seen the man's face during the attack. But they offered no explanation for how I could have gotten out alive if I had. It was only my certainty that if I had I would have ended up dead that shielded me from a regret that would have torn me apart.

before

Fed up with Ray and her mother, Crystal once tried to run away on her bike — her goal being Glenice's house, about fifty miles away. She was maybe ten years old; Glenice would have been nearly twenty-two. Crystal may not have understood how far the journey would be, but she knew how to get there because she had paid attention during weekend visits. She made it to the town of Norway, more than fifteen miles away, before night began to fall and Officer Bob Bell, recogniz-ing the skinny, redheaded kid pedaling slowly along the shoulder and crying, picked her up and took her back home.

By the time she was fourteen, Crystal had grown from gangly to graceful, and her hair had shifted from carrots to sunset. She was already more or less living with other families, sharing friends' bed-rooms, avoiding home for days at a time. She'd started dating, and one afternoon, on one of the rare days that found her at the house, she headed out to meet a boy, but Ray decided he wanted her to stay.

Most of the time, Ray was glad for one less nuisance, but once a week or so, he'd get especially drunk and decide that he didn't like the idea of the kids "running around," even though when they stayed they could never be quiet enough.

Crystal probably told Ray some story about meeting up with Linda, but he wasn't buying it; he told her she wasn't going anywhere. He stared at her from his post near the door, waiting for her to back down or make a move. The boy was waiting; the timing was awful. She grabbed her bag and took long, quick strides across the kitchen, turning her face from her stepfather. Gloria, then twenty-seven years old, was visiting that day, and she sat silently at the kitchen table. She had a miserable look on her face but knew better than to try to help.

Crystal said, mostly to her sister, "Listen, I'll see you guys later. Don't wait up." She tried to sound casual and brave. She had seen her older siblings do this — put their foot down, march right past the old man and let him unload after they slammed the door behind them. The aftermath wasn't pretty, but she wouldn't be there for it. She'd be free.

Just as she turned the hollow brass knob of the door, Ray reached out a strong, wiry arm. He threw it out, really, and Crystal thought that he was finally going to hit her. Gloria saw her flinch. They both knew that if he started, if he hit her once, he'd keep going. He'd been waiting a long time, after all. And she wasn't a baby anymore.

Instead, his hand clamped down, hard, on Crystal's skinny upper arm. He held her there, yelled that she was a slut, told her to go ahead and leave if she couldn't do what he said in his house. He yelled a lot of things, punctuating his points with vicious shakes of her arm. But she didn't hear him very well. His arm coming out so fast, and his hand gripping her so hard, had sent a hot wave of panic through her. He had scared her so much that she peed, standing right there in the kitchen. And then she couldn't hear him. Her shame deafened her.

Finally, Ray let her go and pushed her outside. She stood on the porch for a moment, pants wet, then got on her bike and rode into town.

Crystal became more scarce, while Gwen stayed home and laid low, thinking, *I only have a couple years until I can get out of here and go to college.* She tried to keep out of Ray's way as much as possible — a skill that Crystal never really had.

Gwen missed her little sister, only occasionally catching glimpses of her at school. One day there was a massive food fight in the cafeteria that quickly got out of hand. A boy named Larry threw a chair, and before she knew it Gwen was on the floor, bleeding from the head. She was dazed, but she would always remember Crystal running across the cafeteria, at her side before she could even start to get up. The sisters hadn't spoken in weeks, but that moment of pain reunited them immediately, Crystal bending over her sister, oblivious to the blood staining her beautiful white pants. It was that image of the blood on the pants, Gwen says, that locked the moment into memory.

Crystal helped the teachers on duty press paper towels to Gwen's head while someone ran to call the house, but she couldn't go home with her sister. It was Ray who picked Gwen up, and for some reason he took her to his chiropractor, who made them wait through several other patients before stitching her up. Telling the story, Gwen laughs and says, "Why didn't anybody in the waiting room see this kid bleeding and say, 'Hey, go on ahead of me!'?" Like nearly all terrible stories in our family, this one is told with laughter. The chiropractor used a big, curved needle, and no anesthetic. Later that night, when she lay down to sleep, Gwen reached to the back of her head and felt wetness under her thick hair — she was still bleeding. Finally, her parents took her to the hospital, where the doctor on duty removed and replaced the chiro's amateur stitches. Gwen couldn't wash her hair for some time, so she wrapped a colorful scarf around her head and carried on. She refused to miss a day of school — she had perfect attendance every single year from eighth grade through graduation. No matter what happened, she kept studying, waiting for her chance. She'd go to college, maybe train to be a dental hygienist, like Glenice. She'd get a good job and a decent place to live, and then Crystal would come to live with her.

—

Once they were all adults, most of Grace's children met every Thanksgiving and every Christmas, and eventually gathered once every summer around the pool Carol installed at her house in 1990 — a sparkling, communal luxury. Complicated love compelled them to include Grace in these gatherings, and I wouldn't hear of my grandmother's negligence until I was a preteen. Ray was just a cranky voice in the other room, yelling at everyone to be quiet, until he died of emphysema in the late 1980s. And Howard was a dark ghost, rarely spoken of, his life ended by alcoholism, or a shotgun accident, or suicide, depending on who's telling the story. Next to his body was a list of telephone numbers — people he'd failed to reach.

Now I watch home movies of those annual family pool parties: Grammy waving coquettishly at the camera, Glenice taking center stage with a story, Wendall showing off his skillfully carved watermelon — one year a pig with a curly tail, one year a Bud-weis-er frog. There was always a prize for anyone who could guess the watermelon before he unveiled it. My mother wanders in and out of frame, ever thin and energetic, with a flat-footed walk and a ready smile. Gloria teases her affectionately, Carol's husband jokingly mimes throwing her in the pool, Glenice and Gwen flank her for a photo, arms looped around her thin waist. Almost everyone has a good job, a stable home, a quiet life. There is a lot of love in these videos, a sense of hard-earned relaxation.

It is breathtaking to look back and watch them, so carefree, so young. The parties of recent years are more subdued; there is a sense of lost, irretrievable magic. I can't remember the last time anyone even bothered to make a video. Glenice now says, "We all struggled so hard, and we all made it, and then that happened. We all made it but your mother."

after

Dick Pickett was followed by more cops on that first day, and still more the day after. More than any single conversation, I remember my exhaustion, and everyone else's. I remember my red-eyed aunts coming to me and announcing the arrival of more officials, clearly torn, hesitant to hand me over to the scrutiny of strangers. They explained repeatedly that I had to do my best to help whoever came, underestimating my eagerness to do so. If I just kept talking, I thought, the cops might find the person who had done this. But I did keep track of how often I was interviewed: nineteen times in those first three days. By the end there was nothing left of me; I was only this story of an evening. I felt like life would not continue past that night, beyond this retelling.

The police told me it was very important that I not share the details of what I had witnessed with anyone but them and other officials, because there were things that only the killer and I could know. We had to ensure that if someone other than me revealed any of that information, it would be incriminating. So the killer and I were bound by a dark connection that only the police could see. I didn't discuss the events of that night with anyone in the family, and no one asked me questions. I couldn't figure out if they were trying to avoid upsetting me or if they couldn't handle hearing my answers.

I was also informed that the men who had loved Mom — Tom, Dale,

Tim, Dennis—were all suspects, so I shouldn't have contact with any them, just in case. I wasn't tempted.

At some point, the police asked me to write down what had happened that night. I have a photocopy of this now. I'm struck by the careful, freshly learned cursive, the stiff, formal language revealing my desire for precision. My final sentence is written slightly larger, in block letters, and underlined: "I do not know who committed the crime."

I recently asked Glenice to describe how I looked and acted that first day. When she answered, she spoke in a halting manner very different from the voluble expressiveness I'm used to. She said, "You looked like you hadn't slept in a week . . . I don't know . . . but you just—like your eyes looked, well . . . sunken in and you looked white as a ghost. And you were *sweating*—sweating and hot." I hear compassion in her words, but fear in her pauses. I can imagine that to get closer to me would have been to get closer to what had happened.

—

That first full night, Gwen and her fiancé, Dave, took Glenice and me to their apartment to sleep—we were to share the big brass bed in the spare room. I remember Glenice cracked, worn down, emptied out. When we got to the apartment, she said she had to brush her teeth right away: "I've been crying so much, my mouth tastes like the bottom of a birdcage." It was such a strange and perfect image; I remembered it forever.

We spent the next few days and early evenings at Grammy's, gathering there with her and my uncle Wendall and his wife Jane, who stayed there with her overnight. After sunset, we did our best to numb out in front of the television. We watched *Roseanne* and other sitcom reruns, not speaking much, trying to set our brains on automatic, running the grooves of the familiar stories. But we couldn't escape the teasers for the six o'clock, then the eleven o'clock, news, flashing into view at the very beginning of every commercial break, too quickly for us to change the channel. Even when we grew to expect the footage we would see for weeks, no one got up to turn the knob. We couldn't admit that openly the power those images had over us. It somehow seemed undignified.

The video showed my black-and-white house behind bright yellow tape. It showed men in uniform carrying a gurney out the front door, a black body bag distorted to a shape I didn't understand. There was a strange lump in the middle, and a hollow to one side. I tried not to analyze that shape, just as I tried to ignore the fact that it was daylight by the time the news vans took that shot. I tried not to think of the intervening hours. Of the school bus driver slowing to pick me up that morning, then pulling away. My classmates pressing their faces to the foggy windows.

I didn't know then that the shape on that gurney was the curve of her hip, that she had been carefully lifted and transported as she fell, so her body could tell the story of what had happened to it. All I knew was that it was not the shape of a restful body, that it looked unnatural in a way I didn't want to think too much about. She seemed exposed; all the other body bags I'd seen on the news had been flat. I hated the idea of thousands of television viewers being able to trace some curve of her, as though all the desirous eyes that had followed her in life would never cease looking.

That body bag also featured prominently on the front page of the *Bridgton News,* in a bleak, sad image that took up almost all the space above the fold. I was furious about this, that we could not go downtown without seeing that picture in store windows and on racks next to the checkout line. I've since spoken to the reporter responsible, Lisa Ackley. I was surprised when she mentioned that shot before I even asked about it, telling me how she had fought to have it included. "This is a family newspaper," her editor had countered. "We don't run things like that." But Lisa had refused to pretend nothing had happened, to help cover it up just to make readers more comfortable. "People have to know," she said. "People have to know exactly what this person did." Now that I've spoken with so many people who will refer to the murder only as "what happened," or "the incident," or even "the accident," I understand.

—

Throughout those first weeks, I became fixated on an image: the inside of my head filling with a viscous blackness, insanity as matter, crowding my mind into a tight corner. I knew I had to keep the blackness contained or it would take over; it would suffocate me entirely. I so terribly feared insanity. The part of me that had seen the huge insect in the dark arms of the clock that night, that had heard that sturgeon thrashing on the floor, had to be locked up so it couldn't take over. I considered restraint and control my best defenses. So mostly I did not cry. Mostly I stayed calm. Cheryl, the social worker, said that her teenage daughter thought I mourned "with grace," and I thought that was the kindest thing someone could say about me. I wondered, though, how Cheryl's daughter knew anything about it.

But the Blackness, as I thought of it then, wasn't just insanity. I could feel that what the killer had done had gotten inside of me. I had seen what a person could do and I could never unsee it; I was unclean, poisoned. I looked into my pupils in the mirror and there seemed to be no bottom to the black. Just as much as I feared him out in the world, I feared him within me.

The worst part of feeling poisoned was that it seemed to wipe out anything in me that was gentle and intelligent and funny—all the things my mother had loved about me. I was devastated to think that if she had ever been able to come back, I might already be unrecognizable to her.

—

Despite my attempts at control, there were moments of breakage. One came the night after the murder, or the night after that. We were sitting around Grammy's dining room table—Gwen and Glenice and I, and Carol and Grammy. I was trying to eat something. The idea of my body and its processes still disgusted me. I would look at my calves, shaped just like hers, and they would seem like flesh, like meat, like something that could be dead and inert tomorrow. Grinding an object with my teeth, swallowing its paste, adding yet more to this body — this vulgar, heavy, gross thing I had to carry around — was gruesome. Even showering was difficult: faced with my solid, naked self, having to touch and attend to limbs, belly, to my useless feet, still raw from the run to get help, I shut down completely, stood staring for minutes at a time. My body persisted as a living, warm vehicle, while hers had become a thing under a tarp. The blood flowing neatly through my veins gave me a feeling of horror, a sense of invasion. I didn't feel like I inhabited a living body so much as a temporarily animated corpse.

But I tried. My aunts told me I needed my strength, and I agreed. The meal that night was something I loved, one of my favorites, a leftover from the days of sitting happily with Grammy, a stuffed animal in my lap. Fish sticks and mashed potatoes, maybe. A meal that would have brought joy even a week before. Now I could only eat a bite of it before I had to stop.

Little things can, for moments, carry the full force of tragedy. I looked at this meal and it was all the childhood happiness I'd ever enjoyed and would never feel again, and I started to cry. And as I cried, I thought about how some person — not a tornado or a hurricane or a car crash or a fire, but a person — had taken her away from me, had robbed me of everything, and a great, furious wave suddenly swept over me. "I can't eat! I can't fucking eat!" I screamed. "Why would someone do this? Why! Why the fuck did this happen?! FUCK HIM! FUCK HIM!"

I kept on like this, banging the table with my fist. I could see that my aunts and my grandmother were terrified, and I ran with it. I wanted someone else to be afraid, I wanted someone else to feel everything spin entirely out of control. The fact that I had no face upon which to focus my hatred only intensified it. I raged at my helplessness, and at the fact that no one around me knew what they were talking about. My aunts' attempts to soothe me only made me angrier. "You don't fucking understand!" I told them, although they would have admitted that themselves. But I was beyond being fair. I was nearly blacked out.

Somewhere within me, though, I could see myself breaking down.

As I burned off some of my trapped energy, that calmer, older self came out and shone a light in my head: I couldn't let him do this to me. I could not let the shadow take over.

Just then, Grammy approached me with some pills. I was sobbing but no longer banging the table, and I saw her hand shake as she laid them in front of me. I picked up my glass of water and took them, didn't ask what they were, didn't pay attention to how many. I had always had a childish difficulty swallowing pills, but now I opened up and threw them down my throat. I became quiet immediately, all the fight leaving me as quickly as it had entered. The pills could not have worked that fast; I was just too tired to go on. Defeated. I didn't look at anyone's face. I got up from the table and headed for the living room couch, and as I did, I saw on the kitchen counter the box from which the pills had come. Cold medicine. They truly did not know what to do.

9

before

I never asked Mom about the early days of her marriage; any mention of my father, Tom, upset her, made her irritable and withdrawn. I think she felt that my rare questions about him implied that she wasn't enough on her own. I had a couple of thin photo albums, plastic pages brittle with age, some hazy early-childhood memories, and that was all. They'd divorced when I was five, and Tom and I had only sporadic contact after that, and none after Mom died. And so, after eighteen years of silence, I decided to contact him, to ask him about Mom's youth, about their seven-year marriage. I tried to put her descriptions of him out of my mind. Other people have often told me that my father is a surprisingly likable man, with a disarmingly friendly voice. "Tom's a decent guy," they'll say, "when he isn't drinking."

We arranged for me to pick him up in a pharmacy parking lot. He was the sheepish man with the worn red cheeks. We went to his brother's girlfriend's apartment, a clean, cozy space. He told me he'd borrowed a nice shirt for the day. As he spoke, I found myself smiling at him, trying to put my finger on the familiar quality of his voice. It made me think of stock characters from old movies. A gentle farmer in a drought year. A noble con taking the fall for his buddy. But it didn't quite fit any trope I could call up. I finally had to admit that his voice must have gotten into me when I was new to the world, trusting and fresh. That the exact timbre of it took me back to something simpler, despite everything that had happened.

We both knew I had to be the one to call first, just as we both knew I was searching for her, not for him. But now he calls on holidays, on my birthday. He has my address. We chat about the weather, and job prospects. I try to ignore the sense that I'm betraying her by speaking to him. It is the first thing I have done that I am sure would contradict her wishes. He and I dance carefully around each other, both wondering when I might suddenly feel like throwing a punch.

—

According to Tom, my parents met at a party.

It was at a camp down on the shores of Long Lake, a boxy place covered in cedar shingles darkened by moisture and time, the unheated rooms full of teenagers smoking weed and drinking Bud and Coors, Led Zeppelin on the crackly radio, shirtless boys jumping off the dock out in the dark.

Or maybe it was at somebody's house downtown, parents gone for the weekend, records on a turntable, liquor cabinet busted open, cigarette ash ground into beige shag. High schoolers, dropouts, early-twenties road crew members, little siblings too young to be there.

Or it was in an apartment on Lower Main Street, in the broad middle of a Sunday, afternoon light filtering through clouds of smoke, music cranked up loud, people leaning and calling over rickety porch railings. Calls around to friends for more beer, stocked up: no liquor sales on the holy day. Wild teens, kids scurrying underfoot, adults home, but not from any job. Harder drugs available in the kitchen.

Mom wore high-waisted, faded bell-bottoms, or a ruched sundress in dark blue calico, or brown peg-leg pants and a halter. Tom wore jeans and a dark T-shirt with a pocket. Or a flannel. And boots.

He can't quite remember the details; all of these are equally probable Bridgton stories. But he knows Mom was with another girl, probably Linda. The two of them would have been a beautiful sight, Linda's soft brown curls complementing Mom's bright red perfectly. It was very early summer — Mom's freckles were starting to multiply, and Linda was taking on the brown of what would become a lifelong tan.

But Tom does remember the moment he saw Mom for the first time. He was immediately captivated: she was, as he says, "drop-dead gorgeous." He walked over to her and started talking, about any old thing. She had a great sense of humor, and he was especially impressed by her intelligence, how she expressed herself precisely and fully and didn't dumb anything down, even at a party. He told her, "You are something special," and I can imagine her then, a skinny young teen, pretending not to be overwhelmed by his attention but still impressed by his direct confidence, a rarity in teenage boys. He said, right there, the very first time he met her, that he wanted to be with her. He knew a little about her family, knew there was trouble and unrest, if not outright abuse. He wanted to take care of her. It didn't much matter that she was already dating someone, some guy called Junior, one of the multitude of Knight boys, well-known troublemakers in town. He considered this a minor obstacle.

Tom Perry had the thickest, shiniest black hair Crystal had ever seen. He was a little older — eighteen to her fifteen — with a wide, open face and small eyes that crinkled at the corners. He had friendly round cheeks and the muscular shoulders of a man who reaches under car hoods all day. She could smell motor oil on him, just faintly, a sweet, inviting smell, the smell of a man who took care of things, who could fix what was broken. He looked only at her when he spoke, nothing else competing for his attention.

Tom stole her away from Junior rather easily. He was charming and good-looking, with steady work and his own place. He'd been on his own since he was fourteen. He rented a trailer near the elementary school, close to the Black Horse Tavern, one of the town's nicest restaurants, a place marked with a carved-wood sign that hung from fine chains, where locals mingled with the well-dressed summer people from Boston. He was a way out, a way to avoid living under Ray's roof ever again. She moved into his place a couple of weeks after meeting him.

Tom drank and liked to have a good time, but he had a good reputation in town as a hard worker and a fair man, someone who didn't take handouts and treated people well. These facts compensated for his occasional hell-raising—mostly fighting. Cops were rarely called, and when they were it was only to break things up when they didn't resolve on their own. It wasn't the sort of town where you talked out your differences, and Tom, raised with four brothers in the woods to the north, fit right in.

When Grace called the police, saying that her daughter had run off with this grown man, the cops took a look at the situation: Crystal wasn't the first Farnum girl to start partying, to run from the house and from Ray. Officer Bell, who had picked her up in Norway as a skinned-kneed ten-year-old, was now chief of the Bridgton force, and he and others had reluctantly delivered the girls back home time and again. At Tom's, Crystal was behaving: she went to school every day, got good grades. Chief Bell told her mother, "She's doing fine, Grace. Just leave her be."

Still, Grace kept at Tom. She must have realized that she was going to lose her baby daughter for real this time, and she panicked. She latched onto the idea that the two were "living in sin," her own errant weekends momentarily forgotten. She'd call constantly and demand that Tom return her daughter, so soon enough he drove to her house alone to reason with her.

When Tom arrived, Grace let him in—here was an opportunity to lecture him in person. But she hadn't gotten very far before he said, "Hey, listen. I don't wanna live in sin; I want to marry her."

She had not expected this. "Absolutely not!" she said. "No way! Get outta my house!" If she kept yelling, he'd have to take it back, this ridiculous thing he'd said.

Tom backed toward the front door, square-palmed hands in the air. "Okay, okay," he said. He paused. "Well, just think about it."

But Grace kept screaming, "Get out!"

I imagine Tom chuckling, shaking his head as he started up the car. Ray liked Tom, though. He'd bring his dull brown Oldsmobile to the garage where Tom worked, in the center of town behind the laundromat. They'd talk man to man, share a cigarette. The way Tom saw it, Ray wasn't perfect, but he was doing his best. Grace was so highstrung, and she had so many damn kids.

One day Tom's phone rang at the trailer. It was Ray, a sober weekday Ray: "Come on up to the house. Bring Crystal."

Crystal was quiet on the ride over, tensely flicking one fingernail against the other. It was Ray who opened the door this time; Grace was nowhere in sight. He asked them to sit down in the kitchen, and soon it was settled: Crystal and Tom would get married as soon as possible. She was a minor, so there would be paperwork, but Ray assured them that Grace would sign. Crystal knew it wasn't kindness that motivated her stepfather.

When they brought the marriage papers to her mother, Grace voiced no objections. The men had arranged it, and she knew how eager Ray was to clear the house of children. This would, after all, remove some friction from her life. Crystal would be sixteen in two months, just about the age Grace was the first time she married Ray. For Crystal, pregnancy was nowhere in sight, but freedom was.

Tom and Crystal were married June 20, 1979, in a little chapel in the nearby town of Harrison, on the slender northern shore of Long Lake. There were only two witnesses: Tom's brother Tony and his friend Mike Macdonald. I have no idea what she wore.

—

Gwen never quite forgave their mother for signing those papers. One summer, she and Crystal were painting vacated dorms at Bridgton Academy — a tiny college prep school near their house, a green-lawned alternate universe — earning extra cash, driving each other crazy, playing one-on-one basketball on the abandoned courts. And then the next, Crystal was married at fifteen and on her way to California with a husband Gwen hardly knew. The sisters wouldn't live together, work together, help each other out, as Gwen had hoped. Now she was on her own, and she didn't know what might become of Crystal. In the seventies, California meant adventure and sunlight. To Gwen it seemed like everyone was heading out there, although most would return before long, finding that it wasn't the gold-rush opportunity they'd imagined.

—

Tom and Crystal ripped across the country in a black 1966 Ford Fairlane, a boxy hot rod of a car that Tom had fortified with a police cruiser engine so it could better haul the weight of his tools. They had nothing to lose, and he had family out there. They stayed at campgrounds along the way — cheaper than motels, safer than rest stops.

The Fairlane covered more than three thousand miles in five days, finally rolling up to the house of Tom's father and stepmother. Tom and Crystal just appeared one day at the front door. Tom didn't call anyone to tell them they were coming; he figured that once he arrived, with no money to go home, they couldn't turn him away. Faced with asking permission now or forgiveness later, it seems Tom has always made the same choice.

The family gave them the space they had: a huge enclosed porch with a view of rolling, thickly wooded mountains. They slept under an electric blanket to stave off the Northern California chill. The town was called Brownsville, in Yuba County. To this day, Brownsville is still an unincorporated community, like Milton, with a population of about twelve hundred.

I wonder about Mom's image of California, the fantasies that magnetized all those other kids Gwen knew. Did she picture sandy beaches and desert bluffs, long-haired men and suntanned women in beads, only to land in a flannel-and-jeans, barely there town remarkably like the isolated communities back home? Or was she open to anything that took her a continent away from Maine?

The route from Bridgton to Brownsville is a straight shot across the country, almost the longest line you could draw from one coast to the other. I look at images of restored 1966 Fairlanes, parked in clean deserts with mountains climbing into the sky behind them. It's exactly what I would have chosen for that drive. That car really does look like freedom.

—

Tom found work easily; his father was a logger and a welder and had good contacts. He first worked as a roustabout, an odd-job man, in a huge log-processing mill in Marysville, a larger city about an hour away, down out of the hills.

Tom did a good job, worked hard, and was soon promoted to servicing trucks in the mill on the night shift. The promotion meant that he and Crystal had to move to the city of twelve thousand, and they had trouble adjusting. Tom hated the late hours, and the work was tougher and dirtier than he was used to; he hated smelling like oil and grease all the time. But Crystal studied for her GED at the local high school. The school made her an assistant teacher, and after she aced the eight-hour test, they invited her to teach full-time. Tom still glows with pride, talking about Crystal the teacher.

She was only seventeen when they offered her that job. But she didn't accept. She and Tom had never gotten used to Marysville, where they lived in an apartment complex on the sad fringes of town, a place with a mossy pool in the center, full of drug dealers and child abuse. They soon moved back up into the hills, where life was simpler. Tom's father got him a job as an auto mechanic, and they rented a trailer right behind the garage.

Crystal liked to tease Tom about his motorcycles, an endless series of fixer-uppers that he bought and sold and traded with other young men. One evening she sat on the porch attached to the trailer, surrounded by the warm orange air of a California dusk in September, watching Tom work on one of his bikes. Much of it was brown with rust and the soft dirt on which it was parked, but he knew what he was doing. Crystal thought he might actually finish this one, couldn't wait to sit on the back of it, speeding down a curvy ocean highway, just like on TV. She thought about this while she sat quietly sipping her beer and watching Tom's back muscles move under his T-shirt.

Finally he stepped back and threw the wrench on the ground next to his other tools. He smiled at her and brushed some dirt off his hands.

"Hey," he said, giving her a little smile. "Watch this."

He jogged a few yards away from the motorcycle, then took a running start. He planted his hands on the back of the seat, flipped himself over in the air, and landed, perfectly, astride the bike.

She didn't know he could do that.

"Wait!" she yelled. "Wait right there! I'm getting the camera."

He beamed at her, face smudged, legs splayed out. It was still plenty light out for a picture.

—

But that motorcycle, and all the others, stayed in the yard: Tom never got them in good enough shape to take her out for a ride. Often, he'd take the car and drive off alone, then get in a wreck on his way back, driving drunk on mountain roads. He went through one vehicle after another. And even when they had a working car, Crystal couldn't go far on her own, because she didn't have her license yet and she didn't like breaking the law. It made her too nervous. There wasn't really anywhere to go anyway, and soon she was bored and homesick. Sometimes she picked up shifts at the café connected to the garage, but there wasn't any work around that stimulated her mind. "She went right up the wall," as Tom puts it.

Eventually Tom got his hands on a classic Chevy Impala, a comfortable vehicle meant for long cruises. They scraped together a few dollars and drove back home to Maine—the California experiment had lasted about a year and a half. Of those California days Tom now says, "I was too wild—I wasn't behaving myself at all! I'm positive she would've wanted to come back to Maine anyway. But it would've been better to come back, y'know, not as penniless as we left. She deserved better—I know that now, and I probably knew that then."

I don't doubt that he knew Mom deserved better. But I'm not sure she knew. Not yet.

—

When Tom and my mother returned to Maine, they rented one of Bridgton's many run-down apartments. It was a place of tilted floors and leaky sinks, one of a dozen or so units in a flat-roofed, three-story building, a typical Maine affair with porches clinging to the green chipped-paint sides and crooked stairs and landings running over it like spiderwebs. Mom started work at Pleasant Mountain Moccasin, known as the Shoe Shop, one of Bridgton's two major employers back then — the other was a textile factory called Malden Mills, known as the Mill. Mom worked at the Shoe Shop until her death: twelve years spent standing over a workbench pushing large needles through the stiff leather uppers of loafers, Docksides, and moccasins. She added the thick white topstitching around the toe, the rustic touch that made those shoes so charmingly casual, so magnetic to flatlanders who wore them sockless on vacation. But those stitches also held the shoe together; uniform stitches meant that it would be beautiful, would have a nice, even shape. It was a job requiring skill and precision and strength.

While Mom sped through each day at the Shop, Tom worked on cars and took on some construction jobs. He is a skilled mechanic and carpenter, good at the work but not good at keeping it. He's counted on these sorts of jobs all his life — fixing broken-down cars, working house construction for a day or a week, hired through personal referrals and favors, friends and father figures. Back then, when he wasn't working, he was at the Sulky Lounge, a tiny bar wedged into the main downtown strip, walking distance from their apartment.

Mom wanted to make a nice family, nicer than the one she'd grown out of, so she was thrilled when she got pregnant, and even happier to see that Tom was excited, too. He knew he needed to get his act together, and he reckoned fatherhood was the perfect motivation. He'd clean up some, they would get along better, and they'd be joined by a cute little baby. He loved babies, was good with them. For a while, he calmed down, stayed home more, saved some money. As her little belly got rounder and rounder — friends said she looked "like a pea on a toothpick" — the two talked about the future. But soon Tom went back to partying, once again blowing his cash on old bikes and booze.

Even before I was born, Mom started worrying. She told Glenice she wasn't confident she'd be able to track Tom down when the time came to deliver her baby. "How am I going to get to the hospital?" she wondered aloud. "What am I gonna do, walk?" She didn't think she'd have the cash for a taxi.

Tom says he managed to be there for my birth, but some of Mom's friends have cast doubt on this. He was hidden away somewhere, drunk and unreachable, one woman recently told me, shaking her head. He dropped her off and didn't come back until it was all over, said another. I don't know what's true, but I believe everyone is faithful to their own memory. Tom is just as likely to have shielded himself from regret as Mom's friends are to have created yet another story of failure.

But Mom knew he had it in him to do better, so she waited. She walked the creaky floors at night, calming my cries and listening to Tom snoring in the dark. California was over, but here they could get further ahead; she could contribute more working at the Shop than she'd been able to in Brownsville.

Mom dropped me off at my grandmother's every morning before she went to work and picked me up at the end of the day, taking me home, where we spent hours on the couch, cuddling or playing peek-a-boo. Sometimes she was so happy she hardly noticed that Tom wasn't there, but as time went on, his absence burned her. He missed out on so much, and she had to do everything herself.

Mom grew tired of waiting for Tom to grow up with her. Things got harder and harder. He kept drinking his money. Even when there was some left over, it was difficult to get it from him. He would go straight to Sulky's after work, come home after she'd already gone to bed, pass out, repeat.

One day, Mom came home from work expecting to find cash on the kitchen counter, for basics: baby formula, milk, eggs. Tom had promised. Of course, there was no cash on the counter, no Tom in sight. She called her downstairs neighbor, Ruth, who agreed to babysit for a little while. Although we would leave that apartment when I was still very young, I have a hazy sense of Ruth from those early years: a dark-haired woman with a loud laugh, her kitchen full of spider ferns and cigarette smoke.

That day, Mom pushed open Ruth's screen door and banged out into the street, marching to the bar, getting angrier with each step. She passed someone she knew walking the other way and could barely nod a hello. She yanked the bar's heavy door open, and when her eyes adjusted to the light, she found Tom lined up with the others. She walked over as calmly as she could.

"Jesus Christ, Tom," she hissed. "Where's that money I asked you for?"

"Crystal, listen . . ." he began, his s's gone slippery. "Listen, hold on. Les' talk about this," he continued as he got down off his stool, taking her thin arm in his hand and steering her outside. Too late. They had everyone's attention. The afternoon crowd peered out the door, wondering how it would go down this time.

Mom ripped her arm out of Tom's grasp and starting yelling. "Fuck, Tom, fuck! You don't have it, do you? What am I supposed to do? You have a daughter now, goddammit!"

He leaned toward her, perhaps to placate her. He was bleary-eyed; she'd never get through. As he bent closer, she cocked her fist and punched him right in the face.

Tom was a violent person, and his temper flared especially hot when someone put him down or acted better than him. He was and is given to fights — in bars, at parties — that he can barely remember later. In his late youth, he had the shortish, muscle-heavy body of a boxer; my mother had lost all sixteen pounds of her pregnancy weight, putting her at about five foot five and 110 pounds. But when she punched Tom in the face, he fell down to his knees on the sidewalk and stayed there. He hung his head and shut right up, with all his friends looking on. If he didn't touch her then, he may never have hit her at home, despite the screaming fights that kept their neighbors up night after night. But it's hard to know for sure.

Those fights continued. Ruth and her boyfriend Spencer regularly heard them yelling at each other for hours into the night. They heard plates and chairs thrown. Crystal lost it again and pushed Tom down the stairs. There would be a few quiet weeks, then a huge blowup. A few more quiet weeks, then a series of smaller engagements. This chaos was familiar, and eventually she left it again. She was luckier than Grace; she had the strength to leave, and had only one child to take with her.

I do think Mom may have still loved Tom — at least a little — when she left, although his behavior in the years that followed would destroy any tender feelings that remained. But he wasn't showing her respect, he wasn't helping her, and she could see that he might drag her — and me — down with him. It was hard to give up on her dream of a happy family, but she finally had to admit that wasn't what she had.

But she did have me.

—

As the years passed, Mom's work at the Shop would remain our steadiest constant, the only thing we could really count on besides each other. All through my childhood, the smell of the Shop marked her return home at the end of each day, a sharp smell of leather and glue and dust buried in her hair and in the dye-smudged medical tape wrapped protectively around her fingers. I'd hug her when she came in — the clock reset, the day renewed — and the smell would drift around to envelop me. When I was very young, that smell made me happy but also nervous, although I didn't understand why. When I was a little older — ten, eleven, twelve — it was a reminder that my mother went places I couldn't go, that she wasn't just a mother but many other things, too. Now, when I buy a pair of handmade leather shoes or boots, I bury my nose in them and breathe deeply, and that same smell moves through my body, cell by cell. It's the smell of her hard work, of her devotion to me.

The Shop operated on a piecework basis, with employees paid for each case of shoes completed. Each case contained twelve pairs, and paid between twenty-one and twenty-four dollars, depending on the style. Moccasins were simpler and softer, so they paid less; loafers were stiffer and more structured, and paid more. Sebago boat shoes, named after the most beautiful lake in the area, paid somewhere in the middle. Under this system, speed was rewarded, and there was nothing to keep a determined young mother from working herself to exhaustion.

The string Mom used in sewing came in long pieces, cut to just the right length to weave all around the front of the shoe. There was a needle on each end, and she would begin by pushing one into the leather and pulling it through until the two ends were of equal length. She'd push both needles back in, pulling them out on opposite sides, completing the motion with a firm outward tug to secure the stitch. Then her hands would arc in again to puncture the leather, arc out, tug, arc in. Sitting at my desk now, I pantomime this two-handed motion, shown to me by her fellow hand-sewers and friends. It's like a reverse butterfly stroke, an attempt at flight, at keeping your head above water.

But Mom was known as one of the fastest in the Shop, a naturally skilled sewer who remained dedicated to making the most of a difficult job. She and her friend Penny had benches next to each other, and sometimes they would race, others nearby cheering them on. Penny is a muscular, tough woman, and my slender, smiling mother always kept up with her, beat her half the time. Reasonably talented hand-sewers could do about three cases in a day; Mom usually did four. The annual difference could be up to five thousand dollars.

By a conservative estimate, Mom drew three million arcs through the hot, dusty air over those twelve years, each firm tug spreading tension through her neck and shoulders, each repetition inflaming her wrists. She arrived every weekday at six in the morning and went home at four thirty, starting and ending her day earlier than others so she could be home for me in the evening. She was on her feet all those hours; the Shop provided stools, but almost everyone sewed faster when standing.

To further improve her rate, Mom pre-threaded her needles at home. Each week, she brought home a bag filled with long, white skeins of rough string. The ends were ragged and fuzzy, and each unraveled tip had to be waxed before it could be threaded through the eye of the thick silver needles she used. Sitting on the couch watching TV, or on the porch watching me, she pulled the long tail of each thread across the palm of a hand that held a small cake of soft wax, then pushed the tamed end through a needle. Next she bent the free end back along the string and twisted it into the wax there so the needle was firmly secured. She repeated the process until the bundle was finished, a hundred or more needles clicking together in a sharp bouquet.

Mom could hold a conversation or sing along softly to the radio as she waxed, her hands moving independent of her attention. As I got older, she'd sometimes accept my clumsy help, and I'd sit on the floor chewing my lip, trying to wax with her graceful whipping motion, chunks of wax sticking to the string and impeding my progress or flying off onto the carpet. Another daughter of the Shoe Shop recently told me about waxing with her mother, and I was overwhelmed by a sudden, painful feeling of sisterhood.

For a time, Linda worked at the Shop, too, and Mom must have been happy to have her company. But hand-sewing was too hard for Linda, too painful and tiring, and she soon left. When I knew Linda, she worked for a landscaping company, which tells me something about how hard hand-sewing must have been. She watched helplessly as the Shop wore down Crystal's body, each year bringing with it new kinds of pain.

One day, Mom pulled a stitch taut and felt a huge snap at the base of her neck. From then on, she saw a chiropractor regularly, a tall, thin, gray-haired man with the aspect of an undertaker. He leaned over her small frame, bending her limbs and audibly cracking her bones while I sat in a chair next to the tall table he laid her out on. I didn't like how he smelled — like dusty corners and unnameable chemicals — and my mother's bare skin seemed disturbingly out of place in the brown, closed room, rather than out in the summer sunshine. Near the end of the appointment, he placed two flat plastic pads on her back, then left the room for a while. I sat alone with her for five or ten minutes that felt like an eternity while a rhythmic hum pulsed from a big metal box on the floor, wires leading from it to those plastic pads. I didn't dare to interrupt her trancelike silence and instead sat there sweating lightly and hoping for the humming to end soon. I always worried that the doctor would forget to come back, that I'd have to pull the pads off before my mother was slowly electrocuted as she slept, like an animal gently boiled alive in an increasingly hot pot. I wasn't sure how I would know when I should intervene. I felt a flooding relief when the doctor came back and removed the pads, when Mom pulled her shirt back on and stood up to leave.

I always understood that my mother worked very hard. But it is only now that I can appreciate her determination, that to work as quickly and as consistently as she did meant re-dedicating herself each day, each hour, each minute, to pushing through boredom and physical pain and sometimes despair. She didn't do this for herself; she did it for me. Those years constitute a sacrifice that I could not repay, even if she were still here, but I am bereft that I never got to try. And after she died, the Shop's profit-sharing plan meant that she would support me for years after her death. The Shop paid us better after she was gone than while she was alive.

The Shoe Shop was razed years ago, and now a chain supermarket stands in its place. My aunts and I have all made the pilgrimage, stood in the cereal aisle and wondered where the ghost of her workbench resides. As a child, I went to the Shoe Shop only a handful of times, and wasn't permitted very far into the building. I remember it as a loud cavern full of dangerous-looking machinery and sad-looking parents. Despite her skill and speed, Mom always wanted to escape to something else, a job where she could use her brain, or at least sit down. But Bridgton had little to offer, so she was stuck with the tedious days and the grinding years of the Shop. By the end, she was generally healthy but plagued by her chronic back and neck aches, along with carpal tunnel and migraines. Her hands were whittled down by constant work, fingers bone-thin, the knuckles forever swollen — the only part of her that would ever age.

after

Word of the murder spread fast that morning, like poison released on a wind. Sandy, one of Mom's closest friends from the Shop, was just about ready to leave her house in Casco, two towns to the south, and head to work when her ex-husband, Randy, came walking over from his trailer next door. Randy was a reasonable man, and he and Sandy had remained friends after their divorce, living close to each other so it would be easier on their children — a girl around my age and a younger boy.

When Randy came over that morning, he said a bewildering thing. He said a friend of his, a police officer, had called and told him that Crystal was dead. That she had been killed.

Sandy's disbelief was so pure that at first she didn't feel much at all. "Nooo," she said. "Nah, that can't be. There's been some kind of mistake. Our Crystal?"

Randy said there hadn't been a mistake, but Sandy still didn't believe him. "There must be some miscommunication," she said. He kept saying it was true: Crystal Perry was dead.

Suddenly, Sandy didn't want to go to work. The Shoe Shop was the absolute last place she wanted to go. Because she knew. She knew if she went to work, this would be real.

She sat down for a minute on her porch. The weathered boards were dewy, and she could feel the moisture through her jeans. Maybe she should just stay home today. But of course, she couldn't. She had to go see, to prove this was all just a big scare. She'd go and Crystal would be there and everything would be just as it always had been.

Sandy got in her car and wound up the dirt road leading to Route 302, pebbles crunching under her tires. She forgot to turn the radio on.

She drove over the Casco line to Naples. She drove over the causeway, Sebago Lake on one side, Brandy Pond on the other, and watched the gray sky gradually lighten over the dark water. Last night's bad weather looked like it would stay.

Crystal was always at her bench, right across the way, when Sandy arrived in the morning. Always. As Sandy drove, she kept picturing Crystal standing there, how she would look up and give her that pretty, slightly crooked smile. She thought about how Crystal's red hair stood out as soon as you walked in. In ten or fifteen minutes, Sandy would arrive at the Shop, she'd walk in the door, and Crystal would be right there, sewing away. If she could just walk in and see her, she would know that Randy was mistaken. If she could just see her.

—

Linda's boyfriend, Mike Douglas, left her house that morning at about five o'clock to make the two-hour drive to his job at Bath Iron Works, where he was a welder who helped build massive warships. He left Linda in bed; she wouldn't have to get up for another hour or so. Mike was near the Bridgton–Naples line when blue lights suddenly filled the cabin of his truck. He pulled over, confused, pretty sure he hadn't done anything wrong. The cop who walked up to his window was a guy he knew, Gary Chadbourne.

"Listen," Gary said. He pulled back a little, cleared his throat. "Listen, Mike, Crystal Perry's . . . been killed. Last night. We need you to tell Linda. We need you both to come up to Crystal's house for questioning."

Mike drove straight back to Linda's house. She was in a deep sleep. She heard him as though he was underwater. "Linda . . ." And then, sharper, cutting through the fog, "Linda. Wake up." His voice was loud, urgent. What the hell could he want? Why was he back already?

He told her, the words feeling false and strange in his mouth.

"What?! What?" she said. She was angry, confused. It hit her all at once, made her feel like she was coming apart. She kept asking Mike questions he couldn't answer. He told her that they had to go to Crystal's, right away, to talk to the police. He helped her get up, get dressed. He walked her to his truck and drove her over.

They parked on the side of the road a short distance from Crystal's house. The scene was something out of a nightmare, out of a movie. A fleet of white police cars and other official-looking vehicles lined the sandy shoulder of the road, and Crystal's little car was eclipsed by a large van parked behind it. Huge lettering across the van's back doors read CRIME SCENE UNIT. Yellow police tape glowed in the deep gray morning fog.

Before Linda could get out of the vehicle, a cop knocked on her window, motioned for her to come with him. They sat in his police cruiser; he told her he just had a few questions. She sat in the front, in the passenger seat. Every few minutes, she nervously glanced over at Crystal's house, about fifty feet away.

The officer was Charles Stevens, another in a long line of cops who scrambled to learn all they could in those early days and weeks. Linda began by telling Stevens that she and Crystal were best friends, that their birthdays were six days apart. In interview after interview, she would make sure that her listener knew they were best friends, that Crystal was her only best friend.

She immediately mentioned Crystal's fiancé, Dennis: his quick, fierce temper. She described a call she'd received a few weeks prior. Crystal was crying and frantic; she sounded a little afraid. She and Dennis had gotten into a terrible fight, a screaming match that ended with him grabbing her arm while punching the steel kitchen door. He flung her away from him, then stormed off, leaving her alone in a dark house.

Linda had insisted on coming over, but at this Crystal calmed down, said she was all right. No need to come over, no need to do anything so drastic. There was a limit to how much she would let Linda help. She just wanted to talk. One of her biggest concerns, she said, was that she couldn't afford to replace things that he broke around her house, and she knew that he couldn't, either. But sitting in the police car, Linda told Stevens how hard Dennis could punch.

"You guys have to look at that door," she said. "The kitchen door — it'll still have knuckle prints in it." Crystal must have been looking right at them while she assured Linda she was all right. "He wasn't the right man for her," Linda added, and this profound understatement seems to reveal a desperate wish: that she had been more forceful when trying to convince Crystal to leave him.

Stevens asked about the last time Linda saw her friend, needed her to tell him the exact day. I imagine her haltingly figuring this out, voice shaking: "Um, it was a Friday, a coupla weeks ago, we went out for drinks. End of the month. Maybe it was Sat — No, no, I went to work that day. Friday . . ."

Stevens would have shifted some papers around on the dash, then opened the car's inner console and pulled out a small calendar. Flipped back to April. "April 29th?"

"Yes. Yes, that was it. April 29th." And the date would stay with her always.

Mike had injured his back that day, but he told Linda to go on out and have a good time. She and Crystal went to the three most popular bars in the area around Bridgton: the lounge of the Laurel Lea inn, on the north end of town, then Tommy's, a dive bar in Naples, just to the south near Casco, then Rick's Café, also in Naples, on the shore of Sebago Lake. It was weekly karaoke night at the Laurel Lea, but they weren't singers. They had one beer and left. Tommy's was too quiet; they didn't stay there long, either. Rick's was more lively, so they stayed awhile. A few people would later report that seeing them there was the last time they saw Crystal alive. One, Wendy Avery, the mother of two close friends of mine, asked her if she was still dating Dennis, and she said that she was trying to end the relationship. It wasn't fair, Crystal said, for her daughter to see her and Dennis argue so viciously.

At the end of that night, the two women went back to Linda's house. Linda told Stevens that they talked mostly about me. Mom told Linda that I was doing very well in school, that she was proud of me. She said the school wanted to advance me two grades the next year, so I would skip seventh. On the last day she was alive, she would send me to school with a sealed note giving them permission to do so. I read most of it on the bus, pressing the plain envelope to the damp, rattling window. Without this small transgression, these police notes, reaching me so many years later, would have been the first I'd heard of it. She knew I'd be excited, was just waiting for the right moment to tell me.

In the ambulance earlier that morning, Officer Kate had kept me talking, casually, asking about whatever came to mind. My heartbeat had been wild and erratic, my mind crowded with thoughts, sifting through recent days like the fodder of dreams. One of the first things I told her was that I would be skipping a grade in school. For years, whenever I thought about this, it would strike me as a shallow, self-congratulatory thing to have brought up, but I forgave my childish bragging because I had been in shock. Now, though, it makes sense. I was already grasping at school as a way forward, a way out.

That final night they saw each other, Mom repeated to Linda what she'd told Wendy: that she was going to break up with Dennis, mostly because of his terrible temper. I imagine them sitting together in Mom's little black car. It's past one o'clock — closing time in Maine — and they don't want to go inside and risk waking Mike. Linda faces the windshield but occasionally turns to watch Crystal's expression in the dim light cast from a single bulb mounted on the garage. She can just see her friend's freckles.

Linda and Mom also talked about my plans to go to college — something few people we knew had done. She knew that leaving Dennis would make this more likely; she knew we both needed peace and stability. She wanted to be strong enough to leave him, to improve our life together, make college and other good things more possible.

Mom and Linda would never see each other again. The next Friday, the weekend before the Wednesday night murder, Linda missed a call. Crystal left an answering machine message, saying only that she wanted to talk.

Linda would never know what Crystal had wanted to talk about, or whether she was in some kind of trouble that Friday night. Whether she needed her. And because Linda didn't call back that week, she never got to speak to her again. I wonder how long she kept that message. If she might even still have the tape.

—

This interview is only a glimpse. In his report of their conversation, Detective Stevens did not paraphrase Linda's tone of voice, her tears or lack of tears, her rage or confusion or helplessness. I can only imagine what she said, and how she said it, based on the shadow of the woman I knew so long ago.

But the "just the facts, ma'am," approach that kept Stevens from noting Linda's emotions in his report is unevenly applied. In the wake of a violent crime, people's deepest hopes and desires become a matter of official concern. Privacy erodes from day one. The end of the interview lays both of them bare:

"Both she and Crystal had talked of committing suicide because they have been very low emotionally in the past. Crystal would never do anything like that because she was always there for Sarah." Linda did not expect to be the one left behind.

On the interview summary, there's nothing written next to "End time," but I imagine the sun coming up, the gray light turning whiter and whiter, the rain backing off.

Occasionally, Linda would see a policeman enter or leave our house through the front door, the one we hardly ever used. They still hadn't told her just how Crystal died.

—

Back over in Casco, Penny, the friend who raced Mom while hand-sewing, had just gotten out of the shower, at about five thirty, when she heard somebody banging on her door. She rushed out to her kitchen to see four police officers standing there under her porch light. When she let them in, they immediately started asking her if anyone disliked her friend Crystal. Besides Chief Bell, there were two state troopers and a county cop, which seemed like a lot of people to question one person. She had trouble answering them clearly without knowing why they were asking. They asked a few more questions and finally she said, "What's going on here?"

Chief Bell told her: Crystal had been killed.

Penny's first thought was for me. The cops assured her that I was with my aunts and my grandmother. They asked about Crystal's ex-husband, Tom, and Penny was still preoccupied with me when she answered: "I *know* Crystal wouldn't want Sarah living with him. Just make a promise, right now, that she won't go there."

They couldn't promise her that, of course. They said something noncommittal, moved on. They asked her question after question. Penny's mind raced as she tried to provide clear answers. Finally, they left. The moment they pulled out of the driveway, Dennis appeared at her door. Penny lived alone. He must have been sitting across the street, she thought, waiting until everybody left.

When Penny told me about that day, I asked, "How did you feel, with him standing in your house?" This was a sideways way of asking her if she thought Dennis — who was an old friend of hers — was capable of murder, and we both knew it. She said, "I didn't know *what* he was gonna say to me. But he just pulled me into a great big hug and asked me what he was gonna do with the rest of his life." Still, she was a nervous wreck with him standing there, showing up so suddenly. "I didn't know if he was the one that told the cops to come to my house, and that's why he followed — I just didn't know. It just seemed like he was sitting somewhere, waiting."

For a while, Dennis had worked at the Shop with Penny and Mom, and, like Linda, Penny was plenty familiar with Dennis's temper, his furious explosions when Mom displeased him or the Shop's machinery defied him. When I asked Penny how often he had these meltdowns, she said, "Maybe once a day . . . maybe three, four times a week — *usually* once a day, y'know." Even though I'd heard about these tantrums by then, I'd expected her to say about once a month. Moments later she said, "He *loved* your mother. They were gonna get married."

Penny estimated that Dennis stayed at her house for about an hour and a half that morning. "He just couldn't pull himself together," she said. "He just wouldn't leave."

Penny didn't bother going to work that day. She didn't take her son to the babysitter's. She stayed in her house and wondered how this could have happened.

But she went back to work the next day, and every time she looked up from sewing, Crystal's bench was empty. It was the strangest, most terrible sight. And it remained empty. It was empty during the ice storm of 1998 and it was empty when her son graduated high school. It was empty as the other benches emptied around the last remaining hand-sewers, as shoe production went overseas and the end of the Shop drew near.

before

Mom and Tom were separated for about a year before divorcing, and it was probably during this time that she met a young man named Dale Morton. The meeting itself was unexceptional — two attractive young people, a dark bar, plenty of beer, a careful drive back to his place — but from that night on they fell into step. He had sandy, light brown hair, kind pale blue eyes, and a bristly mustache. He was tan from fishing and canoeing on quiet lakes. He was laid-back and quick to laugh, a mellow drinker who must have seemed like a safe harbor after Tom's volatile outbursts. Their mutual attraction quickly became love, and right before I started kindergarten, we moved into a tiny house with him, on Route 302 near the southern edge of town.

Dale had suffered a back injury while working construction a few years earlier; he lived on state workers' compensation checks while awaiting a settlement from his former employers. He spent his days gardening and fishing and working on a couple of beat-up Firebirds — one dull brown, one metallic speedboat teal — he kept in front of our house. He taught me the function of a carburetor when I was just a little kid.

Dale took me with him on long walks in the woods, teaching me the names of trees and birds, and he cleared a spot in front of our house for me to plant orange and yellow marigolds. That first house, the first place I have real memories of, was so run-down we called it the Dump. It was brown and squat, with an attached garage that was collapsing in on itself, too dangerous to enter and home to a colony of bats that came swooping out against the pink sky at dusk. I fell asleep every night to the whoosh of cars on Route 302, a few dozen feet away. The house had two tiny bedrooms, a seventies-yellow kitchen, and a bathroom so moldy that the floor bowed even under my weight. In the center was a living room and a woodstove, our only source of heat. Mom constantly warned me not to touch the stove's black iron belly, but when I got a little older I was allowed to feed twists of newspaper into the fire, or dig in the glowing coals with a long, heavy poker.

One morning, soon after we moved in, some commotion woke me up and I shuffled out into the living room to find Dale pulling a snake down from a gap between the ceiling planks. I was too sleepy to be scared; he was like a hero in a dream.

We lived in the Dump for about three years. It was where Mom and Dale enjoyed the early days of their love, and where I spent the happily simple first days of my childhood. For my sixth birthday, Mom and Dale redecorated my bedroom, installing rose-colored carpet and putting up dreamy wallpaper I'd picked out myself: puffy pink clouds with V-shaped birds scattered in the distance, an endless beach sunrise. We kept the curtain of bamboo beads that served as my door; I liked the gentle clicking noises they made when I walked through, and the fact that they let in the sounds of the television in the living room. Every night I fell asleep to the *Cheers* closing credits, or the *M*A*S*H* opening theme song. I had a little TV, too — black-and-white, with a big metal antenna — and all the stuffed animals I wanted. During the day I spent long hours playing school — filling stacks of paper with wavy crayon "writing" — or catching caterpillars in the yard.

Living with Dale allowed Mom to settle in, and finally she bought a little black Ford Tempo after saving up for the down payment. That car was so simple, a small four-door in a basic shape, but I thought it was the coolest thing, with its sunroof and red vinyl interior.

When the Dump felt too cramped, especially in the hot, muggy summer, the three of us would go on long drives, in the Tempo or in whichever Firebird was running. We would go to the beach near Portland, spending long, sunburned hours on the yellow sand. I would bodysurf the waves with Dale and take long walks down the horizon with Mom. Or we'd head to New Hampshire and wind along the mountainous roads of the Kancamagus Highway, stopping occasionally to splash in glacier-cold river waters.

Meanwhile, Tom had gone out west, was roaming from one odd job to another, impossible to track down for weeks at a time. Mom filed for divorce, citing abandonment. The fact that he didn't show up for the hearing only strengthened her case. It's possible she began dating Dale before their official separation, but even Tom admits now that he abandoned her long before he left town.

But around the time I entered first grade, he returned to Bridgton and told my mother that he wanted to start seeing me again. Although legally she had sole custody, she agreed to weekly visits, perhaps feeling, despite her frustration with him, that she needed to give me a chance to get to know my father. Besides, he could be charming, and she might not have had it in her to deny him, despite her desire to sever ties, despite his already spotty record of child support payments.

So once every couple of weeks, Mom would drop me off at Tom's apartment, a damp-smelling place in a large, mustard-yellow building on Lower Main Street, considered the seedy part of Bridgton. The people in those apartments didn't seem to have any privacy, crammed together in clapboard apartment buildings and carved-up old Victorian houses. They did not have marigold gardens.

From Tom's apartment on Lower Main, we'd get into his truck — floorboards littered with coffee cups and oily rags and receipts, window cranks too rusted up for me to operate myself. He'd take me out for ice cream, or to a movie a few towns over. He always moved slowly and spoke quietly; he seemed unsure of what to say. I was seven or eight and had no memory of living with him. We talked about school a lot, because I always did well. It was a happy thing to focus on, an easy thing to talk about with a kid. I didn't notice, then, how much we look alike — same small nose, same round cheeks and square hands. It was years before someone told me that we walk with precisely the same gait, each step ending in a little bounce onto the toes. I still don't know quite what this walk looks like on a man.

Tom once took me shopping at the mall just over the New Hampshire state line. At the Hallmark store, he bought me a stained-glass sun catcher with a horse etched into it. When I showed it to my mother, I knew to downplay my pleasure in this shiny, magical thing. I'd heard her talking about him plenty of times, sitting over coffee with her sisters or on the phone with friends. They described him with words that I knew I wasn't allowed to repeat. But I think she was trying to make it work: after a few visits, she pointed out that he'd be happier if I called him Dad instead of Tom. I complied, embarrassed that I hadn't already known to do this, worried that I had hurt his feelings without meaning to. It wasn't clear what was expected of me, how I was supposed to behave with this man I barely knew.

On another visit, Tom bought me an old swing set and we painted it together. He took me to Sherwin-Williams and I got to pick out the colors. I chose yellow and orange, and we spent a sunny afternoon laughing and slinging paint everywhere in his weedy backyard, finally having a genuinely good time. When I got home, Mom was angry that I had so much paint in my long hair — we had used oil paint, so there was really no way to wash it out. She did her best to strip some of it off with turpentine, but I had sticky yellow and orange strands threaded all over my head for weeks. I got a sinking feeling about Tom every time I saw them, as if I'd been tricked somehow.

Not long after, Tom made another mistake, bigger this time. I had the sense that he'd shown up drunk, or late, or not at all, but I didn't dare ask. Mom sat me down and asked me if it was important to me to continue visiting my father. "Not really," I said. "I don't really know him." It was Dale that I saw daily, that I loved. He was the one who was there when I came home from school. He was the one who caught big fish and made Mom laugh and made the cat do funny voices. Tom was just a big man who smelled like motor oil and seemed to want something from me, but I couldn't figure out what.

I'd like to think Mom didn't show that she was pleased with my answer, but I'm sure I knew there was only one answer to give.

—

Years later, I discovered that Tom hadn't shown up late or drunk. He had moved in with a woman named Teresa, who once tried to attack Mom when she dropped me off for a visit, right after I went inside. Teresa had a reputation for violence, unpredictability, and substance abuse that made Tom's drinking look mild. She had a metal plate in her head from a childhood accident involving her father and a gun, the details of which remained murky. She was from Massachusetts, and it was impossible to tell if the mob connections she bragged about were true. To say the least, she was a tough woman, with big opinions. Sensing that Tom still loved his ex-wife, Teresa disliked my mother intensely from the start.

Although Tom insisted that I would have no contact with Teresa, that was hard to guarantee. Mom wanted to be sure that I was no-where near this potentially dangerous person, or anyone else Teresa might invite over to the apartment — she knew that people determined to live in darkness will always find each other. Mom wanted me to go to college someday; she didn't want me around a bunch of people so defeated by life that they spent most of their time drunk and high. After checking to see if I would miss my father, Mom told Tom that as long as he was living with Teresa, he couldn't see me. He ended up staying with Teresa until a few months after Mom's death. By then it was far too late for us.

Still, I carry Tom's last name, because Mom never got rid of it. When I was about ten, I braced myself and asked her why she had never gone back to her maiden name. She waved a hand dismissively, said that it was just easier, she didn't want to deal with the paperwork and hassle. At the time, I didn't question her explanation, but now it seems incomplete. Although she regularly visited her sisters and was a devoted and helpful daughter, I think she wanted to forget the years when she was a Farnum, years of fear and difficulty, years in which she naively hoped that taking a new name could make things better.

—

After the visits ended, I'd see Tom around town every once in a while. He was known for walking everywhere — his drinking meant he rarely had a license — which made him more visible than other people, who passed one another swiftly, in the relative anonymity of cars. To me, he seemed omnipresent but somehow still unreachable, like a vision in the corner of my eye, like a haunting.

But a few times a year, my father and I would intersect, most often at my grandmother's. Her neighbor Bruce was a contractor and an old friend of Tom's. We'd see them together, getting out of Bruce's work truck, the bed crammed with ladders and two-by-fours. I knew this meant Tom was working "under the table," getting paid in cash. Usually, when a father didn't pay child support, the state could withhold his wages, but Tom officially had none, so we rarely received our twenty-five dollars a week. Mom would stick her little rectangular 110 film camera through the curtains and take pictures to prove that Tom was working, the plastic shutter emitting an angry clack, then send the prints to the relevant state office along with long, angry letters. But it did no good. By the time I was ten, we were on a waiting list with eight thousand other single mothers who had petitioned the state to investigate the deadbeat fathers of their children.

Looking back, I can absolutely understand Mom's rage, and I shared it for a long time. But I wish she could have stepped back from the fight and admitted defeat, if only to have had a bit more peace in those last years.

But then I think of her persistence, her unwillingness to let the injustice of the situation go. Even if she knew that winning was unlikely, fighting was sometimes a way for her to maintain dignity. And I'm glad she struggled for more when others would have given up or settled. It taught me how.

after

After days of lending me jeans and sweaters and even shoes, my aunts asked me to write a list of things I wanted from the house, and to indicate what rooms those things would be in. I assumed they would hand the list over to the police, who would comb the scene and bring us what we asked for. It was only recently that I discovered the police hadn't even accompanied my aunts to the house. By then, they had the keys and permission to go in and take whatever we needed. The Bridgton curious would circle for months, driving by slowly to see what they could see, to hover in the epicenter of the dramatic vibration that enveloped the town. Knowing that someone might see them at the house and call the police, Carol called the station to let them know. She also asked if the house had been cleaned, and the woman on the phone assured her it had.

But the house was not clean. The sisters opened the front door and the sun shone through the kitchen windows onto the smears of blood on the linoleum and carpet. The killer's boot prints shone blue-black with forensic chemicals. Squares of carpet had been cut out by the police and taken for evidence, and there were other blank spots in the mess on the kitchen floor. There were parts taken out of the couch, fluff standing up out of the holes. Splashes on the wall, smears on the phone. Our cat Max's scratching post, on the floor near the kitchen, lay sideways, snapped off at the base. "Oh, God," Gwen said upon entering. "Oh, God." Then they silently got to work. Looking back, she will only say, "I had not expected to see that. I had not expected to see that at all."

While Gwen and Glenice and Carol worked inside the house, Gloria stayed outside and out of sight. Later they discovered that she'd dug up one of the little trees in the yard, roots and all. She wrapped it in a sheet and settled it onto the backseat of her car. She wanted to keep something of her sister's that was still living. The tree is now large enough to be Christmas-tree cheery, although the house it stands by is empty: Gloria died of lung cancer a few years ago. The first to go since Mom, her departure reminds me that the others will only follow.

—

The next day, Gwen brought me some of the items from my list, without mentioning what it had taken to get them. She brought clothes and shoes, my diary, a couple of favorite stuffed animals. But my own belongings seemed strange to me; I had the sensation that the real things were still in the house, and those before me were perfect replicas. My stuffed animals gave me a sudden, surprisingly strong feeling of sorrow, because they brought no comfort. I could see now that they had no value on their own. They had just been vessels for Mom's love, a love now gone.

I can never quite place the day my aunts went back into my house, but it had been long enough that there was no chance of saving the tiny rosebush I had given her for Mother's Day, three days before the murder. It had withered and died with no one to water it. My cat, Max, was okay, though — he had been outside that night, roaming, and had found his way over to the Demeritts, who lived behind that first door I knocked on. They'd started feeding him and agreed to keep him. Grammy couldn't stand cats, and no one was sure where I would be living. I was in so much pain I couldn't bear any more, so I resolved not to feel sad about my kitty — it was enough to know people were taking care of him. And it was better that I was alone. Less complicated.

It was around this time that I thought back to Mom's desire to have another child. In the previous year, she had sometimes asked me what

I thought about having a little brother, and I was always opposed to the idea: I couldn't imagine the noise and mess and diapers and demands on her time. I went to friends' houses and saw them fight bitterly with their siblings, saw them constantly trailed by sticky-fingered morons, and came home and voiced my opposition to this hypothetical pregnancy anytime she hinted at it. Now, as I sat in the spare room at Grammy's, displaced among my displaced things, I pictured a little brother, and my thoughts were tender and sad. I saw myself with a toddler slung on my hip, trudging down that dark road, smoothing his soft, rain-wet hair over his forehead and wondering if I'd be allowed to take him with me, wherever I ended up.

A few nights later, I found a silver pendant of Mom's among the things from the house. The pendant was heart-shaped and shiny, relatively new. I held it in my palm, the thin chain draping through my fingers, and I could see it so clearly as it had been just a few days before, sitting on my mother's breastbone. And it was in that moment that I first felt sadness, a pure sadness that had nothing to do with my being left alone or the terror of what had happened. I finally understood the cosmically sad fact that my mother, this beautiful, kind young woman, would never live again. She would never again car-dance or suntan on the beach or drink coffee or play with her cat or watch TV with her daughter. She would never find the love that she'd so badly wanted and deserved. I finally, for just a moment, felt something for *her,* instead of myself. I felt that, separate from the fact that I'd lost someone, there was now that much less beauty in the world. I called my friend Marie and sobbed. I told her I was holding that necklace — she had seen it before, she knew the one — but I couldn't explain the rest. I cried and shook and could barely speak, and a few years later, Marie told me that phone call was the only time she was ever afraid for me: she could tell that, in that moment, all my strength had left me, and she didn't know if I'd be able to get it back.

before

When I was about eight, Dale's settlement money finally came through from his construction accident and he bought a slate-blue house at the end of Otter Pond Road, named for the small, still body of water just beyond its reach. At the time, it was a sandy, unpopulated lane that turned off 302 just a few hundred feet past the Dump, a little farther from the center of town. It cut through a wide field that in summer hummed with insects and gave off the sharp, dry stench of Queen Anne's lace and black-eyed Susans.

The house had a long, sloping dirt driveway and was set into the earth so that one approached it at basement level and had to walk up a long row of porch steps to reach the front door. It was like climbing up into a sanctuary. Inside, the rooms were spacious, the walls were perfectly white, and the baseboards were clean, pale pine. Only one other family had ever lived there.

Dale cleared and planted a lawn that wrapped around one side of the house to the backyard, preserving the bigger pine trees that broke the space up into little glades. The trees were tall and straight like ships' masts, and the sunlight filtered gently down through their long, shushing needles. On the edge of the lawn he put up a dog run for Bear, our new border collie. Beyond that, a snowmobile trail cut through the thick forest that ran down to the pond. A wide window in the living room framed a triangular slice of still water or gray, opaque ice, depending on the season. In the deepest months of winter, I'd fall asleep to the high whine of snowmobiles whipping through the tree-crowded dark.

On cold, short weekend days, Dale would take me down to the pond for ice fishing and skating. I'd sit on the back of a plastic sled behind the big ice auger and Dale would pull me down the snowy trail, looking back occasionally to make sure I didn't tip over. At the bottom, we came out of the woods and into the dome of white light made by the overcast sky and the milky ice. Once we got out near the middle of the pond, Dale would hoist up the auger — a huge screw, with sturdy handles — and twist it into the ice to make a fishing hole about a foot wide while I laced up my high-ankle figure skates. Then we'd spend a few hours together out in the cold — Dale sitting patiently by the hole on a cushion, sipping a beer in a foam koozie and waiting for a fish to spring the red flag, me gliding tentatively over the ice, watching for other fishing holes. If I skated too far off, Dale would call me back.

Dale and I fished in the summer, too, on Otter Pond and on many other calm lakes and ponds in the area. We would pick up bait early in the morning from a dusty old convenience store filled with outdated candy — Zero bars, Charleston Chews, Necco Wafers. I was about seven when I caught my first fish, a decent-size rainbow trout that Mom caught again in a snapshot filtered through the blue of a softly falling dusk.

In my memory, all those quiet summer days with Dale blend together, creating one long, peaceful afternoon. Beyond the sandy shallows the water was flat and navy blue, darkened by the reeds and granite boulders below. The trees were thick and wild, branches bending over the water's surface to snag my line again and again. Dale was always patient when he took my rod from me to jiggle the hook off a branch, or when he waded in to untangle me from underwater grass. I worked hard for the smooth arc that would land my Snoopy bobber out in the sweet spot between the shallows and the deep, smiling when that *swisssssshh . . . plop* sounded just right. There was almost nothing better than hearing Dale tell me I'd done a good job.

As the years passed, there were occasional reminders that I should call Dale by his name; he didn't want to be "Dad," and I'm sure this had more to do with his discomfort than any deference to Tom. Dale spent many hours watching out for me while Mom was at work, but he insisted she make all the decisions about my upbringing. If, say, I wanted to spend the night at a friend's house, I had to wait until she came home to ask her. And although the Otter Pond place was our home, it was Dale's house: he was the one with the money to buy it.

I didn't mind that Dale wasn't Dad; he was a lot more fun than the grumpy, preoccupied men who lived in some of my friends' houses. The three of us had a common refrain: that Mom and Dale would still be together when he went bald. Dale was muscular and energetic. His hair was barely thinning, just getting a little wispier at the crown of his head. And I knew they were still in love because I'd hear the tidal waves of their waterbed on afternoons when I was supposed to be playing outside. We had plenty of time.

—

One summer afternoon, a day when the moisture in the air hung thick and close, I was reading in my bedroom when I heard the sliding glass door to the deck open and close, the rubber seal letting the air in and out like a breath. Mom came to my room and asked me to follow her outside. We thumped down the steps from the deck to the grass, and I saw the garden that Dale had been making on the steep slope toward the pond, finally finished, salvaged railroad ties holding the earth in, lumpy dirt already getting lighter as the topsoil dried in the sunshine. I pictured the tall corn and the waving pansies he had described to me, and I felt a pure, young pride in this man who belonged to me and my mother.

But it wasn't just the garden they were showing me. Dale held up another surprise: a hexagonal crystal, about an inch across, clasped between his thumb and forefinger. Moist, dark earth clung to it. He had found it in one of the sealed bags of soil he'd bought from the hardware store—not a crystal from a quarry but a glass prism with a hole machined through one of its facets, the kind they sold in the knickknack shop on Main Street. It amazed me that they'd found this shining thing inside a sealed bag of dirt. It seemed like a gift from fate, a little bit of preserved light to prove there would always be magic in whatever they did. Dale gave the crystal to my mother, and she ran a length of fishing line through it and hung it from the rearview mirror of her car.

The crystal stayed suspended there for the rest of Mom's life, catching the sunlight and the gray rain light and the refracted colors of everything we passed on our long drives along back roads and our short trips to the grocery store. When she made a sharp turn and the crystal tapped against the windshield, she'd reach out and catch it, smoothing its anchoring string down to center, calming its motion to keep it from breaking.

But one day when I was ten, I came home from a friend's sleepover and sensed a change, as though that light was suddenly hidden by an overcast sky. I distinctly remember that the air in the house tasted different, felt thin and empty, as though its molecules had compressed themselves into a far corner, making way for something large and hard and sharp. People speak of weighted silences, but this one seemed light and brittle, hanging on to that thin air tenuously. I went to my room and read for a couple of hours, willing our house to fill up once more with talk and warmth. Later that night, Mom and Dale started fighting, a rumbling explosion that broke the tension irrevocably. It was fighting like I had never heard before, hours and hours of loud, angry yelling.

For the next couple of months, the three of us fell into a pattern: they would scream late into the night for two or three days in a row while I cowered in my bedroom. Then a tense hush would fall over us all, until, a week or so later, we would gradually come together in a tentative peace. Then, just when I thought the fighting was over, they would break the post-dinner quiet, and the loud, furious shouting matches would begin again. Often when they fought, I sat on my bed and listened, trying to figure out what had gone wrong, why we weren't happy anymore. How I could fix it.

But as the weeks wore on and the fights continued, I got more and more fed up. I'd play cassette tapes on my little boom box to drown them out, or do my best to read intently, to escape, but I could never entirely ignore them. Once, I ran out into the kitchen and yelled, *"Shut up shut up shut up just stop!"* insanely, shrilly. I had mostly been a quiet, obedient kid. But I'd hit my breaking point, and that should have told them something. They looked at me for a moment, and my mother said, evenly, that it was none of my business, to go back to my room.

Maybe a month after their initial outburst of fury, I was in my room with the door shut when I heard the buildup, the irritated murmur that by then I knew prefaced a fight. A high voice, a low one. An accusation, an insulted rebuttal. I started to sweat. I scurried out to the living room and scooped up my cat, Max, and locked him in my room with me for company and comfort. I also wanted to keep him safe; I hated the idea of him cowering in a corner of the living room while they fought. As the volume increased, I sat on the carpet on my floor, holding Max in my lap. Dale was a thunderstorm, a rolling cloud of rage and threat that I had trouble connecting to the patient friend who took me fishing. He called her "bitch," he called her "cunt." I sort of knew what those words meant. His voice was deeper and louder than I ever could have imagined. She returned his yelling with her own ugly snarls, a furious treble. They were in the kitchen, and their voices rang off the cabinets and the hard linoleum. Someone was opening cabinet doors and banging them shut. I heard a drawer pulled out, and the clean cutlery from dinner clattering into it. It was probably Mom, cleaning up, channeling her frustration and energy into the task at hand, refusing to stop to focus fully on the argument. Years later, I would do this when arguing with my own boyfriend, finding household tasks to barrel through while shouting. I did it to keep us both safe, to keep myself from kicking and throwing.

But it didn't really work with Mom and Dale. Someone threw a plate. Someone punched the wall. The ugly words kept coming. I curled up on my floor, wrapped around my cat, tears dropping into Max's striped fur. Then he wriggled out, scratching my arm, and that little pain let the real one come flooding out. I looked into the mirror while my face screwed up and wrinkled into itself, while my skin bloomed red. I knelt there on the carpet, its nubby texture pressing into my bare knees, and doubled over, pressing my forehead to the floor and sobbing hopelessly.

On this night, I knew I couldn't even try to appeal to them. They were too loud. And the yelling and the banging wasn't just noise; it had gotten inside of me. It made me shake and cry, and I knew that no amount of focused reading could take me away from it. I was beginning to feel that if I didn't do something, I would be poisoned by them. I returned my gaze to the mirror and traced my outline, tried to strengthen it by looking.

I slowly wiped my face, still listening to their shouting, and I got out some paper and a pen. I wrote a letter to our school counselor, a woman I had met only once, a few years earlier, when I was evaluated for speech therapy for my lisp. I hated how she spoke to me, with syrupy familiarity that struck me as annoyingly fake. I was so glad when my mother refused to send me to those speech lessons, worried that I would be shunned, no longer considered one of the "normal" kids. But in the midst of all that fighting, the counselor was the only person I could imagine talking to about any of this.

I can't remember if the house quieted down as I finished the letter or if my mother broke off the fighting to come into my room and tell me to go to bed. But suddenly she was there, standing over me, asking to see what I'd written. A sick feeling swept through me, but I handed the pages over. I can remember only one sentence from that letter, something that had been obvious from their fights: "I think she slept with someone else." It must have been this that made her cry. It must have been this that prompted her to make me promise that I would never, ever write another letter like that, that I wouldn't tell anyone about the fighting. I should have been angry, but instead I felt deflated, looking up at my crying mother as she crumpled up that yellow-lined paper.

—

Soon after that, Mom was gone for a while, perhaps a week, no more than two. Dale told me that she was very sad, and needed to go rest for a while under the care of some doctors. I missed her—this was the longest we were ever apart. But those days with just Dale were wonderfully quiet. He made sure to pay a lot of attention to me, and it was a relief, each evening, to know that there wouldn't be a screaming match to hide from. When Mom returned, she was lighter, happier, more relaxed: she said that at first she hadn't liked being away from home, but after a few days it was wonderful to have nothing to worry about for a little while. The doctors helped, she said, but unfortunately, her insurance wouldn't let her stay any longer. I learned most of this by lingering near the kitchen while she was on the phone with her friends. For years, I would think that she had been hospitalized for depression, but Gwen later told me that Mom had called her crying from what was in fact a drug and alcohol treatment facility. Dale had pressured her to go as a condition of staying together. She'd made a big mistake, getting drunk and sleeping with that other man, and he convinced her she had a problem. This turned out to be untrue, or at least a bit of an exaggeration, but it didn't really matter, because he would end it with her anyway.

—

I've always thought of Mom's night of straying as the primary reason she and Dale broke up. It seemed like everything was perfect until then—all sunny days at the lake, fun nights at the drive-in, and cozy winter afternoons building snowmen in the yard. I had no doubt that she had slept with someone else—it was clear both from what Dale yelled and how she responded—but I didn't know much about how it had happened. As it turns out, she went home with that other man after she and Dale had a terrible fight at the bar, a fight so bitter that he got up from the table and drove off, leaving her. She must have been embarrassed, crying, vulnerable. She was probably also furious. The bar would have been a local one; there were bound to be people there who knew her, but it's no guarantee that any of her actual friends were present. Drunk and alone, twenty-seven years old, she might have concluded that her relationship with Dale was over. I was safe at my grandmother's until morning. She needed a ride home, and it seems a friendly, handsome enough Bridgton guy offered that and more.

I have a photo of Dale from that time. In it he is smiling broadly, lit by a silver lamp clipped to a doorjamb. He is young and handsome, and he's holding a small silver pistol, displayed proudly at an angle. His blue eyes are lit up like a summer lake, and look directly into the lens. Behind him is a screen of familiar, jagged green leaves — the side business that augmented those state checks. I spent hours in the basement with Dale while he trimmed his plants, keeping him company in the closet where he kept them, light spilling out onto the cement floor and walls. He and I placed tiny plastic frogs and turtles on little posts among the leaves, like two old ladies decorating their garden with windmills and gnomes.

I had been thrilled when we got a hot tub — it was so luxurious and exotic. Now I realize it was probably a cover for the sky-high electricity bills produced by Dale's grow lights. My music teacher was scandalized, but suspected nothing, when I gleefully sang the chorus to the Grateful Dead's "Casey Jones" on Favorite Song Day. I must never have mentioned Dale's basement garden to my friends, or asked why they didn't have one — it just didn't cross my mind. Maybe I considered it a private family ritual — the cultivating, the fertilizing and pruning. Even the process of drying and trimming had a cozy, secretive feel to it. For years after, I didn't even think about Dale's plants. It was only when I finally ran across this square, faded snapshot that I could make sense of the forest, and see the plants for what they were. But it's not the drugs that bother me now so much as the gun.

I do remember feeling uneasy when I saw Dale in the kitchen, bent over a large mirror, pulling gel capsules apart and mixing them, counting them, obsessing over them. He never talked to me as he worked on the pills, and this made me suspicious and a little afraid. Now I know that despite her love for Dale, Mom was afraid, too. She kept telling Sandy, "What if he gets caught? I don't want them to come take Sarah. Because I have nothing to do with it." She knew better, though. Even if she intercepted every counselor letter, something was bound to happen. She had to have known her time with Dale was limited.

—

These years later, the moment of Mom and Dale's final parting haunts me. It seems to represent the end of some kind of happiness that she and I could never quite find again, and I'd like to know more about why they couldn't make it through. I can't ask Dale; for a while now he's been a hard man to track down. The truth is, I haven't looked too hard: I'm not sure I'd find the same man. Instead I rely on Mom's friends.

A woman who seems jealous of Mom's beauty and youth says that Dale threw her right out after she cheated on him and sauntered back the next morning, unrepentant.

Another, kinder woman says that Mom just made a stupid mistake, and Dale knew that, but he couldn't forgive her, no matter how hard he tried.

Another says that she was just bored with Dale, wanted him to "get off his ass and get a real job," and for some reason, this explanation hurts me the most.

Her Christian friends don't mention the cheating at all, but focus on the drugs. Mom demanded that Dale stop growing and selling, and he refused, so she turned her back on him to take her child out of that environment.

Most all of this is true.

—

One evening during the months of Mom and Dale's fighting, I stood alone in front of the wide window facing Otter Pond, looking down through the trees. Blue evening light was gathering over the water, and all was quiet. After a moment the silence was broken by a shrill scream threading up through the woods. That first lone call was joined by another, and another, until the air rang with an uneven, warbly chorus. Hysteria bounced among the voices, passed around in a cacophony of urgent cries. Each call vibrated in my limbs, echoed in my thumping blood. In my mind, I saw children down there, playing some game gone terribly wrong, plowing through the shallow water and running for the shore in fear. But there was a frenzied power to the sound that told me it couldn't be children, that the voices weren't just reacting but broadcasting. Long before I learned that it was the mating calls of loons that rang out all over the pond, those sounds reinforced something I already knew: that love can sound like insanity and rage.

after

"By the time you're old," Mom would sometimes say, "they'll have fig-ured out how to make people live forever." Still, she admitted that she didn't think scientists would figure it out in time for her. So she was sure of her own death, but not mine. A fact I had tried not to contem-plate. A world without her seemed impossible, immortality rendered unbearable.

So when my aunts asked me what Mom would have wanted done with her body, I knew, from these roundabout conversations about death. She had never wanted me to linger on the idea of her dying, but she had wanted me to understand that someday, many years later, I would have to go on without her. I told my aunts, firmly, that she wanted to be cremated, not buried. I'd heard her mention it a few times.

Carol went to the funeral home to make the arrangements, and Gwen and Glenice took me to the Flower Pot, on Main Street, to pick out flowers for the service. When we got there, we found several news crews in front of the shop — women with sleek, polished, mid-length hair gripping microphones, men with huge cameras perched on their shoulders, one foot planted in front of the other as though ready to pounce.

"Just ignore them," Gwen said, but her voice shook.

"Stay inside until I come open your door," Glenice said, anger edg-ing her words. I did as I was told, and when I stepped out, I pulled my long curtain of hair to one side and hid behind it. The cameras were trained on us, but they didn't approach. They had probably come intending only to get reactions from people on the street, but at the time I felt hunted. They knew who we were.

The Flower Pot was a tiny, cool space, with baskets of green plants on the floor and flowers lit up within tall glass coolers. Little light reached in from outside, and no more than ten people could have stood in there. It had always seemed like an enchanted spot, and I had visited only on happy occasions — Mom and I buying flowers for Grammy's birthday, Dale bringing me in with him so he could get a rose or two for Mom. Now the woman behind the counter looked at me sympathetically — she, too, knew who I was. I was beginning to understand that everyone in town knew who I was, would always know.

Again I was asked what Mom would have wanted, and again I was relieved to have the answer. She loved peach roses, although only gerbera daisies — not exactly funeral appropriate — were available in peach on such short notice. The adults indulged me and ordered them. In a way, it seemed fitting that the funeral of such a young person would be full of innocent, springtime flowers, and their pale petals would complement her hair. I felt so grown up, speaking on her behalf, carrying out her wishes. I wanted to make her proud by doing everything right, as though she had left me in charge until she returned.

Afterwards, Gwen and Glenice and I went to Grammy's house, where Carol was waiting with a brochure of tombstones. I had less influence here — they selected a pink granite stone shaped like a heart, which I considered too sentimental and pretty. The pink heart was meant for a calmer death, someone who had wasted away with a chronic disease or died of old age, someone who had time to say goodbye. Someone who died in a bed, in their clothes, surrounded by love and eased away with the support of machines. I didn't want everything dressed up and made pretty. If I'd had my choice, the stone would have been hard and dark like the death: an angular chunk of polished black marble, or a tall, sharp obelisk piercing the sky. I hated the idea of an unassuming pink thing sitting in a line with all the other stones — well behaved, decorative. Undistinguished.

And then there was talk of caskets, which confused me. It turned out that cremation did not preclude a viewing. I wanted to protest. Hadn't Mom wanted to be cremated so no one could stare at her dead body? But maybe it had just been about not lying in a box in the ground — she had such intense claustrophobia, I think she could have projected it forward even into death. I felt like Dennis would know the answer, but of course I couldn't ask him. Nor could I ask Tim or Dale or my father. I could not risk speaking to any suspects for any reason.

I didn't know exactly why Mom had wanted to be cremated, so I kept my mouth shut. I remember those around me talking about "saying goodbye," which seemed to me just more gentle sentimentality. I had no interest in seeing her. I wanted to tell these people that seeing her dead wouldn't help. I wanted to tell them how unlikely it was that any mortician could get her into viewing shape. But I held back. I didn't want to horrify them. I was learning that there were silences now, unbridgeable spaces between myself and those around me.

Now, I step carefully into the subject of Mom's funeral, asking Glenice just who made the decision to put Mom's body on view. "That's what you wanted," she says. "You wanted to say goodbye. I didn't want to see her that way — it was terrible. I've never gotten over it." When I protest, sure that I'd wanted Mom cleanly burned rather than revealed, she says, "Well, maybe Wendall decided. I don't really know." This sort of tragic miscommunication would happen again and again over the years, warping our love in ways we couldn't even see.

A few days after that initial cautious foray, I call Glenice again. I press further and discover that she and others viewed Mom's body at the funeral home, before the morticians did their work. I am stunned by this, cannot bear to ask any more about it, still have no idea what purpose this viewing was meant to serve. I think about my conviction in those days that I knew more than they did about everything, that they had been protected from what I had seen. I feel foolish, ungenerous, hard. But then Glenice says, "I didn't want you to see her like that," and I feel the old anger: I already had seen her like that. Why is this so easy for them to forget? Their wishful amnesia may come from a place of love, but it makes me feel terribly alone.

—

The funeral was held four days after the murder, exactly one week after Mother's Day. To say it was sunny is an understatement. The spring day that came to receive such sadness and anger from so many people was flawless. It was bright but not hot. The sky was blue — placidly, perfectly blue, the sort of blue that seems to vibrate and pull you up with its boundless energy. It was an expensive blue, like a chip from an ancient vase, like a jewel full of deep light. I kept looking up at it, to check that it was really there. It was impossible that the beauty of that sky had survived that night.

Gwen and Glenice had not yet made that trip to the house, as it was still an active crime scene. So Gwen lent me a dress — bright and flowing, with large purple flowers and a lace collar. At first I fretted that it wasn't black, but Gwen assured me that wearing black to a funeral was just an old-fashioned custom, not really a strict rule anymore. That I looked pretty.

That morning, I stood in front of Grammy's house, surrounded by the handful of family who had gathered there, and peered at my grandmother as she held a flat little camera like Mom's, feet planted, bent forward at the waist, diligently recording the moment. I wore an uncertain smile, confused about why we were taking a photograph at all. Everyone turned out blurry.

We arrived at the funeral home early, and I went to sit on a bench on the lawn. My friend Vicki soon came and sat with me. I remember talking very fast while watching wind blow through green leaves. "I'm sorry," I told her. "I'm just not really feeling anything at the moment." She did me the kindness of just sitting quietly, nodding occasionally to show she was listening. I felt scary and strange, but she just watched the leaves with me, until Gwen came and walked me inside.

There was time in the beginning for each of us to view the body privately. Gwen and I would go in first, even though I didn't really want to see Mom. Her body had been made into evidence, then was cleaned up and sewn back together, and now we were supposed to say goodbye to her through it — the ritual was absurd, but there was no escaping. I knew I would have to see her during the funeral, knew we'd be front row and center, and I wanted to prepare myself. I did not want to wail in front of a roomful of people.

Gwen and I entered the room, and as I looked down the long row of folding wooden chairs I thought, *There she is.* For the second time, I walked slowly toward her. Beethoven's *Moonlight* Sonata was playing — the adagio sostenuto — each high note like a needle sent to pierce my calm, the low notes drawn out and relentless, dragging me inexorably along like my own stubborn heartbeats. The song would haunt me forever, would stop me cold when I heard it in movies or on elevators, or while trapped on hold with customer service. This song, and the beeping of a phone off the hook, will forever hit me from my blind spot.

Mom didn't look a whole lot like herself, and that made the looking a little easier; it was her and not her. But there was a sadness to her disguise: They had put so much makeup on her face that you could hardly see her freckles. And worse than that, her hair had become thin and threadlike, a cloud of pinkish cotton wool instead of her thick golden-red waves. The anchor of her beauty had been ruined, and her face was a stranger's.

Gwen and I stood beside each other, silent. We made ourselves look, and then we turned around and walked slowly back out to the hall. If we spoke, the words are lost. In my memory we are blank to each other; we are, of all things, embarrassed. There was no way to know what to say or do. We weren't there to say goodbye; she was already gone.

Townspeople and friends and distant relatives soon began to arrive, shuffling slowly through an outer room where we sat to receive them. Mom's death was something that had happened to many people, but I remember being furious that there were people there whom I didn't know, who I suspected didn't really know her, who had come to see the murdered woman. I wanted to protect her. I wanted her all to myself.

My father, Tom, and Dale and Dennis and Tim were all conspicuously missing from the funeral. At the time, I thought that as suspects they'd been banned from attending. So I was glad that none of them came. And anyway, it was easier to cast them all out of my heart, all at once, if I never saw any of them again.

Sitting next to my aunts in the receiving line, I shook hands and thanked people, whether I felt like it or not, and, gradually, the buzzing energy I'd felt out on the lawn with Vicki returned. People handed me cards, and I read some of them as they arrived, got distracted and set others aside for later. It was my classmate Jessica, a girl I wasn't even that close to, who had the misfortune of dissolving me. She walked up to me, not looking uncomfortable like most of the other kids who came, but just terribly sad, and handed me a pale pink card — a simple thing with a picture of fall leaves on the front next to a quotation from Thoreau: "Every blade in the field — every leaf in the forest — lays down its life in its season as beautifully as it was taken up." I read it and then my hand dropped to my side and my spine slumped and I started crying, weeping as I felt the weight of everything coming down. It hadn't even been possible to make her look nice for the coffin she probably had never wanted. Those lovely words were empty; Mom had been robbed of her right to die beautifully.

And how very beautiful my mother had been, less than one hundred hours before.

—

The service itself was a brief blur of sonorous platitudes, the whisper of clothing shifting in seats, the occasional loud sniffle from the back row. There was one long pause during which the pastor, a woman, stopped and gave me an opportunity to get up and read a poem. I was known as a writer and had written a poem just a few weeks earlier for my friend Adrienne, whose mother had been killed in a car accident. But for my own mother, for this, I had no words. The pastor gestured to me with a small smile, but I shook my head. I had nothing.

I sat in front with my aunts, head bowed. I wept quietly but obviously, my shoulders shaking and heaving from the beginning of the ceremony to the end, and I didn't look at that strange, inert version of her once, although a voice in my head kept telling me that I should. And I felt ashamed of both of these failures.

before

During the months of fighting at Dale's, Mom and I moved out of his house and into my grandmother Grace's over and over, spending a week or so at her house until Mom and Dale made up, a week or two back at his house until they broke up again. One night Mom packed a few of our belongings and we got in the car once more, headed across town to Grammy's—the same house where Mom had spent most of her childhood. I had pajamas and some clothes in my pink plastic suitcase, and brought three of my favorite stuffed animals along. I hated being apart from the rest of them, and had started to cry when I saw them looking at me from my bed, even as I tried to tell myself that I should be tough, that their glass eyes were empty. I could barely look at our dog, our two cats. I was ten years old, had not yet learned to brace for disappointment. A week earlier we had moved back into Dale's house, and like all the other times, I had thought we were back for good.

As we entered town and the yellow streetlights spilled over my lap, one after another, I glared out the passenger window. I was furious at my mother for calmly steering us back toward Grammy's house, where it was becoming clearer each time that we were a burden. Finally I burst out, "I don't want to go to Grammy's! Why do we have to do this? Why can't we ever just stay at home?"

Just then, we pulled up to the stoplight at the center of town. It was red. Mom threw the car into park, leaned over, and clamped a hand onto my kneecap. "You should be glad we have somewhere to go!" she said, her voice filling the car. "Do you want to be homeless? Do you want to live on the street?" Her eyes were big, and her voice shook with anger. I was shocked: she rarely ever yelled at me, and she never touched me when she was angry. Was Grammy's really our only option? For a moment I saw us wandering around town like the one homeless person I knew of, a man named Ski, who was always thin and dirty, a shambling drug addict who seemed to take pleasure in scaring kids. I imagined Mom's white Keds dingy and gray, my ankles sticking out of pants I'd outgrown, both of us shivering under tattered wool blankets. The scene was Dickensian, melodramatic, and terrifying. We couldn't bring our cats to Grammy's house, because she didn't like them, but we certainly couldn't have cats if we didn't have a place to live at all. I drifted back into the present. I mumbled, "No. I'm sorry," as tears slid out of my eyes again. Mom's grip on my knee relaxed, and her whole body seemed to slump back into her seat. The light turned green. She put the car into drive. And I got a glimpse of how hard everything was for her.

—

When I was younger, I had spent cozy nights at Grammy's while Mom and Dale went out, once or twice a month. Back then, she was a sweet, smushy grandma whose eccentric habits were endearing. Chief among these was her insistence on proper, antiquated names for things; jeans were "dungarees," her well was always her "artesian well," and her monochrome bedroom wasn't purple — it was "orchid." That bedroom perfectly reflected her obsessive personality: the walls, the bedspread, the sheets, the rugs, the picture frames, the silk flowers — absolutely everything was orchid.

But as I'd grown older, in the year or so before we moved into her house, I'd begun to feel a little differently about Grammy. She was still nice to me, but I'd started to realize that she wasn't always so nice to Mom. Grammy had never learned to drive, so we took her shopping almost every single Friday, picking her up and driving over the state line to the mall and the grocery store in New Hampshire, about thirty minutes away, to avoid paying sales tax. We often went over to Grammy's house so Mom could check on various things, and we never missed a holiday, but still Grammy never seemed to thank Mom or do anything much for her in return. Instead she scrutinized her every decision, and constantly accused her of not doing enough to help. Her other nine children, with the exception of Gwen, visited much less often, but she didn't seem to judge them for it.

When we moved into Grammy's, her critical eye focused even more sharply on Mom. She always made sure her daughter knew what a favor she was doing her by taking her in. It was impossible to relax in her house, a tiny landscape of perfect order and personal rituals that we could neither anticipate nor master. Ray had died a few years before, and Grammy now had total control. Clean brown towels had to be tucked around the couch cushions to protect the upholstery that visitors never got to see or sit on directly. Washcloths had to be folded just so. Mom and I lived in a spare room with a twin bed that had a trundle bed underneath, and even though Grammy didn't have any reason to enter the room during the day, the trundle bed had to be tucked away each morning, a tedious operation that made me feel like we were hiding all evidence of our stay.

We had to pay Grammy rent — although it was less than we would have paid for an apartment. We were allotted one tight corner of the basement for our belongings, and had to keep everything under a plastic tarp so the damp wouldn't ruin our photo albums and clothes, or my toys. We had to leave a lot behind at Dale's house, which left Mom, a twenty-eight-year-old woman with a ten-year-old daughter, without a couch or a bed or a dresser of her own. Gwen and Glenice had worked hard to talk Grammy into letting us stay so that I wouldn't have to switch to a lesser school district. Grammy, Glenice says, didn't like how it looked — that her daughter, an unmarried mother, had moved back home. She didn't want her friends to know. Her friends never came to the house, but Grace wanted everything tidy and exactly the same as before, just in case.

Grammy's unsolicited opinions about Mom were relentless. In the first couple of months, when we were moving back and forth between

Dale's house and hers, she wanted to know why Mom couldn't fix their relationship. Without knowing any of the details, she assumed Mom was at fault, although when it suited her she criticized Dale, and Mom for choosing him in the first place. She always pointed out when she thought Mom's clothes were too "flashy." She asked her how much she spent on groceries and how often she was changing the oil in her car — even though she herself didn't know anything about cars. Whenever Mom was in the house, Grammy constantly hounded her. "Crystal!" she'd yell. "Crystal! Why isn't the water jug in the 'frigerator full?" "Crystal, who turned the heat up — what about the 'lectric bill?" "Crystal! What is that *Dale* doing now, anyway?"

When Grammy started to pick fights, Mom did her best to appease. I'd hear her mumble an explanation or response, see the tension in her shoulders when her mother sent her off on a chore the minute she got home from work. I got home about an hour before she did, and I remember my rushing excitement when Mom came through the door, but too often, Grammy ruined what should have been the best moment of the day. And soon I became a target, too. "My, Sarah sure is getting *husky*," Grammy would remark loudly to my mother. I'd be sitting right there on the other side of the dining table, blushing with anger and thinking about how "husky" was the label for the fat boys' section of the Sears catalog. Grace always knew just where to strike; I so desperately wanted to be thin and graceful, and I cursed Tom's stouter genes for making it so I'd never be as lithe as Mom.

Grammy hated that I read constantly, that I mostly kept to myself; she wanted me to make more friends, be more popular, get out of her house. But as much as her comments hurt me, watching her bully Mom was worse. I couldn't stand seeing my normally outspoken, witty mother bow to this woman, and I realized then that their relationship must have always been like this, that Glenice had been right when she'd once told me that my grandmother had been very different with her daughters than she had been with me.

—

One day during this time, Mom picked me up from school about an hour early — a big surprise, as it meant she had left work. I remember all the other kids staring at me as I collected my books and papers while the school secretary stood by the door, waiting. When I got into the car, I saw that Mom wore a thick patch over her right eye, fashioned from gauze and the familiar white tape that also bandaged her knuckles. Someone's needle had broken in half as they pushed it into a shoe, and a jagged end had come flying across the aisle and hit her eye — a strangely common accident. Sitting there in the passenger seat of her little Tempo, I was very close to her. Her attitude was stormy, and the creepy lump of bandage seemed to stare at me far more intensely than the eye itself could have. She had already been to see a doctor at the hospital less than a mile from my school, so it made sense to pick me up a little early, but she wasn't interested in talking. We barely spoke, her loudest expression her hands tensely gripping the steering wheel. I admit I gazed at her more openly knowing that she couldn't look at me closely while driving. I felt like I was seeing something I shouldn't, something that in that moment she didn't have the energy to hide. I wondered what else there was to see.

—

Mom was working tirelessly to figure out how to get us out of Grammy's and into our own place. She didn't want to rent. She visited a realtor's office again and again, trying to figure out what we could buy and how we could buy it. She was tired of shuffling around, of living in spaces owned by other people — a landlord would just be another man to whom she was beholden. She wanted a home of her own, of our own, a place where she and I could settle peacefully, breathe easily. Something simple and tidy, with trees for privacy and a wide lawn in back where we could sunbathe.

After nine months of Grammy's criticisms and my impatient frustration, Mom secured a government loan for low-income, first-time home buyers. With that and some savings she had scraped together, she purchased a plot of wooded land — two acres, not so big for rural

Maine—out on Route 93, a narrow, paved but unlined road that extended from 302 on the northwestern side of town.

Soon after, she stopped by the realtor's office once more and picked up a catalog of prefabricated homes. As soon as she got back to Grammy's, she pulled me into the little bedroom we shared and handed it to me. I flipped through the glossy pages, which detailed three or four layouts and gave options for the colors and finishes of kitchen counters, bathroom fixtures, vinyl siding, and indoor and outdoor lighting. Every surface of the house represented possibility. After months of research and paperwork, her goal finally seemed within reach.

She took the catalog back from me and opened it to a page near the front. "We'll have this one," she said, pointing at the simplest floor plan, its boundaries detailed in delicate blue ink, the trajectories of its doors etched in perfectly curving lines. We were sitting close together on the twin bed; Grammy was out in the garden.

"This will be my room," she said, pointing at the largest one, which seemed fair, since she was the grown-up. "And this can be yours. We'll put your books and an extra TV in the third one, and a little pullout couch in case Glenice wants to come up and visit, or Gwen and Dave want to stay over." By then I wasn't looking at the blueprint anymore but at her face. She looked more lighthearted than I'd seen her in months, and seeing her happy was as exciting as the prospect of moving into our very own house, a brand-new house that no one else had ever lived in before, where we were in charge.

Mom and I studied the rest of the catalog together, and she asked me what I thought about colors and other options. I felt honored, like the house was as much mine as hers. I desperately wanted to add a bay window—it seemed the girls in the books I read were always sitting in bay windows, gazing out into pastures filled with calmly grazing horses. Of course, that option was too expensive. I had a knack for desperately wanting things we could never afford, which must have alternately frustrated Mom and broken her heart. But a wide picture window came standard with our house, and that seemed fancy enough. We settled on beige carpet for the living room and hallway, so we could use whatever colors we wanted for the curtains and furniture. But we picked fun colors for the bedroom carpets — seafoam green for mine, royal blue for hers, and rose for the spare room. For the exterior, we settled on white siding with black trim, cute and simple. In the next few days, I drew a picture of our house in colored pencils, based on the blue-and-white sketches from the catalog. I added a bright green lawn and a row of stately trees out front. When I showed it to Mom, I could tell she was truly happy. The next day, she went downtown to Renys and bought a frame for it.

—

This should have been a time of victory and the feeling of impending freedom. But just before we left Grammy's, a shadow fell over us that would remain until Mom's death.

One night, Mom went out dancing at Tommy's, the dive bar that she and Linda liked, in Naples. She was a worrier, and she had a lot to worry about, but I think when she danced, she felt truly free. I was happy to see her go, dressed up in rhinestone jeans and a billowing white shirt with wide lapels. I wanted to send her out into whatever fun she could have.

A few hours later, I woke up alone and could hear Mom and Grammy talking in the kitchen. I shuffled down the hall, wanting to give Mom a hug and see if she'd tell me anything about her night. The light was on above the dining room table, low on the dimmer, glowing orange against the night-blackened windows. Grammy's voice was high and quavery, full of that manic energy that always meant trouble. Her back was to me, and when she moved aside I saw that Mom's face wasn't right. Her hair was wild, and a purple bruise spread from her cheek-bone up to her eyebrow. The eye was swollen and not open all the way, her lip split, her nose pushed off-center. The damage was all on one side — she looked half herself, half stranger. Her beautiful white blouse was askew. I stood there, speechless, while Grammy took pictures according to Mom's instructions — one from the front, one from each side. Mom's face was expressionless as she turned at right angles, making sure her mother could get the worst of the damage clearly in the frame. Grammy was shaking, but she complied, quieted down for once. The shutter snap echoed into the late-night silence of the house.

Mom took the camera back and I started to speak.

"What—"

"Sarah, I'm okay. I'll explain later."

Her tone left no room for protest. She slept on the living room couch that night, keeping herself away from me.

It was Teresa, Tom's girlfriend, who had attacked her in the bar. Teresa had somehow become convinced that Mom wanted Tom back, after six years of bitter estrangement. Anyone in town would have known this was a delusion. While Mom had known about Teresa for years, this was the first I'd heard of her; I did not know then that it was her arrival in Tom's life that had halted our visits. Mom described her to me: a tall, rugged brunette who would smile at me but not mean it. She told me to avoid anyone who seemed like they could be Teresa; if I was accidentally rude to someone else, that was okay.

Soon after, Mom had Teresa arrested for assault, those snapshots proving more useful than the ones she took of Tom getting out of Bruce's work truck. A judge later ordered Teresa to pay for Mom's medical bills, incurred the day after the attack, and also put her under a restraining order. This only worsened her anger, as Mom knew it would. But she wasn't going to let Teresa push her around without consequences. And she really could not afford to pay the hospital.

Mom's face healed soon enough, but her nose retained a slight bump from the break. I never got used to that bump; I felt uneasy when I caught it in profile. At the time, I didn't understand why this tiny disfigurement bothered me, but now it's clear. It was Mom's beauty that Teresa hated, that convinced her that Mom could disrupt her relationship with Tom. It was her beauty that she'd attacked so viciously, that she'd tried to stamp out. That bump on Mom's pretty face was a reminder that beauty wasn't only power. It was also danger.

after

I would not see my mother laid in the ground. Her body was turned to fire and ash and pebbled bone with no one watching but a somber technician. I do not know what her urn looked like, but it matters little, because the family buried it. Her ashes weren't scattered on a beach or a mountaintop; the funeral was hard enough. Her remains were buried beneath that pink, heart-shaped stone, cast into the darkness next to her stepfather, Ray, in the North Bridgton cemetery, less than a mile from her mother's house.

Some days later, the police visited her grave and found a single black rose. After all these years, we still don't know who left it, or what they could have meant by it. Black roses are the rarest of all, much more rare than peach ones, so it must have been silk or plastic. I like to think of it as a mourning gesture that accidentally slipped into poor taste, but I can't help but feel like it was meant to be a mockery.

—

At the funeral, Linda had sat in one of the back pews. I had a vague sense that this was wrong, but I wasn't able to speak to her — I was in the receiving line, and then I was ushered to the front, and then it was over, a mass of bodies rising from their seats, scattering to their separate sadnesses. There were other friends of Mom's present, but it was Linda I'd thought of while I sat up front with my aunts. She seemed so alone.

About a week later, I visited her. Gwen drove me over in the afternoon so I could have a break from Grammy's house, its dense air of grief. When I arrived, Linda looked as hollowed out as I felt, entirely drained of her bright energy. Suddenly I could see how the years she had spent baking in the sunshine were aging her. She hugged me briefly, then got us sodas out of the fridge. We settled onto her living room couch and turned on the TV. I'd never sat there before — usually the three of us had perched in the kitchen. It was the first time Linda and I had ever been alone, and the silences between our words were cavernous. We didn't know how to be together without my mother, didn't know what our friendship was supposed to look like. Within moments, the Addams Family movie came on.

Linda said, "Oh, geez. Do you want to watch this?"

"Oh, yeah, it's fine. I heard it's really funny," I said. I was fast settling into the habit of pretending everything was okay, of wanting desperately to behave like a normal person. But the coffins and the animate, severed hand and the pale, waxy faces of the characters were sickening, and we watched the entire movie without laughing.

When it was time to go, Linda hugged me at the door, her eyes shining.

She said, "Keep in touch, kiddo. I love you."

I didn't keep in touch. The awkwardness of that visit, all that pain and silence, remained with me, and life took over. I would move many times in the coming years, sometimes voluntarily, sometimes against my will. There were too many people to keep track of, too many to hold on to. But I carried with me a lead-glass cat that Linda had given Mom for her last birthday, moving it from bookshelf to desk to dresser. I would look at that sweet, simple present and think of Linda: her best friend dead, the killer still free, possibly living in her town. I would picture her in her little tan-and-brown house, and I would write her a letter. But the letters never got sent. I folded them neatly, slid them into envelopes. I left them on my desk to await postage, where they got buried in books and homework.

—

Not long after the funeral, Carol and her husband, also named Carroll, took me to stay with them for a few days in the town of Peru, about fifty miles north of Bridgton. Their house could have been cozy under other circumstances, but now it felt dark and cramped, full of worn carpet and brown furniture and marooned in the woods on a poorly paved road that ended, a few miles away, in a narrow lane that looped around a small pond. Carol and Carroll had only one visible neighbor, an old woman who lived across the road. They were two miles from the center of a twelve-hundred-person town: cemetery, schoolhouse, two-pump gas station, one-truck fire station, and one traffic light flashing red and yellow.

Theirs is a small house, their bedroom in one downstairs corner, then the living room, dining room, kitchen, and a tiny bathroom. Upstairs, two small bedrooms with sloped ceilings, tucked under the roof and surrounded by narrow crawl spaces. At night, I watched television in the living room, which shared a wall with their bedroom, numbly staring at the screen with the volume turned down low so I could catch any unusual sounds around the house: a thud on the porch, a screen door creeping open. The distance between Bridgton and Peru insulated me, helped me talk myself out of my fear a little, but not much. I kept my shoes on. When I slept, I did so on the couch. The bedrooms upstairs were too far away. I wasn't sure I'd be able to hear if someone entered the house, and if someone came up there after me, I'd have no way out.

I lay on the couch and tried to convince myself that whoever the killer was, if he had wanted to kill me, he would have done it already. It was a dark thought that I hoped had the substance to hold me up. But every time the wind chimes on the porch tinkled gently in the dark, I imagined a rough hand brushing them, to terrify me. To let me know what was coming.

Back in Bridgton, the police were monitoring any location that had anything to do with Mom, hoping he would make a mistake, show himself somehow. An officer had sat in a cruiser across the street from the funeral, and cops regularly stopped in at the Shoe Shop. Several times each day, a patrolman drove past Grammy's house to check for anything unusual, and the Bridgton Police called Carol and Carroll every few days to make sure I was okay, to ask if we had seen anything strange. The police were sure the killer was someone Mom knew, and anyone she knew would have known that I was in the house that night. "We had no idea who this guy was," Gwen now says. "We didn't know if he was going to come after you." Everyone around me tried to hide or downplay the same fear that kept me up most of every night, a fear that would remain unresolved for years.

A week passed, with Carol and Carroll letting me stay up on the couch late into the night and acting, during the day, as normally as they could. My aunt asked me few questions, other than whether I wanted milk or soda with dinner, and my uncle spent most of his time at work, hauling trees out of the deep woods and delivering them to the nearby paper mill. I was grateful for their pragmatism, their lack of tears. If Carol went to the grocery store, I went with her, glad for something mundane to do. Sometimes we encountered women she knew, and when they looked at me their faces were complex mixtures of concern and forced cheer, struggling under the fluorescent lights of the produce section.

Gwen was supposed to start a new job the Monday after the funeral, sewing microfleece outdoor gear in a small factory near her house in New Hampshire, not far from Bridgton. She had, at most, two dozen coworkers, and they all knew about her sister's murder; the grapevine rumors were confirmed when they watched the nightly coverage on the Portland news, or even the late-night news out of Boston. Gwen's new boss offered to let her take a few days before she reported for work, but she had to do something, had to distract herself somehow, because every unoccupied hour was torture. She was plagued by thoughts of her sister's last moments, unable to imagine them without feeling sick and panicky. She started the new job promptly on Monday. Her coworkers were quiet and kind. And every night, Dave held her, kept her safe. They hoped each day that the police would catch whoever had done this terrible thing. But the days kept passing.

In a strange confluence of fate, Glenice, too, was slated to start a new job the Monday after the funeral, back home in Boston, where those around her had little reason to pay attention to that late-night news item, just one killing among the many. She arrived that first morning carrying a secret, determined to keep it together. She was overwhelmed by a feeling of helplessness, of not knowing what to do, and the best approach, she felt, was to stick to her routine, make sure her mind stayed busy. Both she and Gwen had learned, growing up, that the best thing to do in difficult times was to plow forward, to keep going.

After a couple of days, Glenice did tell her coworkers about the murder — it must have been unavoidable. Outwardly, they displayed the expected compassion, but really they thought she was lying: that she disliked her new job and had made up a dramatic story as an excuse to quit soon. They only believed her when they saw the story in a newspaper. Years later, a coworker would tell Glenice about conversations in the office back then, when she'd been out of earshot: "We were all freaked out. 'Who is this person we hired? Somebody murdered her sister, that's really *weird*.' We thought maybe you were from some really crazy, *crazy* family. We thought, 'What kind of people are they?'"

As though the murder had happened because of the "kind of people" we were. But as the years passed, Glenice's coworkers got to know her and thought, *Oh, Glenice is okay, she's a normal person, she's one of us. That must have been a real tragedy after all.*

The "kind of people" comment is familiar to me. Just a few months ago I told a seemingly caring, intelligent friend about my mother — not only about her death, but about her life, her search for love. My friend replied, "You get to thinking — with all those men — that she had it coming to her." I no longer speak to this person. I cannot trust anyone whose first response, knowing very little about anything, is to blame my mother for her own death.

And I remember, so clearly, the plague of the word "weird" in those early days. When reporters asked people in town how they felt about the murder, that "weird" always came popping out, and classmates kept telling me how "weird" my life had become. Back then, the inadequacy of the word brought me to furious tears. My mother had been murdered, and all these people had to say was that it was weird? Declare something weird and you don't have to think much more deeply about it. It's a word meant to shut a conversation down, push the scary thing away. I didn't have that luxury. Even silence would have been better: to be struck dumb is to be affected. This is the difference between sympathy and empathy.

—

In those weeks following Mom's death, the rest of the family retreated to their separate corners, did their best to stand up to each suffocating, exhausting day. It was disorienting how similar everything was to how it had been before, how the external world didn't change, didn't reflect the fact that none of them would ever again see their baby sister. They drove the same long roads to work, passed the same tall trees on the edges of the same wide fields, were awakened in the morning by the same diffuse sunlight, and all of it persisted, despite the fact that Crystal would never see any of it again.

They made posters, offering a ten-thousand-dollar reward for any information leading to the identification of the killer, and hung them on telephone poles in three counties. Mom's grainy, xeroxed face smiled out at friends and family and strangers for miles. When the late-spring rains came down and melted the signs, the family made the rounds again, replacing them over and over. They each pledged a portion of their savings to the reward, hoping someone would come forward and take it from them. They talked to friends, wondering aloud what possibly could have happened to end Crystal's life in this way. They called and called the cops, checking for progress that did not materialize. But mostly they went back to work. Made dinner. Watched the news. Did their best.

It turns out that Teresa tore down some of the Bridgton reward posters, but she could not keep the word from spreading, aided as it was by car-crash, train-wreck voyeurism, but also by real community concern. For years, my aunts and uncles would meet strangers who knew all about the pretty young woman who was killed in Bridgton, some of whom would mention it before they did. *Have the police come up with anything?* they'd ask once they knew who they were talking to. *How's her daughter doing?*

—

The law can sometimes be blindingly simple, a blunt instrument that can do more harm than good. After Mom died, legal responsibility for me automatically returned to Tom, the father I barely knew. He had been a suspect for only a fleeting moment, and mostly because police always have to examine the ex-husband. But they quickly disregarded him, even before the lab work came back showing that his DNA failed to match any found in the house. His personality wasn't consistent with the crime, they felt. And he was drinking so heavily then that there was some doubt that he could have physically managed the killing.

I am grateful that my family, on my mother's side, knew better than to let Tom take me, and I am grateful, I admit, that he himself knew better. Sometime that summer, a calm, sober Tom, dressed in the best clothes he could find, traveled to the county courthouse in Portland, a stately building so close to the ocean that the air in the parking lot smells of salt water. There, after a short hearing, my father signed power of attorney over to my aunt Carol, granting her temporary custody on the condition that he would no longer be charged the child support he rarely paid. Carol and my other aunts were relieved; as they understood it, if he had defaulted on his responsibilities, and no other legal arrangements had been made, I could have landed in foster care.

Tom says now that he wanted to take me to live with him, but he knew that he was too unstable; he was "still drinking, of course," and he was still with Teresa, who even he knew was dangerous and unpredictable. Teresa wanted him to bring me home, though. She'd scream at him, "Go get her! You're no kind of man!" She craved the warmth of the spotlight. Wanted to be seen as a hero. Less than four years later, she would abandon her own daughter, and Tom would find himself, finally, the more responsible of two parents. Teresa hardly would have done a good job of caring for the child of a woman she hated.

—

Tom remembers seeing me on the courthouse steps with Carol on the day of the hearing, a hundred or so feet away — that I looked at him with a forlorn expression. "I felt I had just added one more sadness to your burden," he says. He wanted to go to me, to comfort me. But this scene isn't possible; I stayed in the car the entire time. I remember that it was warm outside but I felt safer with the windows rolled up. Surely I was sad, but not about Tom. About him I was angry. He could have made Mom's life so much easier. But now when he tells me the story of that day, I simply nod. It's been a long time. Let him keep his myth.

One of my other aunts recently told me more about that day. "Carroll was standing outside the car, watching," she said. Her voice lowered a step. "He was guarding the car." I'd forgotten this long ago. It makes me wonder what other protective kindnesses I've lost to memory. I had also forgotten that as a condition of signing over guardianship, Tom had demanded to visit me before the hearing. A time and place were agreed upon, but he never showed. I don't remember being upset. And now all I feel is embarrassment — for him or for myself, I'm not entirely sure.

When I think about the day of the hearing, I feel tenderness for that girl in the car, those grief-wrecked sisters. We thought we'd be returning to that courthouse soon, to see Mom's killer stand trial. We had no idea how many years would pass.

before

After nine months of bending under the weight of Grammy's criticisms, pushing and pulling that trundle bed in and out, Mom and I finally moved into our new house out on Route 93. It was one story, and just under a thousand square feet, but it felt like a palace. I remember the feeling of our early days there, an overwhelming sensation of space and light and freedom, a feeling that had as much to do with the newness of the place as with Mom's contagious happiness. She was more relaxed than I had seen her in months. She had finally arrived in a safe, quiet place where she could do as she wanted, where she could create a real home for us. Best of all, against all odds, she owned it; as long as she kept making the payments, no one could take it away from her, no one could make her move out. When she'd paid off her little car, she'd called Gwen excitedly and said, "It's all mine!" Owning a house was almost unimaginable. The doorways and countertops were hers, as were the bathtub and the furnace and the line of trees at the edge of the big backyard. I could finish growing up there without worrying, and then when I went to college, I could come home for holiday breaks. And if I ever needed a place to live after that, she could provide it.

We moved in as soon as we got the keys, before we even had beds, happy to curl up in sleeping bags on the short, dense carpet. Grammy called several times a day for weeks, most often with complaints, but

Mom did her best to hold her at a distance. Sometimes, after she'd been on the phone for a few minutes, I'd realize she was talking to Grammy, and walk to the far side of the room and call, "Mo-om!" so she'd have an excuse to hang up. Usually she waved me off and scowled at me for being rude. But sometimes she gave me a shy grin and told Grammy she had to go.

We got a daybed for me, and gauzy curtains to match my green carpet, casting the room in forest light. My new comforter was printed with tropical leaves and flowers—more grown-up than the Garfield one I'd been using.

Twenty years later, I would stay at my aunt Carol's house, and when I went upstairs to the guest room, I found the bed covered in that tropical blanket. It was a sweet, silent gesture, but its effect on me was complicated. I hadn't slept under that blanket since leaving our house that night. I associated it with fear as much as love. It was one of the few things left of that home, a fantasy we lived out for only a couple of years, and one that proved more vulnerable to danger than we wanted to admit.

Mom loved the house and the quiet that surrounded it, the strident songs of chickadees and the twitterings of swallows and the rat-a-tat ramblings of excitable squirrels broken only occasionally by the ocean-wave sweep of a passing car. But the quiet made her nervous, too. She told Linda she felt a little exposed.

The house had been shipped from the factory in two big Lego pieces, trucked in almost completely built — "stick-built" houses were for rich people or for hippies who built with their own hands. When it arrived, the men in charge of settling it in and snapping it together ripped out all the trees in front to make it easier to maneuver the house pieces onto the lot. When we drove by to see the completed house, the entire front yard was unexpectedly barren. Mom had specifically requested that some trees be left standing so that we would have a screen from the road. When she called to complain, the contractor promised to plant new trees out front for free. What we got was two spruce trees no higher than my hip, planted tight on either side of the front door.

Useless little suburban things. They broke up the stark view, but they certainly wouldn't give any privacy.

I was mad on her behalf about those trees, but not really that concerned. Our house faced a chunk of woods, and most people in Bridgton lived on secluded roads like ours. We had only one neighbor in direct eyesight, and she was an elderly woman. I didn't understand, then, that our isolation made my mother even more anxious.

—

Our house was like a diamond Mom had pulled out of the earth herself and now polished regularly. In my adult life, I have never, ever kept such a clean house. Every room was immaculately clean; Mom polished the counters daily, vacuumed every other day, and scrubbed the entire bathroom every week, leaning deep into the bleach-filled tub, squirting that minty-blue gel under the toilet bowl lip. She was drawing a force field around us, creating a magically calm space, free from chaos. When summer came, I liked to run around barefoot in the thick grass of the backyard, or pick my way through the dense woods further down the gently sloping hill. Afterwards, Mom insisted that I rinse my feet off with the hose on the side of the house. And when people would come over to visit, they'd remove their shoes at the door. It was a widely known fact that if you wanted to visit Crystal in her home, you would do so in your socks. The dirt of the world was not to enter.

Buying a house and land were incredible accomplishments for a single mother with Mom's salary. She made so little that I qualified for free milk at school, although when I noticed this and brought her the paperwork, she spurned it. "You're not a free-milk kid," she said. Looking back, I can see that part of the challenge of buying her own home was swallowing her pride to get that government loan, asking a faceless agency to officially designate us "low-income."

Gwen was so proud of her for buying her own house. "You did it, Crystal! You did it all on your own," she said. "See, you don't need a man. Stay away from the men." But Gwen's outlook wasn't really that different from Mom's. All these years later, she tells me, "I wasn't too thrilled with the location of that house. You were all alone out there in the woods, with those logging trucks driving by. All those men who could see you and your mother out on the lawn."

There are dogs there now. A chain-link fence stands along the border of the front lawn, tracing the old police tape. Gwen tells me that the new owner raises German shepherds, and although I've never seen them there when I've passed, as she speaks I can hear them howling, I can see them rushing the fence, jaws open, coarse fur full of cold winter air. No one's getting into that house now. Unless someone lets them in.

—

We moved into the house in November, but even when early winter hung cold and still over the stripped trees, we took regular walks. Once or twice a week, we would head out on Route 93 toward town, moving along the quiet, forested road until the light started to fail and we turned around and headed back to our warmly lit house, the comforting hum of television. If we started early, we could turn left at the end of the road and walk all the way to the War Memorial, passing Linda's house on the way. Once every few weeks, we would stop in to visit, and each time it felt like a special treat.

Linda didn't have kids of her own, so she invested a lot of attention in me. She always had my latest school picture on her fridge, which she kept stocked with my favorite soda — Orange Crush — so I'd have something to sip while she and Mom drank coffee. She asked me a lot of questions, and seemed delighted by whatever I had to say. Around this time I started making beaded glass jewelry — lizard earrings were my specialty — and each time I made a pair for Mom, I made a pair for Linda, too. One night when Mom dropped me off at Grammy's before going out, I presented her with matching ankle bracelets for the two of them; when Linda saw them, she insisted that they put them on right away and wear them out dancing.

Linda had a lot less responsibility than Mom — in addition to being childless, she'd never married — and could remind her to have fun, to unwind. Just as Linda could borrow motherhood for an afternoon, Mom could pretend that she inhabited Linda's relatively relaxed life. More than once, I pictured the three of us living together, no men around, just a swirl of pop songs and perfume and laughter. I always felt so happy in the carefree aura of their friendship. Linda made Mom laugh, and it was her best laugh, the one where she threw back her head, exposing her pale, narrow throat.

—

By midwinter, it was mostly dark when I got off the school bus around four o'clock, and black night would be coming down as Mom came in the door about half an hour later. Our walks suspended, we watched more television. Once or twice a week, we'd ride to the dusty, brightly lit Viewer's Choice Video, at the bottom of Maine Hill, its angled red roof a reminder of the hot fudge sundaes we'd enjoyed there when I was very small and the building was still a Dairy Queen. We'd wander the aisles and pick out a VHS tape or two, then get dinner down the road at House of Pizza, a tiny place that had been there forever — even today, its counter is still green Formica, its menu board still written in white snap-on letters.

We loved romances, and would fantasize, side by side, about future boyfriends and weddings. We also watched a lot of horror films — *The Shining, The Amityville Horror, Children of the Corn* — staring rapt at the screen and then tiptoeing down the hall to our comfy beds when it was over. Mom let me watch almost anything, certainly some things that were too scary for me, but she loved a good thrill and wouldn't watch alone. Scary things were fun for us back then. She couldn't know that we would end up in a horror of our own, that fear would never again be fun for me.

Mom also read a lot of creepy books; she had a collection of old paperbacks about the Jonestown massacre, the Mansons, Ted Bundy. She banned me from these, but I'd sneak into her room when she was out and peek at the photo inserts. The pictures were ghastly: pools of blood showing black on the black-and-white page, thin girls in courtrooms with hypnotized eyes. Scariest of all were the ones where the bodies had been replaced with pure white, the detail cut out of the negative entirely, the person utterly erased.

Next to the thriller and crime novels stood a Time-Life series on the paranormal, tall, black books filled with mystical, silver-printed pictures. Magic took many forms in our house, from star charts to Mom's tarot deck to the ESP experiments I subjected friends to on the rare nights I hosted sleepovers. I'd beg Mom to do a tarot reading with me or to hold a séance with her Ouija board, but she would always laugh me off. Still, she kept these things on her wicker bookshelf, next to a dusty Bible. She also loved traditional holidays, taking seriously the need to decorate for each; she taped paper cutouts of shamrocks on the windows for Saint Patrick's Day, cherubs holding golden bows for Valentine's. When I got a little older and cast doubt on the existence of Santa, she'd say, "C'mon, you can't believe everything those other kids tell you. You know Santa exists!"

On Halloween, my mother's sense of mystery and happy celebration came together. The first year we lived in our house, I was a pirate and she was a vampire, with a cape and fangs and full face makeup. We followed our annual ritual precisely; Dale had never come with us on Halloween night, so this was one holiday that we didn't have to adapt, that remained perfectly the same even after we left him. We began by driving to Grammy's, and she was happy and nice, vicariously playful. Our next stop was an assisted-living facility, where we walked along the warm corridors, knocking on door after door, collecting candy in my pumpkin-shaped bucket. Here we knew most people would be home, and would be happy for a moment of company. The old people loved us, a couple of girls dressed up silly and out on the town.

After the Home, as we called it, we drove along a few back roads looking for porch lights. "What do you think of this one?" Mom would ask as she slowed in front of a well-kept ranch house. "I don't know," I'd say. "Looks a bit dark. But they might have something fancy!" Sometimes when we knocked and no one came out, we could tell that people were hiding inside. We laughed at them, but Mom's message was clear: Don't grow up to be a jerk with no candy in the house on

Halloween. Don't be the kind of person who won't even come to the door.

—

When that first spring came, Mom and I resumed our walks. We walked more often than we had in early winter, and farther. Every few days, the thawing earth smelled stronger and sweeter, and the hard buds on the trees unfurled, the undersides of ash leaves shimmering in the warm breezes, maple leaves like hands opening to cover the empty spaces of winter. We put up a birdhouse, and a pair of swallows quickly moved in; we named them Sunny and Swifty. We visited Linda more and bought a few pictures to decorate our eggshell walls. Mom got some paints and stencils and started adding a border up by the ceiling in the kitchen: red hearts for love, pineapples for hospitality. The project was way more time-consuming than we'd anticipated; it stretched on and on, over many weekends, Mom taking care to make each shape symmetrical, identical, flawless.

One afternoon, she was standing on a ladder in the sunshine, the thickened air of an early-summer breeze coming through the window at her feet, her red hair wrapped in a bandanna, while I stood down below, holding her paints. She looked at me and smiled. "By the time we're done" — she rolled her eyes a little — "we'll have to move or something!" I laughed; I knew we weren't going anywhere. The painting could stretch on forever, and Mom could make every brushstroke as neat and painstakingly perfect as she wanted. We were home. But as it turned out, she would finish the border just barely in time.

after

My family was relieved to have safely ushered Tom out of the picture, but the question of where I would live next was still unanswered. Gwen and Glenice and Carol talked on the phone at night, often about me. Despite all that had happened, I desperately wanted to get back to Bridgton. I loved my hometown and did not want to lose it; I felt like it was all I had left. I wanted my old-fashioned Main Street, my dusty library, my deep lakes. The drive-in during summer. The long grass in the field by the elementary school.

Grammy was my only relative who lived nearby, and my aunts thought she was too old, at seventy-five, to take care of me. And of course she still didn't drive — a real problem in a place with no public transportation. They may also have been remembering their own childhoods: Grace's neglect, her unpredictability. Two beloved teachers offered to take me in, but my family worried that they were just swept up in the moment, that their kind gesture wouldn't hold for the years and difficulty involved in raising a bereaved adolescent. In the end, my former babysitter, Peggy Martin, called up Carol in Peru and offered to let me live with her and her husband, Fred. I had stayed with them in the mornings before afternoon kindergarten and had seen them occasionally since — Peggy was Grammy's Avon lady. But Peggy told Carol that she was my mother's best friend, that she saw me all the time, that she'd be thrilled to have me.

Gwen would have known that Linda, not Peggy, was Mom's best

friend, and if she'd heard Peggy's claim, she might have found it strange. But Carol was the decision-maker, and she wasn't as close to Mom. At the time, she figured my staying with Peggy and Fred would be a convenient arrangement that would allow me to finish out the school year while she and my other aunts decided what to do. Within two weeks I'd returned to Bridgton and to school, and moved in with them.

Peggy and Fred lived in a single-wide trailer on Lower Main Street near Long Lake. Their home was very close to Plummers Landing, a little beach where I'd spent many summer afternoons with my friend Marie. They had long ago built an extension onto the trailer, a sunken room for watching TV, the floor made from plywood that had never been sanded or covered. I remembered that I would get splinters in my feet when I was a toddler. Back then I'd helped Peggy plant pansies and sweep their tiny porch. When she was den mother to her son Jason's Cub Scout troop, I'd been an honorary scout. I spent many afternoons playing in the sprinkler in their garden — sunbeams making rainbows in the spray — and I remembered sleeping in their daughter Kelly's bed years earlier, head to feet, by the blue glow of the radio that soothed her. Now I was given her former bedroom: she and Jason had since grown up and moved out. As a teenager, Kelly had painted the walls a deep red, and done a sloppy job: there were thick red splashes on the ceiling and on the baseboard radiators.

Fred and Peggy told me I could stay with them until I graduated from Lake Region, the high school that pooled students from Bridgton and three other nearby towns. It was the school that Mom had gone to before she'd gotten married, and that Kelly and Jason had attended. Peggy and I went to a play at the high school, and it was the first time I'd been inside. I thought of Mom walking those same waxed halls, past all those years of golden sports trophies. I was eager to follow her there.

I wanted to stay with my classmates, keep getting good grades, graduate head of my class with my friends and all the peers who I was sure expected me to fail, whose sympathy sometimes seemed like vicarious resignation. I was beginning to fixate on the idea of not "becoming a statistic" — I didn't want to end up sad and broken and have people sigh and shake their heads over me, talk about how my failure was understandable, how I'd been doomed. I decided that graduating high school, the same high school I was destined for all along, would be my first big victory over the killer.

I tried to think about the future, but there was a shadow over every moment, an unrelenting, invisible weight. Certain mundane details had become nightmarish. I avoided mirrors. I could not walk on linoleum barefoot. I hated taking showers, because the rushing of the water blocked my hearing. I'd never seen *Psycho,* but I'd heard of it, had seen posters of cinema's most famous stabbing; I'd stand in the warm water and my mind would keep filling with my own shadowy profile behind the plastic curtain. My ears would take the shower's white noise and create vague sounds of threat until I turned off the water and strained to hear if something was happening in another room of the house. I'd stand there naked and dripping, telling myself over and over that all I'd heard was the rumble of the TV, fighting the urge to jump out and put clothes on, until I could turn the water back on and finish washing. To take baths would have required explanation, because of course only small children took baths every day. And I knew how I would sound. I knew I would sound crazy.

Peggy took me to the hardware store downtown and we picked up a couple of gallons of pale lavender paint to cover the blood-red in my room, the stated reason being to make the room seem bigger. She bought a dresser for my clothes, made of perforated and precut cardboard, white with little purple flowers on it. It came in big, flat sheets, and assembling it was a nice distraction. I liked the idea of building something that would allow me to arrange my possessions neatly, make them orderly and controlled. I insisted that purple was my favorite color, but looking back, I realize that it had been Mom's; my favorite color had been red, sometimes black. I'd begun adopting her tastes and mannerisms without even realizing I was doing it. It was a way to preserve her within me.

Peggy even bought me a little purple parakeet from the mall in New Hampshire, to keep me company. I named him Moonshadow, after a

knickknack shop across the way from the pet store, which had a striking neon sign in purple and pink.

—

I was convinced that the killer was probably hiding in town, and
Lower Main Street seemed a likely place for him. If he was a Bridgton
man, leaving would raise suspicion; it would be wisest for him to go
about his usual routine. And while I was often anxious and afraid, I
was also furious. If he wanted to kill the only witness, he could come
find me, I'd think defiantly. Holding on to my hometown seemed the
only way to salvage anything. To fight back.

When I went into town to run errands with Peggy, I imagined con-
centric lines of dark energy with myself at the center. I hoped to snag
him, to sense his location by the pull of our connection. I hoped some
alarm would go off within me if he was nearby. I would run, but this
time, when I reached safety, I'd be able to tell the police who he was.

I went back to school as soon as I moved in. I tried to hold my head
up, plow forward to the end. We had just a few weeks left of sixth grade
before summer began. I'd been a straight-A student, so my teacher,
Ms. Shane, waived most of my missed assignments. Hers was a merci-
fully indirect kind of care; she didn't push me to talk to her, but she
kept watch over me, tried to make things easier when she could. Of
course, she couldn't cushion me from all social interaction. Suddenly,
kids who had teased me for years wanted to be best friends, gave me
the desserts from their lunches, urged me to cut ahead of them in line,
drew me sympathy cards. Some were genuinely concerned; others
made their offerings with a quavery touch of excitement that I was
beginning to recognize as a desire to get closer to the drama. I was
disgusted by this excitement. It made me angry, but it also made me
afraid, less sure of who was really on my side.

One girl was particularly eager to prove our connection: she told
me that her grandmother lived in the big white house across from ours
— the one that shone like a lighthouse — and had heard me knocking
that night but was too afraid to come to the door. This was later verified as fact. Cheryl Peters had already told me that the family next

door, the third house I'd gone to, had also heard me and not opened the door. "They have two children," she said, matter-of-factly. But I was a child, too. Or at least I had been.

I went to my class for advanced kids one day, normally my favorite period, and a boy told me he had heard that Mom had killed herself. As he spoke, he was flanked by other boys, all nodding eagerly as if to confirm the story. I didn't explain how impossible this was. They were just kids, I thought. They didn't understand.

At recess, I stayed inside with Ms. Shane, or I hid in a bathroom stall, crying as hard as I could, forcing the emotion out of myself all at once so that afterwards I could calm down and put my face back together for the rest of the afternoon's lessons. I don't know what I would have done out on the playground.

Some gestures did manage to reach me, though. Ryan Davis, the kind of boy who thought it was fun to push you off the slide or break something precious that you had brought for show-and-tell, sent me purple irises, having heard they were my favorite. They were the first flowers I ever received from a boy, and I told myself to remember them. Whether or not I liked Ryan didn't matter; the flowers were a sign that life would still have some joy in it, even if I wasn't yet capable of feeling it. Romantic love had not saved Mom, but maybe someday it would save me.

—

School, difficult as it was, proved easier to navigate than living with the Martins, which began with tension and worsened each day. Peggy's voice was always loud, and she talked to me in the same singsong tone she'd used when I was four or five. And she insisted that I "talk about it."

"Sarah, listen," she'd start. "Listen, you *need* to talk about your *muh*-ther. I know you must be going through some very tough feelings, and you need to get those *out* there."

"Um, I don't know what to say," I'd answer, trying to keep my voice soft. Feeling anger start to swell.

"Listen, I'm telling you" — getting louder now — "you have *got* to tell me what is going on! It's not good to keep it all bottled up, okaaayy?"

"Uh-huh," I'd say. "It's just . . . I don't know what to say. What do you want?" And then I'd start to cry, which was, perhaps, what she wanted. "What does it change? I can't . . . I can't . . ."

"Now, now. Just try, okaaayy? Just *do* your *best*."

But it was impossible to share my feelings of grief with Peggy, because most of the time it was impossible to feel them. My sadness was overwhelmed by fear and visceral disgust and rage, rage so consuming and aimless that sometimes I was afraid of myself. I was convinced that the killer's fury had entered me, and would never leave.

I knew that Peggy, my soft-bodied former babysitter, with her houseful of Precious Moments figurines, was not interested in hearing about my rage. She wanted to wipe away the tears of the cute little blond girl she had known. She didn't know what to do with my fear and rage, so she tried to will them to disappear, in favor of a gentler, more manageable sadness. One day, exactly a month after the murder, I woke up and found her and Fred getting ready to go to Portland for the day, leaving me alone in the house. When I begged them to stay or take me with them, Peggy told me I needed to "start getting over it."

I discovered later that Peggy and Fred had first heard about my mother's death on the police scanner they kept in the kitchen as a form of news and entertainment, a common fixture in Maine at that time, before expanded cable access and the internet. Murder is a 10-49. They would have heard the code first, a general location, the police channel heating up, local and state cops tensely broadcasting plans and requests framed in bursts of static. Soon they would have known it was her, it was us. Then Peggy called Carol, told her she was Mom's best friend. She may even have believed it herself at the time. I should not have been living with someone who had first heard about Mom's death by eavesdropping on our town's misfortunes. From the very start, her taking me in seemed more about her feelings than about mine.

But I didn't know about the scanner then. I must have thought that my family had reached out to Peggy, not the other way around. I also didn't know that Carol was paying Peggy to take care of me, out of government survivor benefits written in my name. That the bird and the paint and the cheap cardboard dresser were things I'd bought myself, and that any cash left over went into Peggy's bank account. I also didn't know that the original agreement was open-ended, meant to be temporary, and that Carol had no idea Peggy was promising me that I could stay through high school graduation. Peggy misled my family, and we wouldn't realize the extent of her dishonesty until Carol and I compared notes twenty years later.

—

Peggy kept pushing me to share my feelings of sadness, to talk about Mom. When I didn't want to, or didn't know how, she got angry. I was cold, she thought, but spiky and sarcastic when pushed, a combination that I now understand would earn me disproportionate trouble as the years passed. Another fight culminated in her saying, "We take you in out of the goodness of our hearts, and this is how you thank us?!"

"This" meant, as far as I could tell, withholding my feelings, pushing against her nagging, and spending too much time alone in my room.

"The goodness of your heart?" I spat out. "*Fuck* the goodness of your heart!"

My own heart felt black, dead. I hated being so mean, hearing myself yell and swear. Mom wouldn't have liked it; she would have been disappointed. I could have stayed at Carol's, but I was afraid of her house; it was harder to sleep out in those woods than it was in downtown Bridgton. Besides, it was a different school district; I didn't want to leave my friends, or start anew with only a few weeks left. I would gladly have stayed with Gwen or Glenice, but they weren't offering. I'd decided the goodness of people's hearts was their own business. I hadn't experienced any when I was knocking on those first four doors that night.

But I kept trying. I did my homework, I did my best to be nice to Peggy. I thought, *I only have six years left*. I thought about the gleaming floors of the high school, and college beyond. The police insisted that

Peggy take me to a children's psychologist in Portland, and arranged state funding for the appointments. It was an hour-long drive I quickly grew to dread. The doctor was elderly and she kept a big, smelly dog in her office. She looked to me as if she'd never been through anything more traumatic than someone fixing her coffee wrong, and I had nothing to say to her. That doctor lived in the same place my classmates did: an orderly universe governed by safety and logic. Her fancy degrees didn't change the fact that she was living a childish fiction.

After a few sessions, it was decided that Peggy and I would see the doctor together, to talk through our issues. The grown-ups were ignorant, but they outnumbered me. I felt defenseless but still couldn't give them what they wanted — weepy, submissive grief. I couldn't get anyone to understand that my effort at control was the only thing holding me together. And now I know that I had reason not to trust the doctor, who concluded that my silence was sinister. She told the police that my behavior was a "real mystery" and that I could "very well be somehow involved" in my mother's murder.

—

Grief requires imagination: mental images of the one you've lost, of the world that would have been. At school, I struggled to look and act normal, to get all the solace I could out of the distractions of classwork and tests. I threw myself into straightforward subjects, tasks that had clear, simple answers. I was careful not to think too deeply. I did not write stories. I did not draw pictures. I skipped chorus and music class. On the night Mom was killed, I was halted: imagination became a dangerous place, full of darkness and terror. Creativity would have taken energy I needed to survive. And so I could not write, and I could not remember, and I could hardly mourn, only fear.

Ms. Shane gave me extra worksheets and let me plunge ahead on busywork, or she'd recommend a new book to read while I sat inside with her at recess. Reading I could handle; it was still an escape. She also gently encouraged me to join in with my classmates when I could, and on the last day of sixth grade I finally managed to have fun with my friends. We were all looking forward to the coming year, when we would attend Lake Region Middle School, one town away. It was an exciting transition — we would meet all the kids from the other elementary schools nearby, and we would be one step further on our way to becoming grown-ups. We'd be a warm, familiar group — the Bridgton kids — within an exciting larger one.

There was a moment near the end of the school day when I stood in the empty main hallway of the building, sunlight shining on the tiled floor. I thought about the day of the eclipse, only weeks before, and felt an echo of the happiness and excitement that had come over me then. I was glad to be alive. I was full of love for my friends. I was going to make it through.

—

When I got home to Peggy's, Carol was there, putting all my stuff in black plastic trash bags. They looked like body bags scattered all over the living room.

"Peggy called me," Carol told me, "and said you can't live here anymore. She said she can't take it anymore."

I spent that night on the couch in Peru, listening for footsteps.

before

For a brief time, Mom and I lived in a comfortable little kingdom all our own. We belonged to each other, in a way that's common to only daughters and single mothers, especially when both are young. These years later, I sit with a bag of letters and holiday cards that Mom collected, mostly ones I made her. They are always labeled FROM: SARAH. TO: MOM. I LOVE YOU! XOXOXO! My love for her was so strong that no expression ever seemed enough, prompting me to churn out these soft-leaved stacks of construction paper. Now there is no one left to cherish them but me. Young children are naturally effusive in their love for their mothers, but I had a fierce kind of love for her, an every-marker-in-the-box kind of love. A toddler's sort of clinging that held on straight through to age twelve. Of course, no matter what might have happened, the outer world would have imposed itself; we could never have been everything to each other.

Mom, still a beautiful young woman, also wanted more. Soon her friend Ruth, our old downstairs neighbor, introduced her to a man named Tim. I have a flash memory of Tim kissing my mother in our house, standing between the kitchen and the living room. He was tall and thin and boyish, with thick, dark hair. He wore a button-down shirt, tucked in, and he had beautiful hands. When he kissed her, he placed one long palm on either side of her face, his fingers reaching into the soft hair behind her ears. He held her upturned face gently but firmly, like he was drinking from a bowl of water.

When Mom looked at Tim, I could see that she adored him, couldn't believe her good luck. I had never seen her look at anyone like that before. I had never seen her so vulnerable, and it scared me, especially as I watched how he behaved. In his quiet way, he took and took, but did not give. He came over after sunset; he left with the sunrise. He'd disappear for a couple of weeks, and every day she'd get sadder and sadder, and then he'd call her up again.

They had an intense connection, but he wouldn't commit. As she told her friends, he wouldn't say he loved her, expressly told her that he could not say it. He'd been burned by an ex who had cheated on him. He was attending a community college nearly two hours away, training to be an electrician, and would not make pledges until he'd graduated and gotten a job; it'd be another year at least. Even though she wanted someone who would marry her, perhaps have another child with her, and he clearly didn't want that, she kept right on hoping, and he kept right on coming over.

I could feel her tension and desperation; when she wasn't on a high from Tim's love and attention, she was anxious about keeping it. There were times when they would break up for a week or so and she would curl up, catatonic, on the couch, her thin torso looking bent and collapsed, her legs unshaven for days and days. I knew things were bad when I felt those prickly calves against my arm as she stared blankly at the TV, trying but mostly failing to hide how terrible she felt. But then she'd take Tim back, although he still lived far away, still seemed unwilling to alter his life in any way to make her happier. Each time they got back together, I wanted it to work out, for her sake. But each time, I got a little more frustrated.

Mom wanted Tim, but perhaps even more, she wanted a true partner, and all that a partner ideally provides. Companionship. Increased financial security. Protection. Our house on Route 93 was wonderful — peaceful, neat and tidy, and entirely ours. But the nervousness that she had felt upon moving in never really dissipated. She felt better with a man around.

Even then, I understood that although I was there with her, in a fundamental way she considered herself alone. I was a girl: no matter how much I wanted to make her feel safe, I could not. And so she was keeping an eye out for someone who could.

—

Meanwhile, I was edging into adolescence, pulled along by the tide of my classmates. My best friend in those days was a girl named Marie, with whom I'd been close since second grade. She was less of a nerd than me, more artistic than scholarly, blessed with an angelic drawing ability that I coveted. She wore thick, heavy glasses that shrank her pretty green eyes, her teeth were locked behind a heavy grille of braces, and she had hit puberty embarrassingly early. A lot of kids still called me Heifer; it didn't help that in addition to being chubby, I was the sort of know-it-all, teacher's-pet kid who didn't know when to put her hand down in class. Marie and I were probably the only two girls who were allowed to get spiral perms at that age, which only made us stranger to the other kids. We were a perfect outcast match.

Every month or so, I'd sleep over at Marie's, a big two-story home full of knickknacks and old couches. Her mother liked crafting — there were beads and yarn and wooden cutouts of animals scattered on every horizontal surface. I remember watching MTV at their house one of the first times I slept over; Mom and I never had cable. Marie and I caught our first glimpse of both Madonna and Michael Jackson in the same night, and started to sense how much magic there was out there in the world beyond Maine.

Marie lived in town, not far from Bridgton's central intersection, on a narrow blacktop road that quickly ran into the thick woods down to the Plummers Landing beach. On long summer afternoons, we would barrel down that road together, two of us on one bike, headed to the lake to lay out in the sun on a square, floating dock. Marie would stand on the pedals while I clung to the seat, hiding my fear while we coasted through a steep tunnel of green. She was more independent than I was, and would often dare me to do things that I didn't want my mother to know about. She helped propel me forward, her feet strong on the pedals while I peeked over her shoulder.

Finally I started begging Mom for more independence. Our downtown was compact, easily walkable, and I wanted to do something on my own after school while she was still at work, instead of just going home on the bus, sitting on the couch, and waiting for her. After a few tense discussions, I convinced her to let me walk to the library from school, one day a week.

The Bridgton Library was a two-story redbrick building, Carnegie-era, simple columns holding up a small portico. At night, it was lit by opaque globes on iron columns, like something Gene Kelly would spin around. The children's room was in the basement, a cozy area with brightly colored beanbags, but by then I had graduated to the adult reading upstairs. I liked to roam the shelves, pulling down decaying old books of poetry, titles embossed in gilt letters. I always checked the stamped dates on the circulation card, and was especially attracted to books that hadn't been taken out in a while. I had this idea that every book deserved some attention, so I didn't want to read what everyone else was reading. There was also a delicious, heightened privacy in reading something that apparently no one had touched in fifty years, something that was all mine. I stuck my nose into those books and breathed deeply, ran my fingers over the worn edges of the pages. Stories and poetry were best, but occasionally I latched onto a research interest — sharks, horse breeds, mythology, and finally, just in time for the eclipse, astronomy.

One day, on my walk to the library, I was listening to David Bowie, the ringing guitars and strings of "Starman" pouring out of my headphones and creating a translucent curtain between me and the rest of the world. Just before the library, I had to pass a park bench notorious for loud, smoking teenagers, but that day I felt less nervous than usual, shielded by sound. I skirted the group, but one of them jumped out in front of me just as I was passing. He laughed and started walking backwards, and he opened one side of his long black jacket. Shielded by the coat, his hand held a little plastic bag full of white powder. He kept laughing and laughing, then spun and ran back to his friends.

I knew he'd shown me drugs, or pretended to, but I didn't understand why. To scare the young girl? Or was I not a young girl anymore?

There were others who seemed not to think so, like the man who whistled at me from his truck on the street one day. I turned around quickly to see who he was looking at, but no one else was there. Now, when I ran errands downtown with Mom and men called out, I could not be sure to whom they were calling.

After Mom's death, her friend Ruth told the police that I had been spending a lot of time with friends and leaving Mom alone in the house — that I "had a mind of my own," a damning charge for a child, especially for a girl. In reality, for a preteen, I was spending only the usual amount of time with friends — occasional weekend sleepovers with Marie and a few others; long, gossipy phone calls in the evenings. And every single time I went over to a friend's house, it wrenched my heart. When Mom dropped me off, I'd hug her across the car console while she reminded me to be good. I'd linger there, her soft hair falling on my shoulder, and a dizzy panic would wash over me. Suddenly I'd change my mind — more than anything in the world, I wanted her to take me back home so we could watch a movie together, or lie in the sun in the yard. I did worry about her returning to a lonely house, and felt guilty. But my friend would already be waving from the porch. I knew I was supposed to get out of the car, that once I was inside the house I'd no longer feel like crying. So I'd let go, and slam the door, and run up the driveway. I'd perch for a moment on the stairs and blow a big, stagy kiss, my hand sweeping the air in front of my tight throat.

If I felt responsible for her loneliness, if I could barely leave her for a night, and if even her adult friends thought I had a duty to take care of her, what would my love for her feel like today? I am overwhelmed thinking about the hot, dense feeling of that bond, its intense gravitational force. How would I ever have moved away from her? I imagine daily phone calls, worries about her health, about her boyfriend or husband. *Is she eating enough? Is that fatigue or sadness in her voice?* I imagine my own friends and partners finding it all a bit too intense.

I think about the burden of this love, and am grateful, for a moment, for my freedom. And then guilt flashes in my chest like heat lightning, followed by a rumbling quake of sadness.

—

I was probably actually furthest from my mother when immersed in my interior world, where I lived most fully. As far back as I could remember, reading had been a perfect escape, an alternate universe where none of the problems were mine. When I was upset at home or at school, I could always pull out a book, or know that one was waiting for me in the next quiet moment. In first grade, encouraged by my teacher, I'd started writing stories, and this was even better: I could create whatever escape I wanted, include whichever characters I wanted to spend time with. Writing gave me power. As the school years passed, each teacher encouraged me in my writing, and I remember Mrs. Anderson, in second grade, advising me to keep my maiden name forever, so that when I published books, she and others would know they were mine. The idea that an activity that I loved could bring me recognition outside of my tiny town, my rural, isolated state, was exhilarating.

That first year we lived in the house, my teachers arranged for a boy from Bridgton Academy — the prep school where Mom and Gwen had painted the dorms — to tutor me in creative writing. He didn't provide a whole lot of guidance, but the fact that he was hired just for me gave me extra motivation, and, looking back, I am so touched that my teachers went out of their way to hire him. I spent most of my free time in those days making up stories and scribbling them out on the rough yellow paper that I dragged home by the stack, my hands smelling constantly of wood pulp and friction-hot erasers. Even when Mom and I went to dinner with her friends, I would write, pulling out paper and a clipboard when the adult conversation started to get dull.

Late in fourth grade, one of my poems was selected for a national student anthology: a sign to me that, someday, I would be a real writer. I rushed to show Mom the acceptance letter, but her response was uncharacteristically cold. "They just want you to buy that book," she said. In the moment, I was wounded, surprised — she was so dismissive of this thing that was so important to me, that I imagined building my future around. I'll never know why she reacted like that. She could have just been in a bad mood. She could have been jealous of the time and attention I gave to writing. Or she could have realized, as I slowly would, that we had found the first thing we would not share.

—

It is easy for me to remember moments when Mom and I didn't get along, or when one of us said something cruel, because they stand in such contrast to the rest. I still feel pain or embarrassment or disappointment when I think of fights or misunderstandings we had, most of which occurred in that final year, on the forward edge of adolescence. But I'm glad for these memories. They assure me that my idea of our relationship is accurate, not some rosy thing I constructed after her death.

I remember, so clearly, one Thursday evening. Thursday was *Seinfeld* night — we never missed an episode, and we both loved to talk about the show when we saw her friends or sisters. I knew that other kids my age were watching *Beverly Hills, 90210* in that time slot, and I liked that Mom and I had this instead. It proved we were special, somehow more sophisticated.

On this particular Thursday, I was reading in our spare room. Mom let me read almost anything I wanted, and by then I was mostly interested in adult novels. I read with intensity, dropping into a book as if into a deep, cold lake, my pulse slowed, my hearing muffled. That day I was reading a thick romance that had racy scenes I didn't want her to know about. Mom knocked on the door, then opened it and stuck her head in. "Hey! It's almost time for *Seinfeld*!"

I was irrationally, incredibly frustrated. I sighed like the worst parody of an annoyed teenager. "Uhh, I don't know . . ." I said.

"What?" She frowned a little, looked hurt but mostly confused. "Well, I'll come back and let you know when it starts . . ."

The conversation devolved into an argument. I didn't want to be interrupted, Mom thought I had a tone, and so on. Finally I said, "I don't care about stupid *Seinfeld*! Go watch it yourself!"

I know that pushing away your parents is a natural part of growing up, the first step in becoming your own person. I know this. But if I'd known how soon she would be taken from me, I would never have begun the process of leaving her.

20

after

Over that first summer I spent without her, I occasionally went to Gwen and Dave's for the weekend. Their spare, modern apartment on the second floor, with a front door that opened out to the brightly lit interior hallway of the building, felt safe and separate from the rest of the world. And then one weekend, we watched a white Bronco drive slowly up a Los Angeles highway, a murderer hiding in the back. When we changed the channel, we saw the same shot, the only difference a slight shift in color. Redder. Bluer. Redder. All around the dial. Nicole Brown Simpson died one month and one day after my mother. Her daughter was only eight, but I kept thinking she was twelve. Her neighbor found her, but I kept thinking her daughter had. I remember watching that slow-motion chase intently, hoping O.J. would follow through on his threats to kill himself. He entered my life, however distantly, just when I needed a killer upon which to focus my anger.

For years, I remembered the Bronco chase as occurring the weekend of Mom's funeral. I remembered sitting on Gwen and Dave's couch, puffy-eyed and exhausted, the smell of afternoon coffee filling the room, the sound of the news chopper cutting through the air. But of course on that day, Nicole still had twenty-eight days left to live. In the days and weeks after Mom died, time was a movable thing, a fluid substance that pushed the meaningful and the terrible closer together and crowded out everything else.

—

Months earlier, Mom had bought us tickets to fly that summer to Texas, where my aunt Tootsie was stationed in the Army, having finally returned to the States after eleven years in Germany. Mom and I had flown only once before — years ago, with Dale, to Disney World in Florida. This time, it would've been just the two of us. I can imagine her leaning over me toward the little window, looking at the tops of clouds, so solid-looking, like soft hills you could step right out onto. I think now about how excited she must have been while planning that trip. How she would have already arranged to take time off from work, a rare vacation. She'd never been to the Southwest before. She would have loved all that sunshine, all those pretty pastel colors.

Instead, after a month or so at Carol and Carroll's, I flew alone. I wanted to get far away from supermarket whispers and the six o'clock news, put half a country between me and the killer. When I flew, I did so weighed down with a grocery bag of quarters and nickels, dollar bills and fives: the collected kindness of the surviving Shoe Shop hand-sewers. In Portland, I was surprised when airport security failed to find that bag of shrapnel. Only after I passed through the metal detectors did I realize they had been silent, and I was afraid of this silence — it took the place of some kind of necessary witness. I wondered if it would be permanent.

—

I touched down in the middle of the West Texas desert, tumbleweeds and dust devils greeting me. I came in the night, ferried from the airport in my aunt's minivan, and stumbled into a bed made with crisp blue sheets. I woke to bright sunshine and a big, empty room — bigger and emptier than any I had ever slept in before. I could hear my steps swishing on the carpet, and the faint echo of that sound on the walls, which were textured to resemble half-polished stone. I opened the closet door and discovered a space big enough to step into, lined with shelves and many-leveled bars on which to hang far more clothes than I could imagine owning. Tootsie had left stationery on one of the shelves, personalized with my name and bearing a filigreed border of muted purple and brown. In that closet, there was also a small scorpion.

The house itself was spacious and neat, with very little color. White walls, beige carpet, pale linoleum. The living room held a large brown sectional couch, a coffee table, and an enormous, wall-length shelving unit called a shrunk, imported from Germany. There was a brick fireplace, and ceiling fans turned in every room. There were two bathrooms. To me, these people were rich.

The name of the city, San Angelo, was lovely on my tongue, and just exotic enough. I marveled at the short, crooked mesquite trees, at the prickly pear cacti, the armadillo roadkill. The sky, when blue, burned with blue, and, when overcast, hovered white and flat and endless. Once, while walking through the neighborhood, I came upon the flattened, sun-cured husk of a snake that stretched across both lanes of traffic. From the French doors next to the house's fireplace, I looked out over the dry canal, out into the land, a receding line that beckoned patiently. Nearly every day brought a postcard sunset, violent and multihued and spreading over the wide expanse of sky. I did not miss Maine's close granite hills or its towering pines full of shadows. When I heard that on a still night one could see a single candle flame from a mile away, I knew I'd landed where I belonged, in the abundant clear air of the desert.

—

My first days in Texas were spent quietly — dinners with Tootsie and her husband, Jimmy, and their two young sons, Alan and John; trips to Walmart and the grocery store and the pool on the military base. I met the Eilers, next door: Angela and Katie and their parents, Bill and Donna. Angela was my age and Katie was a couple of years younger. Angela and I played basketball in her driveway, took long walks around the neighborhood just before sunset, and poked fun at each other's strange accents. She came to the base pool with us and taught me to haul myself out of the water and salute the nearest flag when the national anthem played over the loudspeakers at four. When she asked why I was in Texas, I told her my mother had been killed, and she did not ask any more questions.

Before that summer, I had met Tootsie only twice: once when I was a toddler and once earlier that spring, when she had visited Maine on her way to Texas from Germany. I have a picture of her and Mom from the evening she came to see us, the only picture I've ever seen of the pair. They are sitting on the floor in between the living room and the kitchen, in the very spot where Mom would die just weeks later.

Though she hardly knew me, Tootsie soon offered to let me live in her home permanently. I had a few weeks to think about this decision, to observe her closely and weigh my options. I had to decide for sure by August 3. When Tootsie gave me this deadline, she stressed the fact that it was the last day we could cancel my return flight without losing its cash value. I still appreciate how careful and ethical she was when handling my money. But I could have used a little more guidance, an idea of how everyone else felt about this decision. She did not say, "We'd like you to stay." She did not say, "Carol would love to have you in Maine."

Tootsie had earned her nickname in the cradle, when her eldest sister leaned down and saw her there, swaddled up and adorable, "just like a little Tootsie Roll!" This did not predict the tough kid who would beat up her younger siblings, or the intimidating, unfamiliar woman I now found myself with. It would be months before I learned that Army women could keep their hair long, that they weren't forced to wear it in Tootsie's unstyled chop. Her face was thin, with a narrow, pointed nose and slender eyes accentuated with slight crow's-feet. She did not wear makeup or make other attempts to soften her image, and I couldn't understand why she hacked off her red hair, which I saw as her only real source of beauty. She was puzzling to me, seemed almost aggressively unadorned; she was a type of woman that I did not yet understand.

Tootsie's husband, Jimmy, was retired from the Army, a tall, broad man with a slight stoop, originally from Arkansas. He kept his gray hair very neat, and he rarely said a word. Tootsie gave the orders: she was a first sergeant, in charge on base and at home. Their sons, Alan and John, ages five and three, were rambunctious, prone to fighting with each other and full of wild energy. I had spent very little time with younger children and did not know what to do with them, especially Alan, a big, blond, square-headed kid who tended to bait his little brother into fights and misbehavior. John, the gentler of the two, was a thin boy with bright red hair who was pretty quiet when left alone. Sometimes, if I sat in the living room and watched TV, he would come and sit on my lap, and the fact that someone so sweet and innocent wanted to be near me was both terrifying and intensely comforting.

Although Tootsie was welcoming at first, buying me books and new shoes and planning family outings for my benefit, I did get glimpses in those early days of the difficulties that were to come. When I first got to her house, I had the occasional habit of talking in a baby voice. This was probably something I did when talking to the cats or to my little cousins, but I won't rule out that I might have done it at the dinner table, joking around. John had the most adorably garbled toddler speech that I've heard to this day. Whenever he said my name — "Tair-wah!" — I felt a pure shot of pain in my chest, a visceral joy that surprised me every time. One afternoon, Angela was at the house and he said something that came out in a really funny way, and we laughed and repeated it the way he'd said it. He sounded so silly! Tootsie heard us and lashed out: "At least when he talks like a baby, he doesn't do it *to be cute.*" I was mortified; shame burned through me so hot that I wished it would singe a hole in the floor so I could drop out of sight. *How could I have been so stupid,* I thought, *to behave like a child in this house?*

From then on, I tried to hide from Tootsie any emotions she might see as too warm, too sentimental. When the family's two cats died suddenly and terribly, within just a few weeks of each other — one choked on a toy, the other was accidentally crushed under my uncle's foot while he was carrying a large, heavy box — I held in my tears, telling myself that after all I'd been through, I wasn't going to get all soft and weepy over some mere animals.

—

The end of summer approached, and Tootsie moved up my deadline for deciding where to live by several weeks. Emotionally, it would have made the most sense for me to live with Gwen or Glenice. But so much had happened, and I'd lost so much, I didn't have the luxury of wondering why the aunts I loved the most wouldn't take me home with them. This fact loomed like a cocked fist in my peripheral vision; if I didn't turn to look at it, I wouldn't get hit.

These years later, I approach this question very carefully. Glenice says, "Gwen lived so close to Bridgton, and we didn't know who this guy was . . . And my place was too small. I thought about moving. But you and Tootsie seemed to have a lot in common. She had been to college; you were both so bright." I can see that they wanted it to be okay, and that my living at Tootsie's made some sense. They were overwhelmed and grieving. I made my peace with this long ago.

I decided to stay in Texas, even though I wasn't sure if I was an escapee or an explorer. Tootsie was unpredictable, she could be harsh and judgmental, but the house and the land were big and airy and sunny. I wanted everything to be okay, too, and would tell my other aunts very little about how Tootsie behaved. My only other option was to return to Peru, and although Carol and Carroll were kind, I couldn't imagine going back to the dark woods and their isolated little house. Plus, the murder was still all over the news; if I went back to Maine, the kids in my new school would surely know who I was. I couldn't stand the thought of strangers watching me struggle, looking for signs that I would crack. I didn't know that the police and many others were glad that I would not be returning, because with the killer still at large, they were worried about my safety. I didn't know that a collective sigh of relief had followed my departure.

before

Dennis Lorrain could have been the one.

He worked as a laster at the Shoe Shop, running a big machine that drove rough silver tacks through leather, holding the pattern onto a last — a chunk of wood shaped like a foot — to prepare it for sewing. He had to wear a headset to protect his hearing — the machine sounded like a gun going off every time he hit it, all day long. Those tacks were everywhere in the Shop, and when Mom wasn't looking, I'd pull them out of the soft soles of her shoes and push them into mine, my sneakers turned to tap shoes, clicking down the halls at school.

When Dennis started working at the Shop in 1992, he already knew a few of Mom's coworkers there, and he was immediately drawn to their beautiful friend Crystal. She was like nothing he had ever seen; he was mesmerized by her freckles, her thick red hair, her pale blue eyes. He saw in her a feminine softness, a delicate manner that was different from those of the women he knew. He loved her voice, so light and smooth. He couldn't imagine her ever raising that voice. She knew just how to look at him, just how to talk to him. She made him feel special. He couldn't take his eyes off her, was always coming up with excuses to visit her and Penny and their friend Richard at the hand-sewing benches.

Dennis's post at the tacking machine was right in Crystal's line of sight. He was tall and thin, but roped with muscle. His hands were broad and strong, and when he moved them she could see the muscles in his forearms shift under tan skin covered in fine blond hair. His eyes were electric blue, his hair light brown and thick and always charmingly mussed. He wore one tiny gold hoop in his ear. When he turned and smiled at her, he looked like a cat: crinkly eye corners, deep dimples, snaggly eyeteeth just peeking over a full lower lip. He smiled at her a lot. He wore tight jeans and took long strides when he walked toward her bench. You could almost hear him purr.

But he wasn't exactly calm. When the tack machine went awry, as it often did, driving tacks in crookedly or getting jammed, Dennis would turn it off, grab the nearest tool — a heavy wrench, perhaps — and bang on the side of the thing in a fury. He was known for these meltdowns. Mostly, people laughed about it. "Get yourself together, man," they said. He was a nineteen-year-old kid.

He was also married. And Mom was twenty-nine, and still dating Tim. At home, the mood of each day was increasingly colored by Tim's behavior — the red of passion, the blue of distance. She knew he loved her, she told Linda; he just needed more time. He was calm and respectful, he was on his way to a good job, and, at twenty-three, he was bound to grow into an even better guy. She couldn't give up just yet. Tim, with his decent manners and his button-down shirts, stood out from so many others in Bridgton: he wanted financial stability, and peace; he wanted to better himself, to rise above a difficult upbringing, and he seemed to know how to do it.

Mom did her best to keep the mood in our house light, taking me out to movies and on special trips to the art museum in Portland. She cooked dinner at the exact same time every night and surprised me with inexpensive gifts that waited on my bed almost every Friday afternoon — pretty hair ties or new books or rings set with big, colorful glass stones. But I could tell when her heart was limping along. I could feel her tension and desperation, and when she didn't feel much like talking because she was sad over Tim, I missed her terribly. I monitored her closely, tuning in to her half of telephone conversations when she thought I was watching television, more interested in keeping an eye on her and anticipating changes in our life than in respecting her privacy. As soon as I became aware of Dennis, I hoped he would push Tim out.

I had no idea Dennis was married, though. I didn't find out until years after Mom was gone. His wife, Janet, was a little older than Mom — in her early thirties. Near the end of his first year at the Shop, Janet cheated on him with one of his coworkers, a man he'd often taken smoke breaks with. This turned up the volume on their already intense fighting. She wasn't a small woman. She was loud, and he once said she punched him in the face a couple of times. Dennis claimed never to have raised a hand to her. He claimed she was the only one cheating.

When Dennis went to work, he relished Crystal's gentle affection, her intelligent conversation. Around this time, when we'd been living in our new house for almost a year, their flirtation became more obvious. Dennis had previously been insulated from the soap opera of liaisons swirling around the Shop — his machine was too loud for him to hear much, and he was, in his words, "country, a farm kid." Now he took his place center stage in the drama — literally. He and Crystal worked right in the middle of the huge building; people observed them from all angles. They were two of the most beautiful people in the Shop.

Dennis didn't live on a farm, exactly; he lived two towns away in Casco, on Tenney Hill, a high, narrow road with dirt lanes that branched off and slid down either side of a ridge. There, he was mostly surrounded by other Lorrains — cousins and aunts and uncles in small houses with rocky, shared backyards. Tenney Hill was also home to a couple of well-known coke dealers, older men you didn't mess with. Crystal, a young homeowner who worked hard for her child, struck him as rare. It seems he was drawn to her for many of the same reasons she was drawn to Tim.

At the time, Crystal really had no intention of dating this very young man, marriage or no, but she couldn't stop herself from talking to him. He showered her with attention, and she had fun gently teasing him in return. As Christmas approached, they joked about mistletoe.

Dennis was still living with Janet then and, by his account, trying to make the best of the shaky marriage. She had two daughters from a previous relationship, whom Dennis said he loved as his own. He wasn't ready to give up just yet. But on Christmas Eve, Janet sent him out for something—a lightbulb, maybe, or milk. The grocery stores were all closed, so he went to Rite Aid. He grabbed the milk and strode up to the counter. Just as he was taking out his wallet, he looked up and there she was: Crystal, with her daughter in tow. He knew just what to do. He grabbed a sprig of plastic mistletoe from next to the register, threw down a ten, and, with a parting nod to the cashier, bounded up to her.

"Hey, can I talk to you for a minute?"

She smiled. She may have rolled her eyes a little. "Yeah, okay. Sarah, go pick out a card, I'll be right back."

They stepped outside into the frigid air. As the glass doors closed behind them with a little suction sound, shutting out the Christmas music and leaving them in the quiet dusk, Dennis held the mistletoe aloft. "Can I have that kiss now?" he said.

And he leaned down and kissed her. And she kissed back, and back, and back.

The next day, Dennis celebrated Christmas at home with Janet and her kids, and Tim came to our house for Christmas after spending the night at his parents'. Gwen and Dave came, and we all opened presents and ate ham and laughed in the glow of the tree. Mom had fun; she was proud to host her sister in her home, happy that her boyfriend and her family were together. But there was a cold undercurrent beneath the warmth of the day. If she and Tim didn't last, she thought, next year would be ruined by the pain of missing him, of remembering him here amid the tinsel and the holiday music.

The glow from that drugstore evening carried Dennis all through the holidays. In the meantime, he and Crystal continued their dance at work. They didn't repeat the impulsive kiss, but they did go to the Black Horse Tavern on Friday afternoons when they got out early. They'd drink coffee for a couple of hours, until it was time for Mom to pick me up from school, just across the street.

Soon Dennis started coming around to our house with Mom's friend Richard once a week to watch *Seinfeld* with us. Richard—a jokey man I called Hairball because of his wild mane and full beard—had always been very kind to Mom, and it was clear that he liked Dennis better than Tim. I took this endorsement seriously, and Dennis was smart about making his case to me. He talked to me, asked me about my interests. He seemed intelligent and didn't patronize me like some adults did. I also thought he was very good-looking, with those long dimples and cute teeth. He was more striking than Tim, it's true, but he was also only eight years older than me. I called him Denny.

Following some depressing natural law, Mom's car had been giving her trouble since the moment she'd paid it off months earlier, and Denny was good with cars. What's more, he was around—she couldn't always afford a garage, and when the Tempo wouldn't start, she had little choice but to call Denny, who always came and could always get it running again. In my diary at the time, I wrote, "Tim just comes and has sex with Mom and then goes back to college. But Denny does things for her, he fixes her car. He fixed everything he found broken around the house. Why won't she date Denny?"

Denny seemed to enliven my mother from the start. I knew, the moment I met him, that first night when he came over with Richard, that my mother was lying when she said they were "just friends." Of course, she may not have been honest with herself about her feelings, either. Denny was full of barely contained energy, and he poured that energy into my mother just by looking at her. I knew he could tempt her away from Tim and his constant disappointments. I was tired of her overwhelming sadness when things with Tim weren't going well, sadness that came upon her like a wave I was powerless to block, a force that drowned us both.

Finally, Dennis walked out on a fight with his wife and never went back. They filed for divorce, and the proceedings moved along swiftly. He went to the courthouse downtown to finalize the divorce during a lunch break from work. When he returned and parked, Crystal had just gotten back from lunch, too, and they walked into the Shop together. As they approached their stations, he was walking ahead of her, and she said, "Hey!"

He turned around, raised an eyebrow, and said, "Yeah?"

And she stepped forward, grabbed his shirt collar, and planted a huge kiss on him, right in front of everybody. People stopped what they were doing to stare.

"There," she said. "Now you can go back to work."

Later, Dennis said of that moment, "It wasn't the day I put a tack through my finger, but it could've been. She just blew me away. All the time, really."

after

Not long after I arrived in Texas, Tootsie took the whole family on a trip to the Six Flags park just outside San Antonio, about three hours away. We stayed at a Motel 6 that night rather than drive home. When she announced that it was time to change for bed, the boys started stripping off their clothes, flinging their tiny shirts to the floor and hop-wiggling out of their pants. I gathered my pajamas from my bag and then stood there, hesitating. "It's okay," Tootsie said. "We're all family." But I hardly knew these people, did not feel like one of them. My uncle Jimmy was right there, and though of course he wasn't looking at me, I wasn't about to change with him in the room. I think Tootsie simply forgot what it was like to be twelve years old, considered me too young to have developed a sense of modesty. I mumbled something about having to go to the bathroom anyway and changed in there, behind the shut and locked door. That moment was when I realized that I was wary of all men, not just those on the official suspect list.

I had a deep conviction that anyone could do anything — knowing that people can kill is far different from seeing the proof. I had learned that humanity itself did not have limits. I knew the killer was a man because of the grunt I'd heard that night; so I knew that men, especially, were capable of anything. That night in the hotel, it wasn't so much that I thought my uncle might hurt me. It was that I didn't want to be vulnerable near that violent energy, however deeply buried it might be, however well checked. I thought it was possible that his shyness was a product of shame, or a subconscious disguise. I was sure there was no such thing as an entirely benevolent man.

In pictures from those first months in Texas, I am a specter: too thin, with bland, utilitarian clothes and haunted eyes. I got thinner and thinner, a project that was as much about denying myself as it was about looking prettier. The blue of my irises had darkened, nearly merging with my pupils, as though the blackness that threatened to fill my head had started showing itself to others, too. The dull clothes were my choice: grays and pale blues, loose-fitting jeans. I had one simple black shirt, my most striking piece. I remember a Walmart shopping trip with Tootsie, shuffling along next to the plastic cart while she pushed, gently touching the soft cotton clothing and occasionally adding a piece to the small pile I would take into the dressing room. As I dropped in a pale blue T-shirt, she suddenly barked at me: "Why don't you ever wear anything that's a real color?" I stammered something; I don't remember what. What I couldn't and wouldn't tell her was that I was looking for ways to disappear.

Although I feared Maine and did not want to return, I still considered it home, and would sometimes think wistfully of the tall pines that I'd left, forgetting that they cast thick, dark shadows that evoked my fear. So I did keep in touch with a few friends. Marie was faithful for years. She sent long letters adorned with beautiful drawings, and cards she picked out from the pharmacy where we used to roam the aisles wasting time, surreptitiously trying on funky nail polish while giving the tourists our best dirty looks. She sent me gossip about our classmates, clearly trying to keep her letters light and cheerful. She asked when I could visit, and we talked on the phone as often as we were allowed. Sifting through her cards and letters now, I see that many of them have disclaimers: "Warning: This note may be mushy or embarrassing!" I am saddened that she felt the need to temper her love for me, the best friend who would never come back to stay. But I was, in a way, put off by Marie's friendship. As soon as I perceived need, I became less likely to write back. Connection to Bridgton had to be on my terms. It was risky. My former home had become a place I could barely look at on a map.

—

As strict as she could be, Tootsie didn't impose a bedtime in the summer, at least not for me. I passed endless hours of insomnia in the same tight grip of panic I'd felt at Carol's, telling myself over and over how far away I was from Maine, trying to believe that meant I was safe. I had a TV in my room — the first time I'd ever had cable — and I watched late into the night, Letterman followed by black-and-white sitcoms followed by hypnotic hours of infomercials, perfectly manicured hands turning and turning sparkly stones against the light, confident men selling gadgets to fix every conceivable problem. I did my best to reach a kind of flatlined numbness. But when I slept, I kept the lights on. And my white Keds.

I always thought about Dennis on those long nights, although I wouldn't have been able to say whether I thought he had killed Mom. I had no proof, I had no specific reason to think so, but his image kept stepping into the blank space in my head where the killer would have resided. I kept an eye out for him, sure that there was no legitimate reason for him to visit Texas — therefore, if I saw him, he was probably coming after me. His face would appear suddenly in a crowd, then clarify into the bland face of a stranger. The world is full of tallish, long-limbed young men with light brown hair. I shook in the grocery store, in the mall, turned away from my friends to hide my suddenly pale face.

—

For reasons neither could remember, Glenice hadn't spoken to Tootsie in twenty years — not one word. Now that I was in Texas, she made sure to call the house every few weeks, and sometimes, before she talked to me, she would ask her sister how I was doing. These years later, Glenice says that early on in my time there, Tootsie complained that I was acting strangely. "She always keeps her blinds closed," Tootsie said. "And I'll get up in the middle of the night and go to her room, and find her in the closet. Sitting in her closet, in the dark! She's acting really weird. Creepy."

Glenice says she shot back: "What do you expect? She probably feels safe in there. You're the psychologist; you went to school. You should be able to handle someone in distress."

Those long nights of brightly lit anxiety still live within me: I remember flipping the blinds up and down and then up again, debating which way made me less visible to the outside. But I don't remember sitting alone in the dark in the closet. The idea is terrifying. And it's disheartening to think that of all the fear I remember from those days, there were apparently hours of panic that were even worse, moments beyond my control or comprehension. I think about Tootsie roaming the house at night, unable to sleep. About her quietly opening my door to check on me and finding my bed empty. I think about cowering in the closet, in the grip of an unthinking animal fear, only to have the door suddenly pulled open to more darkness. And a woman who felt more contempt for me than compassion.

Of course, Tootsie could have lied, or said something that Glenice later embellished without meaning to. It's more likely that I was sitting in the closet with the light on, hiding from Tootsie the fact that I hadn't yet gone to bed. But still it makes sense that Glenice remembers a story of me alone, isolated, trapped in the dark.

—

The night before I started seventh grade in San Angelo, Tootsie came into my room about twenty minutes before bedtime. I was sitting and watching television, or reading—I can't remember. But I do remember how she loomed over me, or seemed to, how she took up all the space even in that large white room. I had laid out everything for the next morning on a blue trunk I used as a bedside table. It was all very neat, very controlled: jeans and T-shirt folded, underwear and bra tucked out of sight underneath. Socks balled up in the shoes I planned to wear, which were at perfect right angles to the trunk. I also had accessories arranged and ready: my watch and the thin silver chain necklace I'd found among Mom's things. I was nervous about the next day, particularly about waking up early and getting ready in time to catch the bus. I hadn't slept a full night in weeks. I didn't want to leave anything to chance.

I was also twelve, and starting junior high, so I wanted to look as pretty as possible the next day. If I attracted a boyfriend, I thought, maybe he would distract me from everything else, the way Angela was distracted by the very idea of dating. My little grid of accessories thus included purple eye shadow. It was a pale, frosty shade that my mother had given me after I'd begged, and then taught me to dust almost invisibly on my lids.

As Tootsie's sharp eyes surveyed the items on the trunk, I saw my compulsive precision through her eyes and immediately flushed with embarrassment. I was still awash in this feeling when she reached down, picked up the eye shadow, and said in a low, derisive voice, "You don't want to look like a whore, do you?"

My response was nothing worth remembering, a passive, shocked mumble. Tootsie put the eye shadow back down, but the message was clear: I was not to wear it. It was useless now, a shameful, secret thing. I remembered then how strange Tootsie had seemed to me that night she visited me and Mom in Maine, strong and direct and plain. She'd worn red cotton sweatpants, tapered at the ankles above chunky white sneakers, topped by a gray T-shirt that said ARMY in block print across the chest. The shirt was tucked into the waistband of her pants, and the bright white drawstring was tamed in a tight knot near the fabric. It was hard to believe that she and my mother were sisters, and I watched carefully when they laughed together, Mom's melodic giggles dancing over Tootsie's masculine rumble. That night in Texas, I sensed that Tootsie's comment was a condemnation of the kind of woman my mother had been, someone foolish enough to care about looking pretty, someone girly. But I couldn't stand to think about this, to face that living in a house where Mom's form of beauty wasn't valued was to begin the process of her erasure.

But that night Tootsie insisted I sleep with the light off, leaving no room for argument. And so I gradually relearned that darkness could be a comfort, too.

—

Tootsie's moods were volatile, her desires a moving target I could rarely hit. She had very rigid ideas about how a person should behave, ideas she usually shared with me only after I had done something to displease her. It is hard, now, to recall examples of what could make her angry; the system of rules was constantly changing, the triggers unpredictable and confusing. I was a relatively good preteen and teenager: I dressed neatly, studied, did not smoke or drink or stay out late. But the smallest infraction could make her explode, yelling until her face turned red, shaking and waving her finger inches from my eyes. I wasn't used to this; this was the sort of fighting I'd only observed, or heard through my bedroom wall. Worse than the yelling, though, was the way she could coldly intone just one sentence and convince me that I wasn't just misbehaving, but inherently bad — silly and ungrateful and weak.

Above all else, Tootsie despised weakness. As the family story goes, she was always hardest on Gwen, her infuriatingly sensitive, quiet, slow little sister. She often repeated her mantra that those who couldn't run a mile, regardless of the reason, were useless. She believed only the strong deserved to live. I wanted to be one of the strong.

Tootsie would go on two-mile runs, timing herself to ensure that she made it in twenty minutes or less, ever mindful, at nearly forty, of keeping up with her eighteen-year-old recruits. She would return red and sweaty from the ninety-degree heat, startlingly soon after her departure, and I was always struck by the idea that if it took that much exertion for her, such a run would be impossible for me. My thinness was from not eating, not from exercise. I had knobby elbows and indented temples; I got winded easily. It occurs to me now that Tootsie could have taken me with her on slower runs, shared training tips and built me up. She could have taught me that strength can be earned and quietly built, not just summoned with a desperate, all-or-nothing force of will.

Tootsie's training as an Army recruiter had taught her to identify weakness and manipulate it, a skill I too often fell prey to. Sometimes when I really did break the rules, she would be shockingly lenient. This disturbed me more than anything else; after enough explosions and judgments, those calm and reasonable responses started to feel like a ploy. I felt real physical fear at the idea of displeasing her. Each time I came home from seeing Angela next door, I scanned the atmosphere of the house, tasted the air to see if Tootsie was wound up, my body tense, my heart speeding until I reached the safety of my room.

Homework was my best excuse to hole up, since the only thing Tootsie and I really agreed on was that I could always work harder. I'd bring home report cards filled with 97s and 98s and Tootsie would ask why, if it was all so easy for me, those grades weren't 100s. If this comment was meant to be a joke, it was impossible at the time to differentiate it from her often outlandish criticism. I did not allow myself to think about how my mother would never have said such a thing, and tried not to dwell on my conviction that Tootsie wouldn't speak to her sons that way. I told myself that I needed a place to live, period. And I was not interested in replacing my mother.

—

About four months into my life in Texas, I came home from school on a Wednesday afternoon, exhausted from sleep deprivation and the effort of speaking and moving and smiling like a normal teenager, from answering questions in class and listening to my classmates talk endlessly about crushes and movies and unfair parents and skateboards and their hair. I set my heavy backpack down in my room and noticed the silence in the carpeted house. I walked the length of it to the garage, which I found blissfully empty.

I walked back through the house toward the bathroom, pausing for a moment to stare out the glass doors. My eyes traced the flat line of the canal along the horizon, just above the shallow-pitched roofs of the neighbors' houses. The sky was white with heat, even this late in the year.

Tootsie and Jimmy timed my showers to keep me from running the water bill up too high. I had gotten up late that morning, too late to shower, and I was now hoping for one that was unmonitored. It was there in the soothing water that I could actually relax. I could cry and not worry about Tootsie appearing and seeing my contorted face — she had made it clear that "we don't lock our bedroom doors around here," so I often felt self-conscious falling apart even in the supposed privacy of my bedroom. Of course, it was hard to enjoy the refuge of the shower when any moment could bring her hard knuckles rapping on the door, gruffly declaring, "Time's up!"

But as I turned the tap to hot, I heard the heart-sinking, burring noise of the garage door sliding up. As I stepped into the shower and heard the boys tearing through the house, yelling at each other and banging on their toys, as I heard the murmur of Tootsie and Jimmy's typically passionless exchanges, my legs started to buckle under me. I sank to the hard plastic floor and drew my knees up to my chest, putting my hands over my face and biting the heel of my right hand to silence the sobs rising up through me. My hair hung heavily along my sides, swollen with water, the ends lying on the bathtub floor. I thought about how my mother would run hot, soapy baths for me when I came home from school crying, upset about some slight from a friend or a bad grade on a test. I thought about the quiet stillness of those baths, how I could linger there reading a book until the deep water cooled around me and the bubbles deflated and disappeared, while she cooked dinner. I would call out to her then and she'd come wrap me in a big fluffy towel, playfully scrubbing my head, then sit me down on the toilet seat cover and gently work the tangles out of my long hair.

My tears ran with the scalding water, my sadness a live thing within me, physically painful and clawing to get out. Almost worse than the sorrow of missing her was the fact that Mom's death had revealed everything to be meaningless. So much of what I'd thought was true had turned out to be an illusion. I saw the people around me living by these illusions — that love and safety could be counted on, that life had meaning and the future could be controlled — and I did not feel that I could ever again share their suspended disbelief. I was swimming against a strong, cold current: I could see them there, playing on a sunny beach, but I couldn't rejoin them. Continuing the struggle seemed not only incredibly painful but, even worse, pointless.

I picked up my shaving razor and cracked open the plastic head with a practiced movement, freeing the blade. I held the strip of sharp metal between my fingers, which were suddenly steady, and I stared at the beautiful, sexual gleam of the thing. A deep calm came over me as I thought once again about lying back and letting it all flow out — pain, loneliness, strength, everything. I was so very tired.

But then I thought of those little boys somehow finding me there, in the bathroom I shared with them.

And I thought of my mother, how disappointed she had always been when I gave up on something hard.

And then I heard a sharp knock on the door.

—

The thought of suicide stayed with me, in the shower, in my darkened bedroom, in the backseat of the minivan on the way to the grocery store. It hid behind the smile I forced at school, it cast a pale shadow over each happy moment. Sometimes suicide was like a door in my peripheral vision, a potential exit that I could step through at any time. I felt better and calmer just knowing it was there, that I wasn't trapped. But most of the time, it was an object of desire, a thing with its own weight and texture, a deeply magnetic object whose pull varied in strength but rarely ceased.

Sometimes, the scary thing about suicide was that it seemed inevitable, the only logical end to everything that had happened. My mother's death had shown me what the world really is: a constructed thing, made of elaborate social rituals and ties of love. To live in the world, I realized then and still believe, you have to participate, you have to make relationships and meaning for yourself, because there is no ultimate design. You have to pretend that it is impossible for a killer to come in the night and destroy everything. I will never forget that improbability is not the same as impossibility.

In those first few years, I participated — I hit all my marks, I shuffled through all the steps — but it was more a march than a dance. The charade was exhausting. But although much of what I'd known had proven to be false, there was still one thing I knew with absolute certainty: my mother would not have wanted me to die. So each day I found a new reason to keep living.

23

before

Denny finally prevailed over Tim, and during the first few months of their relationship, he proposed to Mom countless times. But Mom wouldn't even think about saying yes until Denny had a ring. He couldn't just talk about getting married; she needed concrete proof he was committed, that this wasn't just an infatuation. But this condition was also a stalling tactic. She had serious doubts about getting engaged to such a young man, one she had been dating for only a handful of months, who was recently divorced. And she was starting to worry about his temper, about the fights they were already having, fights that were increasing in regularity and volume.

Naturally, Denny focused on solving the easiest problem first. So when the three of us went out shopping, he would drag her into jewelry stores. Mom would look at colorful gemstone rings and earrings while Denny tried to steer her to the engagement rings. I tried to keep my smudgy fingers in my pockets, hovering over the glass counters, all filled with rows of bright promises. I grabbed brochures by the handful, learned all about diamond grades, trying to use knowledge to bring the fantasy closer. I thought that if we could only get a diamond onto Mom's finger, the engagement would fix everything. She wouldn't have to worry so much about money. Tim would never return. Denny would love her and stay with her. There would be no more periods of disheveled sadness, when she didn't even bother with her customary blue eyeliner, her bare eyes naked, exposed in a way I wasn't supposed to see.

After his divorce, Denny had moved into a friend's basement, but he was constantly looking for a place of his own, and often took us with him on the search. We would climb into his truck and he would play us country music — Travis Tritt, Garth Brooks, Patty Loveless. Tales of strength in the face of sadness, of devoted love that withstood time, of faith that flouted reason. To me, those songs were lovely daydreams. These trips could last all afternoon, the three of us wedged onto the truck's bench seat, winding along dirt roads to drive slowly past Denny's prospects. He would talk about moving us into the beautiful houses we peered at, while Mom deflected his stories and I swooned, oblivious to what she would have had to give up to move in with him. On the way home, we'd stop to pick blueberries in fields loud with grasshoppers, or buy ice cream from tiny roadside stands.

—

Denny finally bought a respectable B-grade, quarter-carat, marquise diamond, shining but not stunning, set on a tapered yellow gold band. He showed it to me secretly and told me how much it cost: $161, steeply on sale. They had been together for about six months. In my diary on August 14, 1993, I wrote, "Denny is going to give Mom the ring on the twenty-third, Mom's birthday! That's so romantic!"

When Mom left our house that birthday morning, she turned out of our driveway and onto Route 93 to see black balloons tied to a telephone pole. She drove another quarter mile, and there were more dark spheres floating in the morning air, dull with dew. On High Street, there was a big, hand-lettered sign — HAPPY 30TH, CRYSTAL! — next to more balloons, which appeared at shorter and shorter intervals the rest of the way to the Shoe Shop. When she arrived, there were still more black balloons and crepe paper tied to her workstation, plus a card signed by her coworkers, who spent the rest of the day joking about how she was becoming an "old lady." No one could know that this would be her last birthday, that she would never be old.

Mom drove home from work that day happy, her balloons making gentle bumping noises in the backseat. So many friends had gone out of their way to show her how much they loved her, had gotten up extra early to make a fuss. When she got home, she tied the balloons to a leg of our kitchen table, started dinner, and waited for Denny to come over. I had a card for her, and a present, a pewter figurine I'd seen her admire in a store downtown. It was a warrior woman, a tiny, curvy lady with a drawn sword and a dagger in her boot, a jewel set into her prizefighter belt.

When Denny came, we all sat down to dinner and cake. He seemed to be in a ruffled, edgy mood, and I started to wish he hadn't shown up. Sometimes he was so fun and sweet, and other times he was like this: moody and fuming, just on the edge of an explosion. It was clear the proposal would not be happening that day, and I was smart enough not to bring it up. I went to bed early, for once putting up no resistance, and quickly drifted off to sleep. I awoke soon after, as their voices rose into an escalating argument. A high voice, a low one. Soon they were screaming at each other. Mom sounded frustrated, mostly, but Denny's anger had a commanding quality about it, scarier than in their previous arguments. They were in the kitchen, and their voices rang out against the hard surfaces of the linoleum floor, the steel refrigerator, the Formica counters. Finally I heard a loud bang, a hollow sound punctuated by a crack that resounded in the thin walls. I sat up tensely in bed, listening to the thick silence that followed. Then I heard our side door swing open and slam, echoed by the sound of Dennis climbing into his truck. I heard Mom stride down the hallway, shut her door, and start crying. I snuck out to the kitchen for a glass of water, and stood next to the sink drinking it down, looking sadly at those black balloons floating in the dark.

—

It would take Denny three more months to overcome Mom's reservations, months during which we both saw many of his good qualities. He took us on long walks through the woods, and he made me a bow and arrow from a sapling and then taught me how to shoot it, explaining that you had to aim higher than your target, because time and distance would pull your arrow down. He told funny jokes, and he never seemed bored by my long descriptions of the books I was reading. We drew up plans for a tree house he would build me, once he had extra money for the lumber.

One Friday night, Denny stayed home with me while Mom went out dancing with Linda. We watched movies, and at some point we went outside, then turned off the porch light and gazed at the stars while he smoked and I pointed out the constellations. I told him about the Big Bang theory. He listened, then thought aloud, "But what came before that?" He was sure that beyond any observable phenomena, there must be some guiding force, an idea I found beautiful and reassuring, even if we couldn't identify exactly what that force was. I felt so safe that night, standing in the darkness with my friend and thinking about the universe.

When Mom and I watched romantic movies, I imagined her and Denny in the lead roles. They were more thrilling to me than any movie romance, and like a movie romance, they seemed inevitable. I knew that their age difference was one reason Mom kept saying no to Denny's proposals, but I think we both saw that his youth was also an asset. He was still a work in progress, and among other things, he wanted to be defined as the man who loved Crystal Perry the most, who took care of her. I could see he had flaws, but he showed up. He wasn't some flaky college boy who messed with her emotions, like Tim, who I knew was still sending letters to our house. Dennis was composed mainly of potential and passion. If that passion occasionally translated into bouts of temper, well, his impetuousness went hand in hand with his spontaneity, his energy, and the urgent rustlings, the caught breath, the buoyant laughter I heard from her bedroom when he stayed overnight. I forgave him his tantrums, just as she did. I kept thinking they would disappear. Maybe if she just said yes, I thought, he would calm down.

Then one afternoon not long before my birthday, during a happy week, Denny took Mom's hand and led her to her bedroom. He shut the door behind them, then casually handed her a paper bag, twisted shut at the top. "Look what I got Sarah!" he said, with a *ta-da!* smile. When she uncoiled the bag and reached in, she found that simple ring Dennis had bought her months earlier. She finally said yes. I know I was excited that day, but I can't remember if she was. As she later told a friend, she was reluctant even to show her ring to anyone.

—

The engagement didn't bring the sudden change I'd hoped for. Dennis kept exploding, then making amends. She kept taking him back, and I didn't want to hold grudges. I wanted to believe in them. She wanted him to be the person with whom she would finally make the family she'd been dreaming of; she wanted him to make her feel safe.

But Dennis's presence did little to protect us from threat. Teresa — who still lived with Tom — started calling us. The phone would ring, and Mom would hesitate before getting up from the couch, giving the receiver a suspicious glare. She'd pick up, and I'd hear a few moments of Teresa's grating voice spill out before Mom slammed the receiver back onto its wall-mounted cradle. Sometimes she would miss, and the receiver would bungee to the floor. She'd replace it more gently, then turn back toward me, run a nervous hand through one side of her hair, and come sit back down on the couch. The restraining order must have timed out — I don't know if Mom ever did call the cops again, but they took no further action against Teresa. A known loose cannon getting wasted and calling her boyfriend's ex, threatening to kill her, wasn't much of an event in Bridgton. Through all those months when I'd forgotten about Teresa, Mom must have been waiting for the day she'd resurface.

I knew Mom was afraid, but she wouldn't say so, and although she encouraged me to hate Teresa, she also told me to laugh her off. "Don't take her too seriously," she said. She thought it was beneath us to be intimidated, no matter what Teresa was capable of.

Teresa's rage worked in combination with cold, precise instinct: she told Mom over and over that she was going to burn our house down. She'd catch us sleeping and we'd die in the fire and she'd have destroyed something that must have made her terribly jealous. Teresa, living on state disability checks and making death-threat calls from a pay phone, could never hope to buy a house.

The kitchen's ringing phone became a fraught thing: impossible to tell if it was a cheery bell announcing a friend's hello or a shrill siren that could cast fear over the rest of our night. For a few months, I wasn't allowed to answer it at all, but one time I forgot. The phone rang and I skipped over to it, thinking it was Marie, and stuck the receiver to my ear.

"Hello!" I said.

"You fucking cunt! I'm going to come over there and—"

I jumped and hung up the phone. Mom made me tell her what Teresa had said to me. I stammered and blushed and felt like I was the one who was making her mad, saying that word.

Sometimes Tom called, too. I don't think he made any threats—mostly he was just drunk and maudlin. "I'd like to see my kid," he'd slur. "C'mon, Crystal, just let her see me." As though she were stifling some desire of mine.

Mom would say something like, "If you care so much, why don't you pay some child support?" And then she'd hang up. She knew that once he sobered up, he'd know better. And it's true that he never asked for anything when he was sober, knew he didn't have the right. But he didn't make any efforts to straighten out, either. He often started his first six-pack in the morning, job or no, and he didn't leave Teresa, didn't even stop her from calling us.

—

I don't remember ever seeing Teresa face-to-face, but apparently I did. After Mom's death, several of her friends would tell the cops that one day, the week before the murder, Teresa had come up to us on the street. She must have seen Mom suddenly, or sought her out, then rushed up to her, confronting her before she had time to take me away.

"You can't have him now," Teresa said. "I'm pregnant! I'm having his baby—whaddya think now?!"

Mom took a second, then hissed back, "Well, I'm pregnant, too. I don't give a shit about you two." It was a sad lie: she very badly wanted a larger family, but she wasn't pregnant.

Teresa wasn't lying, but her pregnancy didn't stop her from toasting Mom's death three days after the murder, sitting in the cab of her friend Mary's pickup, drinking down a bottle of cheap champagne and laughing.

after

The school months in Texas stretched on, and I was grateful for the routine of classes and band practice. Angela had convinced me to join marching band with her, where she played flute and I played clarinet, and for the first time I felt at home again in a pack of kids. The classes were more challenging in Texas than they would have been back in Maine, which turned out to be a relief. When I first arrived, I'd gone to a school counselor and told her that I was supposed to skip seventh grade. "Just call the office in Bridgton," I said. "They'll tell you." But skipping was against my new school's policy, which seemed terribly unfair. I complained loudly, arguing that I was being forced, essentially, to attend an extra year of school. But I think I was actually upset because skipping had felt like my mother's final wish for me, the last one I could identify, and I could no longer fulfill it.

Despite the comfort of routine, school could still be a minefield of inadvertent cruelties. My French teacher was a jolly Québécois who liked to play us the pop music of his homeland — he had that embarrassing "buddy" style of teaching. One day we were having a class discussion about families, and he posed a question to me about my mother. "Umm," I said as the rest of the class waited expectantly. He sighed and prompted me with something, thinking I didn't have the words to answer him in French. *"Non,"* I said. *"Non, je . . . Elle . . ."*

"Comment?" he said, growing impatient.

I could have lied to this teacher. I was pretty good at French at the time. I could have said that my mother sewed shoes or that she lived in Maine, that she had red hair. I could have told him her age or said she was thin, or even said she was divorced. But I didn't want to say any of these things; none of them were true anymore, and I wasn't willing to lie, in any language, just to make people more comfortable. We hadn't yet studied past tense, and if I had referred to her in the present, it would only have underscored her absence. I thought for a moment, and could only come up with a blunt answer. *"Ma maman est morte."*

"Comment??" he said, loudly.

"Ma maman est morte," I repeated, cheeks burning. *My mama is dead.* The room was suddenly completely silent.

"Ma mère est morte," he said. *My mother is dead.* Then he looked at me, eyebrows raised, and swept his hand out in a "Go ahead" gesture.

"Ma mère est morte," I whispered.

—

Toward the end of the semester, just before my first Christmas in Texas, I received a card from Dale. He wrote that my photo sat on his desk every day, that he would never forget me. "Hope to hear from you when you're ready. Love, Dale." The card was postmarked not from Otter Pond Road but from the state prison. Although he didn't explain in the note, I heard he had gotten in a terrible car wreck with a woman who had been paralyzed as a result. He had been driving drunk or high or both. I considered it a tragic accident more than anything else, unable to face the true extent of his culpability.

In my heart, I knew that Dale had not killed Mom, could never have, and even Gwen and Glenice were comfortingly convinced of his innocence. But a voice still whispered within me, reminding me that anything was possible. I thought I remembered the police telling me he was a suspect, but I wasn't sure. I wanted to know if he had already been in prison when Mom was killed: then it would have been safe to write back. I didn't know who I could ask this question, and it made me feel shy — it seemed somehow inappropriate to want to be in touch with him. And although Dale had visited me every few months in the years after he and Mom broke up — taking me fishing or out for ice cream — now I couldn't help but think about how viciously he had fought with her. I didn't write back that Christmas, and unfortunately he never wrote again. Now I wonder if my friendship could have made a difference. But I wasn't ready.

Just a few years ago, when I was preparing to find him again, Dale and an accomplice were arrested for pistol-whipping a young man into unconsciousness, then attempting to throw him out a window, in what appeared to be a drug deal gone wrong. Glenice sent me the article online. "So disappointing," her note read. "I never would have thought Dale would end up like this."

—

That Christmas morning at Tootsie's, I sat on the carpet near the tree, handing presents to the family. I opened mine as I encountered them, slowly, letting the boys open three in the time I took with one. Eventually I pulled out a solid rectangular gift that could have been a hardcover book. I flipped up the tag. TO: SARAH, it read. FROM: MOM.

I looked at Tootsie, who met my gaze with a small smile. I flicked my eyes back down to the package, then carefully pulled back the paper to reveal a solid brass frame, two-sided and folded like a book. Inside were six photographs of me and Mom, each carefully trimmed and set within the matting that came with the frame. On the right side was a five-by-seven, beautifully lit and composed, no doubt taken when Tootsie and Jimmy visited us when I was very small, as they were the only people in the family who owned a high-quality camera back then. In this photo, my mother and I sit in uneven sunlight. I'm about four years old. I hold a Barbie doll and look straight into the camera with a serious expression, blond hair in pigtails. It's a face I still make — friends often recognize it when I show them this picture, laughing as they point it out in a chubby-cheeked kid. Behind me, my mother wears a flowing top in a 1980s calico print and her signature blue eyeliner. She is twenty-three.

As I sat next to that tree, I imagined Tootsie calling other family members so she could corral all the other pictures in the frame for me — snapshots from later eras that I knew she wouldn't have owned.

I thought of her hovering a pen tip over the gift tag, wondering what to write. And I wanted to thank her, but I didn't know how. She had done a lovely thing for me, but hadn't acknowledged that she had done it. We had no script for tenderness between us. I set the photo frame aside and dug through the presents, looking for something else to distract Alan and John.

I still have this frame; it is the first thing I unpack when I move, and if I go on a long trip I bring it with me. It's heavy, but it has crossed many miles of land and ocean. There are five photos in addition to the one taken by Tootsie or Jimmy, all arranged in the left-hand side of the frame. A studio portrait of mother and infant, in sepia tones. A snapshot from the Halloween two years before Mom died: me as a princess, Mom as a gypsy. The two of us eating sandwiches on a stone wall, legs sticking straight out before us, then sitting on a sunny hillside surrounded by tangled blueberry bushes, wind blowing our hair. And then a moment from our final Christmas: Mom and me standing in front of a glowing tree at the last family party she would attend. In it, my mother is wearing the suit we selected for her funeral viewing, chosen for its solid structure and high neckline. Tootsie couldn't have known this; she'd been absent from both the party and the funeral. That photo resonated differently for me than it did for her, like almost everything else.

before

I didn't have the full picture regarding Denny, and Mom was too unsure to act on what she saw. A few months into their relationship, his temper got him fired from the Shop. I now know that he became more controlling after he left, perhaps because he couldn't monitor Mom all day anymore. Her friend Sandy recently told me that she would often see him pull Mom aside, talking low into her ear and scowling while tears came to her eyes. Sandy couldn't hear these exchanges, but she gathered that they were over little things: Crystal smiled at a male friend and Dennis took it the wrong way, or he was simply having a bad day and she hadn't given him enough attention.

Shortly after he found a new job at an auto parts store, Sandy said, Dennis made Mom cut her hair. I was surprised to hear this; despite everything she put up with, it's hard for me to imagine her taking such a specific order. But I admit I can see her giving in after he hounded her about it over and over, reasoning that, well, it's just hair, after all, and hair grows. But her hair wasn't just hair. Her hair was the most powerful emblem of her beauty, and it seems he wanted it reduced. He wanted to be the only one looking at her.

—

Soon after that, Mom realized that she had made a mistake getting involved with Dennis, that the relationship was unsalvageable. He kicked the side of our house so hard once that he broke the siding and had to replace it. Another night, he left our house so angry, he crashed and totaled his truck. He broke a shovel in half, wielding it aimlessly in a tantrum. He grabbed Mom's arm once, hard — at least, once that I saw. She kept trying to leave him, but he kept pulling her back in. By early spring 1994, the Shop's hand-sewers made a joke of checking Crystal's finger for the engagement ring each morning — she pulled it off and pushed it back on that frequently.

Secretly, I had started to worry that Denny would go over the line, push one of his and Mom's screaming matches too far. I thought of this line like a physical thing, a definitive landmark that I would recognize when we came to it. We had watched all those horror movies and made-for-TV dramas: I knew that violent men only got more so after marriage, after the woman was trapped, and that sometimes even nice guys turned out to be psychos. This fear stalked the edge of my mind.

But then he'd be back: the same funny, smart, cute guy I knew, arriving at lunch with flowers for her, maybe a stuffed animal for me. I knew he was the same man who yelled at Mom in the night, who called her a slut, who would furiously accuse her of not loving him enough, as though that were the worst possible sin. But in the daylight, it was hard to believe it.

So I kept renewing my faith in him, making excuses. Denny was under a lot of pressure, after all — he had wrecked his truck, and then sprained an ankle weeks later while running around playing tag with me in the yard. He was also having money troubles, although I didn't know at the time that this was because he had gotten himself fired from the Shop. I thought it was possible Mom had gotten nervous after the engagement was official, might have become more exacting, harder to please. I knew how frustrating she could be, how stubborn. She never, ever said she was sorry for losing her temper.

I pushed away my concerns. *You've watched too many movies,* I'd say to myself. *Denny will get better. Everything will get better. They just need more time.*

But there was no time. On a Sunday in mid-May, the three of us celebrated Mother's Day at my grandmother's house. By Thursday Mom was dead, and Dennis became the prime suspect.

—

The police came to Dennis's house at a little past four in the morning that day. He heard a loud banging on the front door, next to his bedroom, and as he shuffled out into the living room, he saw his mother. She was in her nightgown, and edged backwards as the cops moved in, filling the small entryway. There were at least four of them. One was Gary Arris — the family knew him, but that night his face was still, professional.

Dennis's mother pulled her nightgown tighter around her. She wasn't quite awake yet and couldn't understand why anyone would come at such an early hour. Her husband stood behind the bar of the kitchen, blinking in the light, and the police started asking her son questions. He was twenty years old, standing there in pajamas. A couple of the cops looked very big.

"Did you go anywhere last night? Did you see Crystal Perry last night?"

Dennis was direct: "Is she all right?"

He didn't get an answer, but another question.

"Dennis, were you at home last night?"

And then he panicked. Instead of answering, he asked another question. He says it was "Is she alive?" The cops say it was "Is she dead?"

She wasn't alive. His mother caught him as he fell.

When Dennis came to, he was led out to a police cruiser for questioning. A couple of the cops stayed in the house to talk to his parents separately. He was not handcuffed. He walked through the rain and sat in the back of the car. He did his best to provide answers, alternating between numb disbelief and a frantic, instinctive desire to get to Crystal, to do something. He had gotten home from work, he said, just past eight o'clock. He remembered because that was when he called Crystal on his parents' house phone. The microwave showed 8:07 exactly. She was upset. He was supposed to have been at our house at eight, but he had stopped to check out a car that a friend was selling. A brown 1968 Mercury Cougar. He was seven minutes late by then and twenty minutes away. He admitted that he and Crystal had argued over the phone.

"I'll come right over, right now. C'mon, Crystal, don't be that way. It's okay, I'm on my way right now."

"No," she said. "No, don't even bother. I'll talk to you on Saturday."

It was Wednesday night. Dennis usually came over on Wednesdays and Saturdays. So when I first heard fighting that night, I'd assumed it was Dennis she was fighting with. I'd forgotten he hadn't been there when I went to bed. I didn't even wake up enough to form these impressions into full thoughts.

I hate to think that as I drifted back to sleep, I might have felt exasperated, frustrated with Mom's inability to leave this man who was causing us so much trouble. But I may have — I was so tired of their fighting by then. I certainly figured that I couldn't do anything about it. *Let her stand up for herself,* I might have thought, had I been more awake, had it really been Dennis.

I didn't know until many years later that she had gotten irritated and told Dennis not to come over, that she *had* stood up for herself. She didn't care what he wanted; she needed to sleep. And despite his temper, it would turn out that it wasn't Dennis I heard — he had respected her wishes and stayed home. He wasn't in our house that night. He wasn't the one. And so she had no one to protect her when someone else came knocking.

—

Dennis once failed a polygraph examination. When asked if he felt "responsible for Crystal's death," he said, "No," and his body went haywire. Responsibility can mean many things. I wonder how my heart would have responded to such a question.

after

They flew down to Texas as a trio, a small flock of carrion birds: Chief Bob Bell from Bridgton, plus Dick Pickett and Dale Keegan — a new detective — from the Maine State Police. In Pickett's notes from that long weekend, there's a section, perhaps written while on the plane, where he coaches himself. His bubbly script, *i*'s dotted with little circles, contrasts with its content. "Appeal to her sense of justice. Don't want it to happen again," he writes. "Smile ... also be serious when appropriate." He adds, "Mother may have been an embarrassment to her. She may have wished it happened."

They landed at Tootsie's house after dinner on a Friday night — to see where I lived, to say hello. Angela came over, too: she was curious, she wanted to support me, and the cops wanted to see what sort of friends I had.

Chief Bell was gray-haired and quiet; he hung back. He had an almost grandfatherly air to him. He was there to represent Bridgton, of course, and to consult with Pickett, but it seems to me that the chief of police wouldn't normally fly halfway across the country to help out with an interview from a case already nine months old. I believe his presence speaks to his dedication. To his memory of that sad little redheaded girl he once picked up when she was running away on her bike, back when they were both so much younger.

I didn't appreciate any of this at the time. I just saw three men, come to question me. I still didn't like Pickett very much, was still put off by his attempts to ingratiate himself with me. The way he spoke seemed calculated, false. Even while supposedly making friendly conversation, he would ask questions and then not listen to the answers; there was no natural flow. He still seemed to think I was purposely hiding something. I was glad to hear that I would spend most of the weekend with Keegan. He was younger than the others. He chatted with me and Angela in my room, and complimented my large book collection. Later, she and I agreed that he was reasonably good-looking, in a forgettable sort of way. He had, it turns out, recently been trained in new interrogation tactics at the FBI Academy in Quantico.

On Saturday morning, Tootsie drove me to the Holiday Inn downtown to be officially interviewed by Detective Keegan. We were silent in the humming elevator and walking down the hallway. He greeted us effusively, all smiles as he swept open the door. After brief hellos, Tootsie left to meet up with Pickett and Chief Bell. I let her disappear from my mind. I didn't want to think about her talking about me, about Mom.

After some small talk, Keegan and I got settled. Thinking back on it now, I don't know how he was alone in a room with a minor, but I suppose Tootsie must have consented. This is one of the many things about the investigation that doesn't make sense to me, no matter how many questions I ask or how hard I think about it.

There was a hotel desk chair for me: heavy wood, padded vinyl. Keegan sat down in another, handed me a Coke he'd fetched from the vending machine down the hall. I took it and glanced out the window through the gauzy curtains. I could see the occasional car or truck working its way down the wide, pale streets, moving slowly across the pane of glass like a drop of water, silent at this height.

Keegan began slowly. What was my relationship with my mother like? What sorts of things did we do together? Did I know her friends? Was it true what people said, that we were like sisters? All weekend, he would alternate between friendliness and pressure, acting as both good cop and bad. Sometimes he insisted that I had repressed memories from that night, that if I just thought hard enough, and felt re-laxed and open enough, I would be able to give him the information he needed. At other times, he spoke as though I was hiding information on purpose. And although I didn't want to admit it, because the idea seemed too far-fetched, it also seemed as though he was trying to de-termine if I had something to do with Mom's murder.

Despite all this, and my well-entrenched suspicion of cops — the general feeling of distaste and disappointment that swept through me each time I saw a blue uniform — I resolved to cooperate with Detec-tive Keegan. I was willing to turn myself inside out for even the small-est chance that I could help find the killer. I actually felt a little bad for him, sent down here to shake up the orphan witness, to do Pickett's dirty work. I hated that his name was Dale, though; I didn't want to associate him with anyone I had loved. Since he insisted that I call him by his first name, I avoided calling him anything at all. But I took each Coke he offered, thanked him and drank it, until I was jittery from caffeine and the strain of making nice. When he pressed me, asking the same question over and over, I stayed as calm as I could, even if all I really wanted was to pick up the lamp and hurl it through that tall window.

Now, I listen to recordings of that long weekend, captured on a stack of black cassette tapes. I had to buy a tape deck to play them, and the outdated little device feels like a kind of time machine. The sound quality is uneven, having degraded over the long years; some sections are warped and slow, others manic and anxious, and whole stretches of interview are missing. But much remains, and as I listen, dutifully typing out each word, I often feel like a voyeur. The girl on the tapes is exactly me one moment, and in the next she's someone else entirely. Her voice is high, her Maine accent still prominent, shot through with fresh bits of Texan twang: "ten" sounds like "tay-en." Even when she is sobbing, she is agreeable; she tries very hard to deliver what is asked of her. I hear no trace of the angry girl I know lurked within, the girl with the window-breaking rage. The girl who didn't want to answer the same damn questions over and over and over. But she's in there. She's the one who resisted Keegan's theories and implications, who would not let his desperation for answers twist reality, erode and damage my sanity. She's the reason I'm still here.

I remember, on top of a stack of paper on the bed, a hand-drawn diagram of my house. It magnetized me. It was so orderly, clearly mapped and neutral, completely unlike the dark chamber that had grown inside my head. Keegan noticed me staring: "I've got some diagrams of your house we're gonna go over — I can see you looking at them — and some pictures. No bad pictures." Later, when he first pulled the diagram close so we could examine it, he said, in a jokey, game-show tone, "This is *your house!*" I don't think he understood that even the diagram gave me a heavy feeling in my chest, or that calling the house "mine" only made me think of how very *not* mine it now was, how I would never return. A home can become a crime scene, but the reverse is impossible.

—

On that first day, I took a polygraph examination. Although the Supreme Court would later question the reliability of polygraphs as courtroom evidence, they were then and still are a useful tool for police. A polygraph report can reinforce or invalidate different lines of inquiry, help a detective see the path to truth more clearly. It's a divining rod; it's not the water.

This test would examine only one question, which Keegan intoned with deliberate pauses: "Do you know for sure . . . that the person who killed your mother . . . was" — and here he inserted one name from a list of seven: Dennis, Dale, Tim, four other male suspects from Bridgton, and a control, Cheryl Peters, the social worker who had first come to Grammy's house. An additional query was "a name I have not mentioned," which would mean that I had seen someone but did not know or would not reveal that person's name. The base question had been carefully written — I could only say that I did not know it was a certain person, not that it definitely wasn't that person.

Keegan told me about the fight-or-flight response, explaining that the body is faithful to truth: anything else sends it into alarm, raising the blood pressure and quickening the heartbeat and the breath, as though responding to physical threat. He hoped my body would tell him that one of these people might be the killer. "The thing is," he said, "if you did see someone, your heart's gonna know." This combination of the literal and the figurative now strikes me as beautiful.

To take a polygraph examination is to be restrained. Before the test began, Keegan strapped me into the various measurement instruments, explaining the function of each. The first two were black cords across my chest, one high, one low, to measure my breathing. I remember how careful and solicitous he was while putting those on me, and can now imagine how uncomfortable he must have been, alone in a hotel room with a young girl, moving in close. I hear him now on the tape, laughing nervously and saying, "Oh, you're so skinny!" I rolled my eyes when he said this, not believing him. But once the cords were in place, a serious feeling descended upon me. They exerted a slight pressure that made me feel like I was breathing abnormally. It was a slightly out-of-rhythm feeling, like the pause and stutter of observed footsteps. A tangle of wires sent impulses to a machine housed in a black metal box, where they were recorded by a spidery inked arm scribbling my breath onto the pale blue grid of a rolling cylinder of graph paper. I tried looking at it. I tried not looking at it. I took a deep breath and watched the spider arm go haywire.

Next came the blood pressure cuff—familiar enough. I had always been a good patient. Then two metal caps—one for my left index finger, one for my ring finger—to measure the conductivity of my skin, which would increase if I broke out in a sweat, however subtle. Keegan attached each finger cap with a long, winding strip of black Velcro, holding my hand carefully. His hand was hot and dry and muscled, his touch awakening the fear that lay so close to the surface then. *Oh, calm down,* I thought to myself, sternly. The cold metal began warming to my body temperature, bent over the pad of my finger like a thimble, an ironic echo of protection. I remembered, briefly, that Mom had never used thimbles at work—they slowed her down. She preferred her leathery callus, her body's natural response to her difficult work.

As Keegan sat back down and got his notes together, I tried to breathe deeply and evenly, tried not to think about the sensors on my fingers broadcasting my electric sweat to a second scribbling metal arm. I could hear it scratch against the paper, like a fingernail on a door.

Keegan asked me to keep my feet on the floor, to look straight ahead. The inked metal arms scraped at my ear, tempting my neck to twist. We began.

"Do you know for sure . . . that the person who killed your mother . . . is" — he took a breath — "Cheryl. Peters."

"No," I replied. Then there was a fifteen-second pause, to allow the machine to recalibrate.

"Dale. Morton."

"No." Long pause.

"Dennis. Lorrain."

"No."

He ran the test three times, shuffling the order of the names each time. I felt like a sleepwalker, intoning those no's against the silence. It was a slow call-and-response litany, a two-person ritual. It was as though we were casting a spell together, trying to conjure the answer we both so desperately wanted.

Keegan spoke softly, and rather slowly, throughout that weekend. In almost all moments, he radiated kindness and concern. He had a comfortingly familiar, but not jarringly strong, Maine accent. But the cumulative effect of his words wasn't comforting. Once I was free from the polygraph, we began what felt like an unending interview about that night. He thought I had something to say, and over the course of the weekend he became increasingly determined to get me to say it.

He asked the same questions over and over, changing the wording slightly, or the angle; he pretended to explain himself clearly while constantly contradicting himself. When I became confused, he blamed my grief, my fear, my guilt. He looped his theories and stories around me, trying to see what he could squeeze out.

I'm not trying to put words in your mouth or anything . . .

Not to accuse you of lying or anything . . .

Is it possible you know who did this? And if you don't want to tell me, that's fine. Tell me that. If you don't want to tell me who did this . . .

There's some things you're telling, that you could have only seen, not heard. The words you use, there's more there. Almost like pulling teeth here; you're telling us more. And there's more than you're telling us. For whatever reason, you don't want to tell us . . .

Yeah. I'm just trying to sit here and think, if I was in your shoes — if I knew who did this — why wouldn't I tell? Huh. The only thing I can think of is fear. Fear of the person. I think you're scared . . .

I think something like this would be something you wanna try to get out. Just like anything, you don't want to do things you don't want to . . .

Is it possible you walked out there, and you saw an attack, and you ran back to your room? . . . I'm not trying to put words in your mouth, okay! . . .

If you saw the attack going on, you got scared so bad . . . It could've happened to you. It would have been a double murder, would have never been solved . . .

Can you describe the guy? . . .

If you don't wanna say, you can write it to me. Tell me what you saw . . .

Anyone who did this to your mom is still out there. And it could happen again. You don't want that man to be that violent again. You don't want that guy getting away with murder . . .

Do you know who the person is? . . .

On the morning of the second day, before Keegan launched back in, he left to get something from his car, and Tootsie came into the hotel room. She rushed toward me as I stepped backwards, startled by her frenzied energy. "Listen," she said, raising a bony finger and pointing it in my face. "Stop wasting everyone's time. We all fucking know you're protecting someone. Now just tell them who it is. Tell them who it is! You're driving the family crazy."

We stood about a foot apart, looking into each other's eyes. I had almost grown accustomed to her sudden accusations, but this one proved that she could still shock me. What actually hurt, what took a second to process, was that "everyone." That "family." I imagined my other relatives standing behind Tootsie in an angry crowd, a force with her leading the charge. As though Carol and Gwen and Glenice, Webster and Wendall and Wayne, even Betty and Gloria, all thought I knew the answer, all thought I loved a murderer more than them, more than my mother, lost now forever.

"I don't know," I said, the words edging past my closing throat. "I'm sorry; I really, *really* don't know who it is."

Tootsie put her finger down and turned away with a disgusted snort. And then Keegan came back in and continued.

I'm sure you did a lot of thinking last night. Do you remember anything in more detail? . . .

I'm sayin', I'm not tryin' to put words in your mouth. There's just certain details here that don't add up. I truly believe that you heard more than you said . . .

'Cause, when people tell stories to us — not you — especially the bad guys, they'll try to tell lies to protect themselves. Not that you're telling me a lie, but you don't remember. And you're not a bad guy here . . .

I hardly believe that there's all that screaming going on, that your mom didn't scream a name, or didn't tell you to go hide, or the bad guy didn't tell your mom to shut up or any type of thing . . .

And the thing is, we're not trying to say that you're crazy or anything like that. We're just saying that — you gotta admit — something is happening in the next room, all the yelling and screaming, that probably you heard something. Okay. And you have a reason that you don't want to tell us, okay? . . .

I don't want to just sit here and go over and over and over this. I'm not gonna do that. But I'm gonna be quite honest with you. There's more there. I believe you did hear more . . .

Did your mom say anything? Scream, "I'm gonna kill you!"? Or did the man say, "I'm gonna kill you!"? Even to protect herself. Your mom could have gone to the kitchen, gotten something, to protect herself. And then the man took the weapon away. She was trying to protect you . . .

I'm not trying to put ideas into your head. We're just going on different theories of what happened. If any of this stuff is coming back to you. If you didn't see it, don't tell me you did, okay? But if you saw something happen . . .

Did she see you standing there? Did she not see you standing there? She could've thought the bad guy was gonna get you or something. You look at the bloody footprint here, there's almost an indication . . . that the bad guy started down the hall towards your room, and came back. For some reason, he stopped . . .

Don't try to make things up to make it — ha! — look good for yourself, y'know? . . .

What do you know? Ha-ha . . .

I wanna make sure you don't come up with anything and say, "It must've happened this way," y'know? Did you hear your mom say Dennis's name, or anything like that? Or Dale's name? Did she say, "Stop it, asshole," or anything like that? "You're hurting me"? . . .

If you were a betting person . . . You must have strong feelings . . . who would you bet did this? It's up to us to prove it, now. Let us do our job . . .

In response to Keegan's questions and theories, I answered "I don't know" at least sixty-two times. Sometimes I said it calmly, sometimes with a lilt of curiosity, sometimes through sobs, sometimes with a monotone, flat dejection.

Keegan told me a story about another girl, a girl who knew more than she had at first admitted. "We had a case up in Maine — this is true; you'll probably think I'm making this up, but I'm not — there was a girl, twelve years old, saw her mother kill a man. And she helped bury the body. She was twelve years old." He told me that he had talked to her again and again, for years, and she would not tell him where the body was. Suddenly, after eight years, she came in and told him. "Do you know something?" he asked. "You will not feel good, today, if you tell me. But in the long run, you will feel better."

Unfortunately, I would not feel better, because I didn't have anything to tell him. It was like I was trapped in a locked room, and he kept saying that all I had to do was turn the knob, but I didn't have the key.

"We asked that girl, 'How close were you two?' 'Oh, kinda like sisters.'" Keegan looked at me closely, as if he were peering behind my eyes: "There's more details there."

This story did not convince me I had more details. I did not feel a kinship with this girl. I felt jealousy. She could visit her mother in jail. That man had probably been violent, abusive. If I'd had the opportunity, I would gladly have buried whoever came to our house that night.

—

I would like to say that my sixty-two *I don't know*'s meant that I held firm, entirely faithful to my original story of that night, to my own true memory in Texas, to the night as I remember it to this day. But I did not. Near the end of the second day, after a short break, I looked within my mind, and in the rainy mist of that night, in the weak white light reaching from that one streetlight, a car appeared in our driveway. It was a blue car. Parked right behind Mom's. A blue car, like, well, Dennis's. "I don't know if I'm just seeing it in my head, or if it really happened," I told Keegan, through tears. To his credit, he did suggest that maybe this image was from another night. But then he led me back inside my house, to the moment when he was convinced I had seen my mother struggling with someone. "Can you describe him at all?"

I said, "I don't know if I saw the person." I didn't say, "I didn't see the person." Deep within me, I knew I really had not, but here Keegan was, so convinced that I had. After so many hours of questioning, I now doubted myself at every turn. I was so broken down and frustrated that I was hardly sure of my own name. Suddenly anything seemed possible, and my story felt like just that: a story. Malleable, expandable, expendable. The story of a little girl. Of a girl.

Eventually I said I might have seen Dennis in the house. But when Keegan posed follow-up questions, I could not provide any details. The blue car dissolved into the mist; the supposed figure of Dennis melted into the shadows. When I couldn't say anything more, I realized that these were just visions, not memories. I was young, after all, still capable of magical thinking—just a year earlier, I'd believed in witches. I was thirteen years old.

When I brought up Dennis, Keegan said, "We're working on the blood samples now, to see if they match him. We're looking at him . . . I'm sure you've heard about the O.J. Simpson trial, all the blood tests they're doing." I wasn't convinced Dennis was the killer, had no clear reason to think he was. But I did still fear him, in part because I had no other face upon which to focus my fear. I could say I had not seen him that night, but I could not confidently say that I thought him incapable of murder. I had seen his temper.

And so Keegan, and Pickett, too, revived this fear, which grew in the nights following their departure. But they neglected to tell me that Dennis's DNA had, a full two weeks before their visit, failed to match that found at the crime scene.

—

Late that Sunday, Tootsie, Pickett, and I went to the San Angelo police station to have my hands inked for comparison with certain smudges left at the crime scene. I pressed the rivers of my palms to the paper and hoped they wouldn't match, so we might have the mark of the killer. But the smudges, and the other finger and palm prints at the scene, would all turn out to be mine: the meaningless, careless marks of a child. The erratic mountain ranges of the polygraph reports were unreadable, inconclusive. My words had not helped us, nor had my hands, my fingertips, my heart, my breath. I was nothing more than what I did not know, what I could not tell.

27

---

meanwhile

After Mom's death, our town went on without us, forever. Summer came to Bridgton, the misty rains of May replaced by long, clear daylight. The vacationers from Boston and New York returned to their cottages lining Long Lake and Highland Lake and the ponds, and word spread among them of that pretty young woman's death. It was the last thing they would have expected of the town they came to as an escape from the world, that escape now exposed as an illusion.

The people of the town talked about the murder in the grocery store, over coffee while their kids played in the backyard, while sitting on the sandy lakeshores. They shared suspicions. They began locking their doors at night.

But the essential rhythm of Bridgton remained the same. The Shoe Shop hand-sewers took their places each morning at their benches, either turning from or gazing over at Crystal's empty one. Construction workers and contractors and masons continued work on new houses and repair on old ones. The clerks at Renys greeted the same customers, over and over. The Fourth of July fireworks went off without a hitch, exploding into the dark sky above the elementary school ball fields.

And of course, the summer was full of parties. Parties were a good place to talk about the murder, to conjecture and exclaim. Especially late in the night, when some dark and nasty things were said, about Dennis and other suspects, and about Crystal. One of her friends said that Crystal "basically dressed like a prostitute," a false claim surely born of cruel jealousy but also stifling fear. It was safer for certain people to think she'd had it coming to her; it made it easier to believe it wouldn't come for them.

Those months had a nervous, hectic energy to them; the murder lurked in the back of everyone's mind, an anxiety waiting to be let out. The killer could be sitting there next to you at the lake, in line behind you at the bank. He could be at any party; you could brush up against him while pulling a beer from a crammed-full fridge. You could go home with him. You wouldn't even know.

A central figure in the Bridgton party scene was Donnie Martin. He worked at Tommy's, drove a blue-black Thunderbird, and had long, flowing hair. He was known as a pretty boy and a cokehead. He had previously worked at the Shoe Shop. Several people said that during that long, strange summer, he had a habit of getting fucked up and claiming that he had killed Crystal. He'd say it with a proud swagger, and then forget all about it by morning.

The police questioned a young woman named Miranda White, who shared a number of mutual friends with Donnie. When the cops spoke to Miranda, they focused on one particular night that summer. She and Donnie had both attended a party at my uncle Ray Perry's house — Ray's wife, Stacey, was Miranda's boss at the Subway sandwich shop. She told the cops that she hadn't really talked to Donnie that night, or couldn't remember having done so. But, knowing who Crystal's ex-husband was, she had another story she thought they might find interesting.

When Miranda got to the party, the place was busy, the living room and kitchen and the basement full of people, including Tom Perry. She grabbed a beer, then worked her way through the smoky crowd to sit on a couch in the living room. She didn't see Donnie, but Tom was right next to her. She was nineteen; he was thirty-three. It was still early in the evening, but she could see immediately that he was very drunk. At first, he bristled when she sat down, but there was nowhere else to sit, so she stayed put. Eventually he started talking about Crystal.

He was convinced that everyone thought he had killed his ex-wife. He was feeling sorry for himself, and got pretty worked up as he spoke. He claimed that even his own mother thought he had killed Crystal. He hadn't, he insisted.

He clearly wanted Miranda to sympathize, soothe him. Once his laments wound down, he started being really nice to her. Asked her if she needed anything, and eventually started coming on to her. When she didn't indicate interest, a switch flipped. He told her to shut up. He called her a bitch.

Tom got more and more drunk, until his brothers Ray and Danny asked him to leave. It was a crowd of big drinkers, but he'd outdone himself. He was ranting and raving, and it was too early in the night for his bullshit. He didn't want to go home, though, because he was fighting with Teresa. That was why he'd come in the first place: to hide from her.

Ray and Danny finally just pushed him out the door. Tom ran down the porch steps in a rage, seized a car battery, and hurled it through the house's picture window as everyone leaped back out of the way. The forty-pound box hit that expanse of glass like a bomb going off, and shards flew through the living room like a gust of rain. It cemented the night in the memory of everyone who was there.

—

Teresa, too, felt the dark pressure of the murder, like an insistent hand pushing her mind further out of shape. One night that summer, she had to leave her infant daughter with friends overnight because she was hallucinating blood all over the kitchen, was screaming and could not be consoled. She often rambled to friends about Crystal's injuries, and several found her details so chillingly specific — although ultimately false — that they went to the police. One even recorded Teresa's phone calls and took notes. It is both disturbing and heartbreaking to read them; the shaky handwriting seems to telegraph panicky fear.

On another night, Teresa went to the bar, with no plan for getting herself home. The man who ended up giving her a ride spoke to the police a few months later. Teresa had kind of invited herself along, he said. He couldn't really say no. They left the bar and started talking in the cab of his truck, and she brought up Crystal Perry's murder. She asked him to drive down Route 93, to that house. "We sat in the door-yard for a few minutes," the man said. "She couldn't stop thinking of her friend, I guess." After a few minutes they pulled out, then drove around in aimless loops, passing the house several times. A few hundred feet from our house, they pulled over again, onto the shoulder of the road. The man left the radio on, and the two stepped out onto the pavement and stayed there for a while, dancing slowly in the dark.

28

after

Gradually, I let my life in Texas gain some traction, distract me from everything I'd lost in Maine. I got to know my neighbor Angela better, and we soon became very close friends. She was petite and stick-thin and hadn't yet hit puberty, but she was already plucking her eyebrows and shaping her thick brown hair with a curling iron that steamed and hissed when she hit it with her styling spritz. Her weightiest concerns involved which boys liked her or didn't, and whether she would make the junior cheerleading squad. It was she who initiated me into those rituals of feminine polish that I had seen my mother perform, those things I craved and Tootsie disdained. Angela had the passive-aggressive honesty of a sister, but she kept me from alienating myself with strange clothing or hairstyles. I kept returning to the idea of suicide, obsessing in the shower instead of using that time to bathe, and once, when I hadn't washed my hair in five days, Angela said, "Wow, why is your hair so greasy?!" I was shamed into compliance, but at least shampooing and conditioning my waist-length hair was a healthy distraction. Sometimes life just doesn't leave time for misery.

I was a few inches taller than Angela, and stouter, even at my thinnest; I mostly felt large and ungainly next to her. She had an easy, compact cuteness that, for a time, I attempted to emulate, wearing flowered skirts and polo shirts rather than my usual ripped jeans and loose tees. Her ideas about beauty and behavior were, at the very least, a track I could follow. Being around her sharpened my desire to be small, harmless. I ate less and less: another way to practice restraint, to banish that little girl called Heifer. I'd finally gotten thin — 108 pounds at nearly five-six — and it's hard now to tell if I was trying to be more beautiful or if I was still trying to erase myself.

I quickly grew to prefer Angela's house to Tootsie's — it was a relaxed, comfortable place where I could borrow her easier life for hours at a stretch. Her mother, Donna, was the first true stay-at-home mom I'd ever met. She was like a blond, Texan Sally Field, with big, highlighted hair and a twangy voice. She had competed in beauty pageants "as a young lady" and now kept very busy raising Angela and her quiet little sister, Katie. I remember eating cookies in Donna's spacious kitchen while she asked me about school, about Tootsie and her little boys. Angela's father, Bill, was in the Air Force, but he had an ease that was alien to both Tootsie and Jimmy — he liked a beer after work, he watched action movies with us, and he was a big Cowboys fan. He had a cheesy mustache, and he gave great hugs. Bill told me that his branch of the military was generally more laid-back than the Army, a sentiment Tootsie once echoed, but with scorn.

The Eilers were like a television family, and I found their bland rituals both fascinating and comforting. The neighborhood itself was soothing in its uniformity and order; for months I'd had to count the houses from the bus stop to be sure I'd come home to the right one. On cooler nights, Angela and I camped in a small tent in her backyard, talking late into the night. We talked so much, in fact, that we unwittingly developed a sort of twin speech, wherein we could listen to each other and speak to each other simultaneously with little confusion. Angela felt like a little sister to me, because she had been sheltered from so much of what I'd witnessed and experienced. I already had my period, and she was terribly jealous. I clued her in to the general mechanics of sex, which I had divined from movies her parents would have forbidden, plus the overheard, quiet shufflings that had emerged from behind my mother's bedroom door. But I kept my knowledge of grief and terror to myself. I didn't want to darken the sunny childhood that she was still enjoying. When I discovered that Pickett had briefly interviewed her when they came down, I felt defensive of her. "They asked if you were ever cruel to animals," she said. "It was so weird. You love kitties!" She didn't seem to understand that this question meant they could be evaluating me as a suspect. Still, I watched her carefully, looking for signs of fear.

—

January 1995 approached, and I thought of it as merciful. I held tight to the idea of a new beginning, or the possibility of one, someday. But this would be a shadow year, too.

On January 24, the O.J. Simpson trial began. I still felt like I contained a great darkness, poison that I didn't want anyone to see, and now the outer world was a gauntlet of blood-spattered tiles, accusations of Nicole's infidelity, and those terrifying black gloves. Everyone had an opinion, from kids in my math class to adults I overheard in Walmart. Murder was everywhere, the sexiest thing. I couldn't hide from it, so instead I hid myself. I saw again how excited people got when they talked about a killing, and I didn't want them turning that excited interest upon me. I listened mutely while people went on and on, and I said nothing. The police in Maine collected DNA samples from more men and sent them off to the FBI lab in DC, while much of the country learned about this technology for the first time.

The O.J. trial was a mess from the start, but at least they had the guy. All they had to do was convict him. It was just a matter of time — he was right there, it was so obvious. Both cases were missing the murder weapon, which I understood to be no small challenge for a prosecutor. I had to see that this detail could be overcome, once a viable suspect was identified. I needed to see that he was the only missing piece, that when we put him on trial, he'd be convicted. The man who killed Mom wouldn't have the benefit of a high-powered legal team, money, fame. As a white girl from an overwhelmingly white state, I had little understanding of how race factored into the trial, and thought more about how men dominated women, how the rich dominated the poor. Like most of America, I was focused primarily on what the O.J. trial meant to me. If O.J. went down, I reasoned — even while knowing that my reasoning was fanciful — Mom's killer would, too.

I didn't want to see O.J.'s face every day, and I got tired of seeing Nicole's bloody patio and the door that could have kept her safe, if only she'd known not to open it. But Tootsie and Jimmy were captivated; it seemed that whenever I passed the living room TV, there was O.J. I saw his lame pantomime when he tried on the gloves found at the murder scene, the smirk that pulled at the side of his mouth. In the days that followed, I kept waiting for someone — a reporter or commentator — to wonder why, if he was supposed to be innocent, he hadn't at least feigned sadness or disgust at handling gloves covered with the blood of a woman he had once loved. But I never heard anyone make that point. I even mentioned it to a friend once, but she just shrugged. It seemed that nobody was much interested in Nicole. To America, O.J. was special, whether or not he was a murderer: he was charming, famous, and physically heroic. Nicole was just another beautiful woman.

When the verdict came, acquitting O.J. of murder, everyone in my classroom jumped up and cheered. Everyone but me.

In that moment it was abundantly clear: even if the police identified the man who killed Mom, even if we waited years for that glorious day in court, we might be disappointed. The law was imperfect, vulnerable to human whim. I could not wait for justice to come heal me.

always

From this distance, I can look back and see, objectively, that Mom was not model-perfect. She was thin, with flaming hair and pretty eyes, but she also had pale eyebrows and crowded teeth. It takes my sharpest concentration to see these imperfections; like many daughters, I will always consider my mother to be the pinnacle of beauty. And she was truly striking. In the small town of Bridgton, many people agreed.

After Mom's death, when the police interviewed Earl Gagnon — a friend of Tom's who worked at the Shop — he said, "A lot of guys looked at her — pleasing to the eye, you know." The full record of interviews, and the stories of other townspeople, back him up. There are too many to detail in full, but here is a partial list of men who, in the days and weeks and years following Mom's death, were known by police or rumored by others to have been attracted to her:

BRUCE INGALLS, a contractor who lived next door to Grace, who helped Tom avoid his child support responsibilities by paying him in cash.

SCOTT MITCHELL, Mom's friend Valerie's husband, who looked just like Tom Petty.

GLEN KNIGHT, her friend Kim's husband, a self-righteously pious born-again Christian who now works as a prison warden.

DONNIE MARTIN, the one who had that habit of bragging that he'd killed her.

ERIC HARNEY, a former hand-sewer, who once pointed to his head and said, "I've got her number, right here."

FRANK MANZER, whose wife, Noelle, was a slender redhead. Once, after the murder, he pinned Noelle to the bed and stabbed the mattress with a kitchen knife, over and over. She waited until he was dead to tell the police that she suspected he had killed Crystal Perry.

RONNIE FOSTER, who stared at her so intently at the Shoe Shop that she had to move her bench.

MICHAEL HUTCHINSON, a young guy who worked for his father's masonry company.

A MAN IN A WHITE CAR, NAME UNKNOWN, who once followed her all the way to New Hampshire. She told Dale about it but wouldn't let him investigate.

AN ELECTRICIAN NAMED DONALD CALLAHAN, who once slept with her, then complained when she scolded him for sharing the details with anyone who would listen. The day after she was killed, he was doing some scheduled work at Chief Bob Bell's house and told him, "Crystal was a real bitch."

HER FRIEND AND COWORKER RICHARD TURCOTTE, benevolently in love with her still.

TERRY OULLETTE, who once fixed a sink at Grace's house and was rumored to have a "fatal attraction."

RYAN NOVAK, a Bridgton police officer. He became "John Doe" after a fellow cop retrieved his cast-off cigarette for DNA testing.

DAN LAGRANGE, a gray-haired neighbor who occasionally hired Mom to clean his house when she needed extra cash.

PETER KNIGHT, who lived out west somewhere, and called Mom out of the blue the month before she died. He was a registered sex offender by then. Previously known as Junior — the boy she dated before Tom.

LLOYD POULIN, who mentioned Mom's death from the back of a Bridgton police car after being picked up for being drunk and disorderly. He asked the cop, "How old is her little girl now, sixteen or seventeen? Crystal was a slut, wasn't she? That daughter is a sweet little thing."

—

Bruce Ingalls, Grace's neighbor, is one of the most interesting of these men. When Grace married Ray for the second time, the family lived in an apartment for a few months before moving into their house in North Bridgton. Gwen was nine or ten at the time, Crystal seven or eight. In the apartment next door lived a teenage couple: Bruce and his girlfriend. Years later, Gwen would find it strange when Bruce ended up buying the house right next door to Grace and Ray's, on the other side of town, as though he were following them. After the murder, she found it even stranger. It made her a little suspicious.

Bruce, though, doesn't seem to have been a bad guy. Despite his established attraction to my mother, I'm convinced that his close proximity to the family in two separate locations was a coincidence. He hired Tom and paid him in cash, but Tom was his friend, and what he did with the money was his business. He figured that was between Tom and Crystal.

Tom now remembers an afternoon when he was on a carpentry job with Bruce, sometime around 1992. They were driving down Main Street near the bank, and they slowed as they saw Crystal entering the crosswalk. She stopped there, in front of the truck, smiled at Bruce, and, as Tom puts it, "did a little dance thing, right in the middle of the road . . . he-he, a little . . . dance thing." Then she turned and walked away, laughing over her shoulder. "She was playful," Tom says. "But reserved most of the time."

When she stopped traffic without even meaning to — literally or figuratively — she knew how to use the moment to quietly get the upper hand. If she sensed that someone saw her beauty, she could add a smile to amplify it. She used what power she had.

It's fun to be attractive, and I'm glad Mom could occasionally throw a man's desire in his face, with a lighthearted you-wish taunt. But I also think about her moving her bench away from Ronnie Foster, about her need to tell Dale about that white car that followed her to New Hampshire. I think about the incredible mental pressure of being the target of so much attention and desire, even if she was aware of only some of it. I think about Gwen's concern about us living all alone out on Route 93, and I remember how mad Mom was when the contractors cut down all those trees in the front yard.

Shortly after the murder, a neighbor of ours named Eric Thibault spoke to the police. We didn't know Eric well, but I had swum in his pool once or twice. Eric had a theory. "Maybe somebody's truck broke down," he told the cops. "And then they went to Crystal's to use the phone. When they got inside, they would've seen how beautiful she was, and tried to rape her. And then I guess she put up a fight, and they killed her." In this story, the truck breakdown isn't even a ruse, some premeditated lie to gain entry. It just sort of made sense to Eric that a man could be driven to spontaneous brutality by a woman that good-looking.

And while Mom truly was beautiful, I believe a similar investigation would reveal a similar web of desire around any reasonably attractive woman: a network of men, some benign and respectful, some objectifying and aggressive. Some of the men surrounding Mom were ones she'd dated or otherwise encouraged; others she'd turned down, and still others she'd gently ignored, to spare their feelings. One of them decided that he had the right to take what he wanted. And he became very angry when she said no.

I still maintain that Bruce Ingalls wasn't a bad guy, as far as I know. But he once demanded of Linda, "Tell me what Crystal's got against me," because she had so many times spurned his advances. As though she owed him something.

—

It is often simply easier to give men what they want. I once said yes to a man because I was positive that if I said no, he would rape me. He was aggressive and pushy in a way I'd never encountered, flattening me painfully against a cold window when I tried to pull away. In that moment, I saw that if I continued to resist, he might not listen to me, and then there'd be no going back. I didn't want to take a chance. I didn't want to be a victim, so I made the best of it. I decided to be agreeable, pliant. It is not always possible to make this decision, but in this case it was. I talked my body into it. I sort of wanted him, but mostly did not.

And I let some men into my apartment recently. I could have said no, but didn't. The whole time they were there, I was haunted by what could be happening.

I was sitting home alone, middle of the afternoon, in Brooklyn. My building was quiet. Carlos, my friendly upstairs neighbor, the only male neighbor I know, wasn't home — I knew because his footsteps are always heavy on my ceiling.

Everyone was at work. I work at home.

A knock came at my door, and I got up to see. As I walked across the kitchen, I pulled on a button-up shirt over my tank top, because I wasn't wearing a bra. I was barefoot. I used the peephole. There were two men standing there, one tall and broad, with a smaller man behind him. My door is heavy and you can't really talk through it; the door chain is broken. It's not the safest neighborhood.

I opened the door a little and the big man explained that they were there to check the water. He was wearing a plain white T-shirt, dirty and worn thin. His face was relaxed, but his friend looked shrewder. The friend also wore no uniform.

I was confused. "There have been complaints," he said, "about the water in the building. It's not always hot?"

This is true. The water occasionally goes lukewarm in the middle of a shower. But the building management is lax; unless it went ice-cold for days, I wouldn't have expected them to come fix it. I hadn't bothered to call and couldn't imagine anyone else in the building calling about such a relatively small thing. We were still trying to get them to fix the front door, so people couldn't walk in off the street. The latch had been broken for weeks.

"We did some work downstairs," the big man continued. "We need to check to see if your water's hot."

They weren't wearing uniforms, but the management hires all kinds of under-the-table men.

"Okay," I said. I opened the door all the way.

My hallway is narrow, and suddenly I realized how big this man was. Huge, really. And there were two of them, and one of me.

"You're the only one home in the whole building," the big man said.

I flushed. I pressed myself to the wall so they could walk past me and I pointed, way across the apartment, to my sink. "There it is," I said. "Over there."

They were in now. I stayed in the doorway. I put my back to the swung-open door. My right hand hung in the free air of the hallway. Let them steal if they wanted.

The smaller man — not actually a small man — looked at me. He didn't say a word the entire time. A slight smile appeared on his face. I could see him thinking, *She's afraid*. I could see him laughing at me. In that sort of situation, only the man can laugh. Only the man knows whether something terrible is about to happen. And even then, he might take himself by surprise. My vigilance isn't unique.

The big man turned on my faucet, the hot tap only.

"Come over here and see," he said.

"No, I'm good," I said. "I trust you."

Steam rolled out of the faucet, coiled over my cabinets. The big man laughed. "Come over here and feel it."

The small man smiled some more.

"No," I said. "No, thank you."

I shook for hours after they left.

after

I'd noticed Anne Harris on the very first day of eighth grade, in gym class. As I stood next to my locker, pulling itchy green uniform shorts over the thighs I considered far too big, in walked this person in a black leather jacket trimmed with toothy silver zippers and accented with shining buckles. She was tall and long-limbed and moved with the loping gait of a boy. Anne's hair was the color of sand, the top half pulled up into a ponytail held by a fluffy red hair tie, the lower half shaved close to her head. I had never seen hair like that, nor had I ever seen a girl shuck off torn, oversize jeans to reveal boxer shorts. She was very slim under all those clothes, but clearly strong, her hands long and wiry, her eyes smudged in black. I planned to stay out of her way.

Later that week, though, Anne fell in step with me and a girl named Amber as we ran laps outside. Between halfhearted attempts to jog through the dusty heat, Amber bemoaned the death of Kurt Cobain. She had just started listening to Nirvana, and Kurt had died about a year and a half earlier — not long before Mom — but as Anne drew up to us, Amber was dabbing at tears and gazing wistfully into the distance. I remained silent as Anne asked what other music Amber listened to and she fumbled for a cool answer. Anne smirked a little, looked into my eyes, and moved the conversation on to something else.

I still had my Maine accent then, and Anne asked where I was from, what had brought me to Texas. My mother had died, I said. Amber responded with silence, her glossy brown hair falling over her face while she stared at the ground. But Anne asked some more questions, real questions, and my answers slowly revealed a sketch of what had happened: Mom was murdered, I was there, the guy was still free. And then I told a lie. I said that before I'd left Maine, my family had put me in a mental hospital for a while. It was the sort of lie that you don't realize you're about to tell until you hear it coming out of your mouth. The sort of lie you yourself believe immediately. And like many lies, this one revealed a wish. How lovely it would have been, I thought, to have had some time just to sink into misery. To not have to deal with family or school. To be surrounded by people whose job it was to keep you safe from your suicidal hand. And to have the circumstances of your life truly reflect what had happened to it. A mental hospital seemed to make a lot more sense than neat rows of chairs and desks, than football bleachers, than that white-lined running track.

I didn't say much else that day, but by the end of class, Anne was insisting that I spend the upcoming weekend at her house. We quickly became closer, and I'm sure that within a few days or weeks, Anne realized that I'd lied about the mental hospital. But she never called me out, never even mentioned it. I have always been grateful for this generosity. I think she understood what I was trying to tell her. That I was tired. That I needed some help.

—

That Friday was the first of many that I would spend with Anne, increasing the distance that had started to grow between me and Angela. She and I really only saw each other at band practice by then, and at the football games where we played halftime shows. I tried, but I couldn't share her excitement about popularity rankings and homecoming rituals. I was in honors classes that year, and I could see that she thought my new friends were weird and nerdy. My life quickly became Anne, band, obsessive studying, and attempts to avoid Tootsie's terrible moods.

Anne and I spent most nights in our friend Nick's run-down classic Mustang as he sped up and down the freeway, outracing his headlights into the desert dark, whipping around the other cars, killing time. I sat in the backseat on the passenger side, pushing my fingers against the melted rings of cigarette burns on the vinyl upholstery, thinking often of Dale's Firebirds. Anne sat next to me, and I breathed in ribbons of her cigarette smoke as they uncurled from her hand. In front of me was our tall friend John, four years older than me, a country boy with long hair and a quick wit. I mostly let everyone else do the talking while the cool, dark air rushed into my face, leaving me clean and free, floating above the highway until it was time to head home.

When we weren't riding with Nick, John and Anne and I would hang out at a pool hall called Corner Pocket. It was a gathering place for the happily unpopular: grunge kids in flannels, kickers in Wranglers, and artsy outcasts in black long sleeves. When I think of those nights, the jukebox is on a five-song repeat, and today those songs bring me John's long fingers in an elegant bridge, his crooked smile; Anne's warm, thin arm around my shoulders; the weight of her leather jacket when she let me wear it, the snaps and big lapels pressing against my heart.

I was special to them — the youngest among our group of friends — and they were protective of me. When some older men came in and started hitting on me, John and Anne made it clear that I belonged to them. When a mutual friend offered me weed, they seemed glad that I declined. If I lined up a shot that didn't look quite right, one of them would bend around me and correct the angle of my cue, the pitch of my hand. Or drift to the other side of the table and point at the exact spot I should aim for on the moss-colored bank, fixing squinted eyes on me and giving me the focus I needed to land the ball in the pocket with a satisfying *thunk*.

At the end of the night, the three of us would emerge into the dark air of the desert, and I'd feel the space stretching out all around us. We'd climb into John's gray pickup truck, nicknamed Lucky, and make our way into the denser lights of what passed for a downtown. When we reached Anne's house, she would slide out first and I'd leave the middle seat reluctantly, still a bit awkward even after the closeness of the evening, then John would depart in a loud rattle of loose metal and muffler.

In Anne's room, we sat cross-legged on her king-size bed, draping the soft old sheets over our laps. Anne was only fifteen, but she had already fit in a few years of partying, chasing chaos that she was now trying to put behind her. Befriending me was, I think, part of moving on, because I had never partied, never sought out additional trouble. She told me stories from that time, usually to demonstrate how foolish it all was, to tell me not to waste my time, and once she even took me to the church parking lot where an older man had assaulted her, perhaps to remind herself she'd gotten through it. We were similar: too old too early. *Here,* I thought, *is someone who gets it, someone who's been through some shit.* She understood my need to sit back for a while and listen, to let others confide in me while I took them in, provided what advice I could. I needed to be of use; I needed a break from myself. And whenever I did feel like talking, I didn't have to shield her from anything. We said we were putting her "on the couch," but really the therapy was for me.

We'd stay up late into the early morning, three or four or five o'clock coming on unnoticed. We listened to Anne's extensive collection of 1980s cassette tapes. We sang, *Heaven isn't too far away.* We sang, *Sweet child o' mine.* I nervously shared my mother's Rod Stewart tapes with her, worried she would think they were dorky, and then laughed when she knew all the words. We sang badly, out of tune, but in unison. When we watched TV, Anne put her head in my lap and I combed my fingers through her hair, over and over. We wound down the hours, and when we slept, she took my hand in hers. I could feel her thin fingers and her calluses and the tension she never put down.

These rituals were enacted over months of weekends, each wrested from Tootsie with a meek request for her permission. I loved Anne more than I had any friend before. I wanted us to trade all of our stories, every possible song; I learned a lot from her, and felt she always understood what I told her. But also, I needed to be physically near her, and I was terrified that Tootsie would sense these feelings and confront me about them. I was afraid of what she would do, how she would react, worried that she might throw me out. I also didn't want her to make me think too deeply about this friendship. I didn't want to have anything in common with Anne's neighbor, a girl our age whom Anne had scornfully referred to as a "dyke." So I pretended to everyone, and to myself, that Anne was merely my best friend.

Her mother kept only half an eye on us, reasoning that teenagers needed some space to find their own way and could have that space, as long as they were smart. Of course, she hadn't told Tootsie this, and sometimes I'd tell her stories about my aunt's strictness and we'd all laugh and laugh. Anne's mother referred to her as "*Toot*sie Dearest."

With Anne, I worked on finding my strength again, not feeling so beset by my circumstances. One day, we watched *Léon: The Professional*, and in Natalie Portman I found my perfect hero: a twelve-year-old girl seeking revenge for the murder of her family, conveniently perpetrated by an enemy cop.

For Anne's sixteenth birthday, I snuck into her house while she was out and cleaned her disastrous bedroom. I scraped away years of black mildew from the sink and shower in her attached bathroom, inches of dust and ash from her immobile ceiling fan. I excavated through layers of term papers and fanzines and tape cases and costume wigs and bootlaces and fishnet stockings and family Christmas cards until I finally found the soft carpet of her floor. Once I had, I dragged out her mother's ancient vacuum cleaner and went over it twice, the tracks of lifted tufts like a freshly mown lawn. I went through shoeboxes filled with junk and found about a dozen broken black eyeliner pencils, stickers from her childhood, postcards from other Texas cities. I held my breath as I dumped out four or five large lead crystal ashtrays, and blackened my nails scrubbing them in the kitchen sink. I cleared her packed shelves and dusted them, I washed her sheets and remade her palatial bed. I found her journals, but had no need to read them; I was sure I knew everything she'd written.

Anne came home just as I was finishing. I was covered in sweat and dust, and glowing with satisfaction. My right foot bore a razor-thin cut from where a submerged coat hanger had caught it, a tiny wound that would turn into the bright scar I still carry. She smiled at me, looked around, and said, "It won't stay this way for long, you know." I knew.

What mattered was that I had given her some breathing room for a while, a small break from the chaos she was so adept at creating for herself. What mattered was that she let me take care of her, if only for a while.

—

While I spent nearly all of my free time with Anne, Tootsie's house remained much the same, full of tension and recriminations and occasional, disorienting displays of kindness. I had been there about a year when she and Jimmy began the process of legally adopting me, something that I hadn't given much thought to. Although I hadn't grown any more comfortable in their house, once the discussion began, I became attracted to the idea of security. If I was adopted, no one would have to worry that the state — any state — could come and take me, or that Tom would suddenly decide to challenge Carol's power of attorney. I'd be spoken for, and I could stay there in that sunshine I loved, my weekdays filled with satisfyingly challenging classes and time spent in the friendly crew of marching band, and my weekends with Anne.

About a month after Tootsie first mentioned the adoption, though, she came to me in my room, shut the door behind her, and said that Jimmy was having second thoughts. She didn't tell me why he was reconsidering, but she said that if he didn't agree, I would have to go back to Maine right away. I couldn't discuss any of this with him; it was tacitly forbidden. Over the next few weeks, I tried to identify what he might not like about me, what I could tone down or compensate for. I tried to be extra nice without being obvious about it.

Jimmy had always been a mystery to me. He'd been a cook in the Army, and it made sense to me that his job hadn't involved direct combat, so adept was he at avoiding it at home. In the years I lived in that house, I had just one real conversation with him. He told me he could make almost anything out of cake, and for special Army celebrations he had re-created famous battlefields and monuments. I could not imagine him doing anything so whimsical or imaginative. He seemed so serious; he smiled so rarely. Usually, my only sense of how he felt about anything came from Tootsie.

Eventually, Jimmy apparently agreed to the adoption, and the three of us went to the courthouse in downtown San Angelo for a short proceeding before a judge. I would never discover what his resistance had been about, or if it had maybe all been fabricated by Tootsie, a manifestation of her own uncertainty, or an attempt to make me feel indebted to her for winning him over.

All the paperwork had been completed and reviewed in advance, and the hearing had the feeling of a technicality. It was important to the judge, though, to know what I thought about being adopted, if I felt that it was in my best interest to stay with Tootsie and Jimmy until I was of age. I wanted to stay, as I had in Bridgton, so I agreed to the adoption, happy to be officially consulted, happy to be spoken for and settled in for the next four years. We would all work out our difficulties, I thought, or I would work around them, in the tight spaces of freedom they left. And anyway, things might get better. After all, we did celebrate the adoption with a nice lunch out.

But if I really expected paperwork to bring about any dramatic changes, to make Tootsie gentler or Jimmy more communicative or to make me feel closer to their kids, that was not to be. I may have relaxed my guard a little, but the strained, tense aura remained. Every weekend I could, I went to Anne's, where I felt accepted and loved by her and her mother, who hugged me hello and goodbye.

Tootsie had become increasingly suspicious about the time I spent at Anne's house, though, convinced that I was smoking and possibly drinking. When she picked me up, my clothes filled her car with the reek of cheap cigarettes, and I'd have to tell her, again, that although Anne and her friends smoked around me, they probably wouldn't have let me smoke even if I'd wanted to, and they would have been disappointed if I drank. There was no way to fully explain to her how protective they were of me. What I now understand as their instinctive compassion made little sense to me then.

After hearing about Tootsie's interrogations, Anne's mother tried to drive me home on Sundays as often as she could. Reluctant to hand me off to my aunt, Anne would come along for the ride. One late-spring morning, she walked me to my door, then leaned in and gave me a small kiss on the lips, as she often did. I felt a quick bolt of happiness spiked with nervous fear, because I knew that kiss didn't mean to Anne what it did to me, or if it did, she would never have admitted it. And then my flush deepened and a nauseating fear took hold of me as I saw Tootsie's shadow pass behind the cut-glass panel of the door. Anne didn't seem to notice. I remember her stepping backwards into the sunshine, smiling, then turning to walk back to her mother's waiting car.

I turned the brass handle of the door, sweat breaking out on my palm as I wondered whether Tootsie had seen this kiss. This meaningless thing. I tried to duck into my room, but just as I rounded the corner in the hallway, I heard her voice at my back, its low, gruff tones tinged with disgust. "Is Anne always quite so friendly?" she asked.

I turned toward her; her face looked both angry and amused, prepared to mock weak explanations. "Anne? Oh, she's just like that. She's just very, um, affectionate," I said. Tootsie had me trapped: if I said anything more, it would reveal that I knew what she was talking about. I had to pretend that it had not even occurred to me that the kiss could be romantic. "I see," she replied. We stared at each other for a moment. When she didn't say anything more, I gave her a shaky smile and escaped to my room as slowly as I could.

Within days, Tootsie had banned me from going to Anne's ever again. Her only explanation was that she thought I wasn't telling the truth about what happened over there, that Anne's mother wasn't as careful a parent as Tootsie would have liked. It still shames me that I obeyed her. I tried to explain to Anne, and she repeatedly asked me to lie, to say I was elsewhere and to come over as I had before, but I couldn't risk it. I was too afraid of Tootsie; I felt anxious just thinking about it. Looking back now, I can also see that part of me — a small part — was relieved to be out of Anne's orbit, the overwhelming pull she had on me, a magnetism I didn't want to understand.

—

Once the era of Anne had ended, marching band filled some of the newly empty space in my life, and I spent many hours practicing in the evenings with Angela, who welcomed me back unquestioningly. We began tenth grade, moving up to the large, well-funded Central High School. I took every Advanced Placement class possible and felt like I was on a steady path to some kind of success. I was fifteen, and had always thought that the age of sixteen marked the beginning of adulthood; I was on my way. I had never been much of a performer, but I took an acting class and joined the debate team, feeling strong and ready to participate in things that other people cared about, ready to take risks, to be seen. Central had a selective creative writing program, and I planned to apply the following year, when I became eligible, even though the idea terrified me, as I'd written very little since Mom's death. I met dozens of people and was interested in everyone, open to new friendships. My nights of fear had mostly disappeared by then, like a fog burned off by the Texas sunlight. I could see ahead more clearly, to college and my steadily approaching freedom. Things were even starting to get slightly better between me and Tootsie — she and Jimmy were divorcing, and once he had moved out that summer, she had started to seem a lot more relaxed.

Two months into the school year, I was riding home in a charter bus after performing in the first halftime show of the year with the marching band in El Paso, a six-hour trip each way. I watched, headphones on, as the sun disappeared below the unending horizon line and the glowing blue descended upon my friends, falling asleep around me, one by one. I remember feeling a calm, immense peace as the bus shot across the perfectly flat desert. I looked out at that land and felt a deep sense of belonging.

I got up late the next morning, having gotten home after midnight. As I brushed my teeth, Tootsie knocked hard on the bathroom door and said, "We need to talk." I spat into the sink and paused. I made a neutral face in the mirror. "Okay, just a minute!" I wondered what I had done to irritate her this time. I wiped my mouth. I walked to the kitchen to meet her, determined to remain calm and defend myself as best I could against whatever accusation she had dreamed up.

She said, "Your aunt Carol and I were talking last night, and we agreed that it would be best if you went back to Maine."

Something twisted inside my chest, answered by an immediate and powerful urge to fight that weakness. I didn't want to react until I'd had some time to think. I said only, "When?"

"Well, you can leave this week or you can wait until the end of the semester." She said this as if the options should have been immediately obvious to me.

"Well," I said, "I'll have to think about that."

I spent the rest of the afternoon at my friend Loren's house, returning home a few hours later to gather some of my things. I found Tootsie in the kitchen and said, "I'm staying at Loren's tonight."

"Excuse me?" she said, raising an eyebrow.

"May I stay at Loren's tonight?" I said, as softly and evenly as I could, trying not to give that "may" sarcastic emphasis, inwardly furious that she could upend my life and still expect courtesy and submission.

"Well, what's your decision?" she said, standing up to her full height and looking down at me.

"Well . . ." I began. I hadn't really thought yet about when I wanted to leave. It had only been about four hours since she'd told me I had to. "I've been in school for two months already . . . and I only got to do one halftime show in marching band after practicing all summer, so . . . I'd like to stay until the end of the semester."

She crossed her arms and looked at me for a moment. Then she said, "No, the sight of you is pissing me off; you're leaving on Wednesday."

It was Saturday. My mind froze up in response to this. I retreated to my room and stared at the wall. *Think*, I thought to myself. *Figure it out*. She seemed to be bluffing, hiding something. If I could identify it, maybe I could stay. A memory of all those long, sleepless nights at Carol's edged into my mind. I had to try to stay. I could not go back to Maine. But over the next few days, my attempts to get an explanation from Tootsie were met with a wall of anger I could not penetrate. It took me years to realize that there was probably never a choice, that she must have bought that plane ticket before she told me anything at all.

—

Tootsie and I mostly kept out of each other's orbits in those final days, speaking as little as possible. She bought me a cheap three-piece set of luggage and I found myself in the ridiculous position of thanking her for it. But as the hours disappeared, so did my restraint. On Tuesday night, I came out into the living room where Tootsie was watching the news and told her that I thought it might be illegal, what she was doing. I had been in the courtroom when they processed my adoption, when the judge decreed that she take care of me as her own. You couldn't just go back on a legal promise like that. She turned off the TV and rose from the couch. "You don't know what you're talking about," she said. "I'm just your aunt," she said. "The adoption was only so you could have health insurance."

I was astonished by how much this hurt. I'd tried to harden myself against her, but I knew then that she would always be stronger. I felt like a fool for seeking reassurance in the judge's words, for remembering them at all.

But after a pause, I pushed further, still confused and disoriented by the speed at which things were moving, and she pushed back, getting louder and louder. Anger rushed in and replaced my sadness, held me up. Soon I could no longer hear what she was saying. After three years of trying to maneuver around her, I abandoned all caution and strategy. I started yelling back louder than I ever had before, my nervous system going haywire, the ringing in my ears blocking sound. I can't remember what we said that night; I only remember the swift climb from sadness to fury, my words coming faster and louder, my mind frantic, Tootsie moving in close. I stayed like that for a few moments, burning hot, until a little switch went off in me with an almost audible click. I fell silent. Then I was coasting, cooling down. I tuned back in; could hear her yelling again. I realized that I had been staring at the hard, knobby prominence at the top of her cheekbone with the intent to smash my fist into it. I had failed to hit her through no control of my own but rather through sheer dumb luck, and I almost laughed aloud thinking of how brutally she would have retaliated.

And in this sudden clarity, I had a fine idea. I looked at her squarely and, in a low, controlled voice, said, "I don't think it helps to scream and get so upset." I had never responded to anyone's anger like this, with cool logic that was meant to subdue. I may have learned it from her, the times when we clashed and she opted for detached contempt. I said again, "I don't think it helps to scream," and repeated it two or three more times as she continued to shriek at me, my outward stillness enraging her further. Eventually she ran out of steam and backed away, looking spent and old. I turned around, went to my room, and tried to calm my shaking hands.

—

I flew back to Maine the next day. Tootsie and I were silent on the two-hour drive to the airport. As I stood in line at the gate, ticket in hand and waiting to board, I still wanted to salvage something. Maybe if I said the right thing, her reply would make me understand. So I told her, "I'm sorry things turned out this way."

She shrugged. "Fuck it."

I turned away and walked down the jet bridge, stunned and blind.

PART TWO

FORWARD, FORWARD

31

Fear was waiting for me at Carol and Carroll's house in Peru, behind the gloomy wood paneling of my attic bedroom. The house felt no different than it had three years earlier, right after the murder. Texas was nothing more than some sunlit dream.

My aunt and uncle went to bed early, around nine o'clock, and I'd say good night with a smile meant to hide the anxiety I felt at filling the remaining hours of night. I watched TV for an hour, until ten, when I was expected to go to bed. Once upstairs, I'd read until the quiet of the house broke my concentration.

Darkness filling the house, darker woods surrounding. A creak from downstairs. A tiny shuffling within the walls. Each sent a jolt through me, bigger every time, until I'd respond even to silence, a hyper-ready live wire primed to run. *It's nothing*, I'd think, flushing doubly with adrenaline and shame. *I'm safe, it's fine, it's fine.*

And then that hard-line part of me, that flinty older sister, would speak up, a fully formed voice in my head that I could not control. *But maybe he knows, now, that you're here. News travels fast, and he's probably still in Bridgton. Of course he could find you — anyone could.* She told me that readiness was more important than happiness, more valuable to survival.

I knew I was supposed to accept a new reality: one where a killer entering the house was unlikely. But I had no proof.

And so the fear would grip me colder. But I'd find something to hold on to, a way to keep myself out of the abyss. I'd focus on the fact that my uncle would awaken if anyone were to enter the house. My uncle, territorial protector, with guns.

But then the voice would remind me that Carroll was getting older. That maybe someone had come in and quietly strangled him, snuffed him out a couple of hours ago, before my hearing had been sharpened by fear. My aunt could be sitting down there right now, staring into the eyes of the killer, unable to warn me for the knife at her throat.

My heart rate would increase, rushing through my body with more and more force. Sweat would gather on my upper lip. I'd reach up slowly to wipe it, careful not to make the sheets rustle, should the sound reveal me. Careful not to breathe too deeply, should the rushing air be heard downstairs. I had to convince myself that the sound of my pulse, loud as it seemed, was contained within my body.

No one was down there. The killer was down there. This could be my last minute before dizzying terror, and the end of my life. This minute. These past five minutes. This hour. Two.

Finally my fatigue would win out. If tonight posed no threat to me, if I was going to live, so much the better. But since I couldn't stop thinking I might die, I'd prepare by letting go. I'd think about the killer bursting in at any moment, imagine myself crazed with fear and begging for my life, and decide to go down more quietly. Dignity might be possible, I thought. I'd picture myself greeting him with a calm face. Standing still while he gripped my arm and showed me his knife. Nearly falling down with relief. A kind of joy at finally knowing the ending.

At this point, the fear would let go of me, and a great sweeping freedom would take hold. My hands would unclench, and I'd free-fall down into sleep.

Morning brought light and life, and the day brought distraction. Nightfall returned me to the fight.

Morning again. Day. Night again. For months.

—

I didn't tell anyone about those nights. I was too proud, and was convinced that no words could erase my fear. In school we read Faulkner, and our discussion of Vardaman's "My mother is a fish" went on and on, and all I could think about was the wet, thudding sturgeon that night, in that house only an hour's drive from my classroom. I sat silent and ill and desperately hoped that the teacher wouldn't call on me. But I would not leave the room. I would not reveal myself.

Although I felt less safe in Maine than I had in Texas, Carol and Carroll were much easier to live with than Tootsie and Jimmy. I knew they loved me, even if they didn't seem thrilled that I'd be sharing their home for the next three years. When they picked me up at the airport, we'd all seemed awkward, uncomfortable — the situation was foisted on them as suddenly as upon me.

Carol had a no-nonsense attitude, but with her curly blond hair and musical laugh, she was approachable and warm. She was forever trying to lose ten pounds, going on wacky diets involving cabbage soup or grapefruit. She did heavy work at the paper mill, working eight-hour swing shifts that sometimes ran through the night, but complained only rarely. At dusk, she would open the door and sing "Kiiiitteeees!" to call her cats inside from the cold. I knew she had a hard edge within her, but it was buried much deeper than Tootsie's.

My uncle Carroll worked in the woods, cutting trees for that same paper mill. He had the same curly blond hair, and had been with Carol since they were teenagers, back when he was her brother Wendall's best friend. He was silly around little kids and cared deeply for animals, who seemed magically drawn to him. Still, he also carried a flinty anger within; some days he would be unaccountably silent, and I'd constantly feel like I was annoying him.

Peru was familiar, but disappointing. It's a typical Maine town, but even smaller: fewer than two thousand people living on thickly forested land that winds between a river and a ridge. It's about an hour north from Bridgton, an hour that makes a big difference. Four other small towns feed into the high school, which sits across the wide Androscoggin River in Dixfield. The school is called Dirigo, the Maine state motto — Latin for "I lead." When I attended, Dirigo led in girls' basketball and sometimes boys' wrestling and not much else, and had a student body of about 250. I had dedicated teachers, especially in my English and history classes, but I learned calculus out of a textbook from 1963. The entire first floor was gutted; most of our classes that year were held in church basements while the old building was being renovated, and I couldn't pronounce the French I learned because I could barely hear my teacher over the band saws in the next room. The wide, slow Androscoggin was beautiful, but when we wanted to swim we had to go upstream, past the paper mill in Rumford. This was not a land of sparkling lakes; the summer people did not come here. The shadows of tall, dark pines loomed over me. Sunset happened early and far away, beyond the prodigious mountains.

I was isolated by my anger, an indignant rage that made me turn further and further within myself, convinced that no one could understand me. Carol and I would have some minor clash, and I'd head up to my bedroom and kneel on my bed and scream, high-pitched and breathless, shoving a pillow into my mouth until I could hardly breathe, drool and tears wetting the pillowcase. I can still feel that peach-fuzz cotton on my tongue, taste the baby powder and faint detergent. My body rigid, I'd drive my head into the pillow over and over, angry not at Carol but at Tootsie — so angry that when I heard she had moved to Washington State, I imagined a hundred-foot cedar falling on her. Even in the moment, I knew the image was silly and cartoonish, but I wanted something unfair and horrible to happen to her, and the image was perfectly diffuse and indirectly violent, like a spinning house crash-landing in Oz.

Carol and Carroll were mostly reasonable and calm, and they did truly care about me. They did a lot for me over the couple of years I lived with them. But there were some blunt reminders that their responsibility for me went only so far. I arrived shortly before my sixteenth birthday, and I'd already had my license in Texas, under a special "emergency" provision related to Tootsie's military work. In Peru, the nearest town big enough to have a movie theater was forty-five minutes away, and no people my age — in fact, few people of any age — lived within walking distance. But when I asked Carol how we would go about securing my Maine license, she said, "I don't think that's such a good idea. If you get in a wreck, somebody could sue me and take my house. You'll just have to wait until you're eighteen." I could live with them, but they would not take any risks for me, however far-fetched the potential consequences. The fact that this made sense didn't make it less painful.

I knew that if I'd been born into another family, I could have ended up in foster care after Mom died. Or, perhaps worse, with my father and Teresa. I knew that taking me in wasn't easy, that Carol and Carroll — whose son was now thirty-three — hadn't planned on housing a teenager in their later years. I tried to be thankful that they had accepted this burden. But I didn't want to be accepted. I wanted to be wanted.

I was desperate to conceal myself, to seem placid and normal, because I knew that I'd reached the last place that would take me. I could not show my rage, as I had at Peggy's. I could not feel for any other girl the sort of affection I had felt for Anne, or at least I couldn't do anything about it. But I knew that neither of those things had been the reason I'd been told to leave either of those homes. I knew it wasn't that simple. It was hard not to suspect that there was a catalog of things about me that were annoying, offensive, hard to live with. Sometimes I wished that someone would just tell me what they were.

—

Dixfield got a new chief of police a couple of months after I arrived. It was Dick Pickett. I felt followed, plagued. I was working to put that time and that town and that girl behind me — I built a barricade of the lakes and rivers and mountains between Bridgton and Peru, mentally exaggerating the distances. Dick Pickett sitting in an office just steps from my school seemed like a sick joke. I didn't want him or anyone connected to Bridgton anywhere near me. I fantasized about acting out, drinking at a party somewhere, getting arrested and hauled in and then facing Dick down, asking him if he and his boys couldn't do something better with their time. Like solve my mother's murder.

I ignored the fact that the state criminal division was a separate entity from the Dixfield Police Department. And I didn't know that someone new was taking over the investigation, someone smarter, far less arrogant. That he and his partner were analyzing every word of Pickett's files, were tracking down dozens of potential suspects. That in the next couple of years, they would draw blood for DNA testing from so many men that they would come to be known as the Vampires.

I went silent again, as much as I was able. I spoke to people only when I had to. A girl named Carrie, whose grandmother lived in the only house visible from Carol and Carroll's, was asked to help me settle in at school. There was only the one building, plus those church basements; there wasn't much to show or to explain to me. Sometime during the first week, she introduced me to a few friends of hers, and the first thing I said to them was "Sorry, I'm not going to remember any of your names." I wasn't interested in making friends after learning all those names at Central, names of people I would probably never see again. After all that work, my grades hadn't even transferred.

I planned to wait out my last two years of school, graduate, and go back to Texas. Anne and I had started talking on the phone again and writing long letters. I understood that this mirrored my first days in Texas, when I longed for Maine forests even as I was falling in love with the desert, and once again I felt I'd forever be dreaming of a place other than the one I was in.

I did my schoolwork well, still seeing college as salvation. My teachers paid close attention to me, and I didn't realize how depressed I was until the guidance counselor asked me into his office and said that several of my teachers were worried about me. They knew why I'd come to the school, why I lived with my aunt and uncle; I was one of the few new students in a fifty-two-person class that had been together since kindergarten. "I'm fine," I insisted, ashamed that my unhappiness was so evident. "Really. But thanks."

Still, I agreed to be paired with one of a handful of teachers who had offered to listen, informally, to students' troubles. I got the youngest one, a good-looking guy who must have just gotten out of college. But I couldn't tell him anything. The problem was that I'd noticed, while he was writing on the board during Humanities, how much his hands looked like Mom's — freckled, with long fingers, strong palms, and large knuckles. I was scared of those hands, of their unnatural persistence in the world, but I also wanted them on me. When we met after school to talk, all I could do was look at those beautiful hands of his, folded on his desk. I could have leaned over and softly kissed his full mouth. I could have burst into tears. I sat there, carefully not moving, unsure which impulse was more likely to seize me.

—

That first winter back rose to greet me like a dog that had been chained and waiting, lean and cold and beautiful and full of teeth. The snow came down relentlessly, and as I waited for the bus in the morning, the air was so dry and harsh that I could feel it rushing down my throat and into my body with each breath. But I had retained my thick northern blood: each morning I woke in the dark and showered, and I would stand out by the road in a canvas jacket over a T-shirt, the long ropes of my hair freezing around me.

In January, the night before we were to return to school from winter break, a light drizzle of freezing rain began, sparkling in the spotlight mounted on the garage and pinging against the windows. The next morning I awoke to the pure silence of lost power, the absence of refrigerator hum and furnace kick. Even my uncle's police scanner was silent. My alarm had not sounded, and I had no idea if I was late or early. I walked downstairs in a disoriented haze, and when I looked outside I saw that two inches of ice had covered everything in the night; the glassy layer on the porch railing was so flawless that I could see right through it. The rain was still coming down fast, a solid silver sheet. The ice on the porch grew to three inches, four. Carol's rosebush, towering out of the snow, held slabs of ice on every twig.

The ice came down for two full days. We were out of school for two weeks, out of power at our house for three. I read every book on that semester's English class list, from dawn through candlelight. I drank cups of hot chocolate and wrote in my journal and looked out at the bright whites and soft shadows of snow polished under the glare. We had heat for a few hours a day, when Carroll ran the generator. I'd step out onto the porch now and then, just to listen to the gunshot crackle of trees breaking under the weight of the ice. Many of them died under that weight, but others held strong, sending forth green leaves when spring finally came.

The melting of ice works by acceleration: slow at first, then faster and faster. As the warmth returned, I thawed out, too; I felt purified, lighter. I was grateful for Carol's simple meals, served every evening at six o'clock precisely, and for the neatly folded laundry she left on the stairs for me to take up to my room. My purple parakeet, Moonshadow, had stayed at Carol and Carroll's while I was in Texas, and every few nights Carroll would take him out of his cage and give him a bath in the kitchen sink, the two of them saying "Good little bird!" back and forth to each other, Moonshadow boxing with Carroll's thumb.

Things kept improving, gradually, life nudging me along. I got recruited to the math team and started practicing with the tiny, misfit marching band. I even joined the tennis team, although I could barely play. I applied for and was accepted to a summer program for students who would be the first in their families to attend college. I wasn't a runner, but I let my friend Jen talk me into joining the cross-country team so the girls would have six members and thus be eligible for state rankings for the first time in years.

I felt the same pull toward Jen that I had toward Anne. I tried not to think about it, to deny it, but of course volunteering to run miles through the steep, rocky woods every day after school was just the sort of stupid thing a person does to win a girl's affection. But I knew our friendship could go only so far; my uncle hated "queers." More and more celebrities were coming out in the late nineties, and related news coverage never failed to spark a vicious rant from him about how "all those pedophiles should be locked up; we should just shoot 'em." I wanted to think that none of this applied to me, but could not ignore my body's panicked reaction each time I heard him say these things. In addition to my worry that I'd be thrown out, I didn't want to lose his love; I didn't want him to hate me. I did not want more loss.

Conveniently, I liked boys, too, and I soon fell for one — Jen's best friend, Jason — so I dated him. It was easier and safer to be like everyone else, or seem to be, just as it had been easier and safer to hide my past in the time of the O.J. trial. I became skilled at ignoring my own desires, focusing less on what I wanted to do and more on what I was supposed to, on what was expected of a smart, college-bound girl. I could not take risks, and it seemed foolish to make myself more vulnerable than I already was.

My school tour guide, Carrie, and her friends Danielle and Nicole became my close friends, and to this day they love to repeat my opening line to them — "I'm not going to remember any of your names!" — while bursting into laughter. We four girls were a relatively innocent group: we liked to stay up late watching funny movies and swim in Danielle's pool and play billiards in the rec room above her garage. We could make one another laugh at any stupid little thing. We didn't party or drink or smoke weed; I felt safe with them.

But when I was alone I felt different, far apart. Very late one night in my bedroom, I turned to a random cable station and began watching a movie called *Freeway*. In the movie, an orphaned, fifteen-year-old blonde is driving to her grandmother's house when her car breaks down. A nice-looking man in glasses picks her up, but soon she figures out that he is a serial rapist and murderer, one she's heard about on the news. She eventually manages to shoot the man several times, by being tough and nasty and smart. I watched this movie in a state of hypnosis, not just cheering this girl on but becoming her. I was in that cab in the night: I could feel the busted springs of the grimy bench seat, the forward-sweeping motion of the truck, the weight of the gun in my hand. And I felt, in my body — in what had become her body — the desire to kill. *Oh, if I could kill some man, one of these men who prey upon us.* It wouldn't even have to be the one who killed Mom. Any violent man would do. My hands tightened into fists; I was a torch upon my bed. When the movie ended, I didn't know what to do with myself. I didn't dare leave my room. If I did, I might take all the glasses and dishes from the cupboards and throw them to the floor one by one, just to destroy something. I stayed up until sunrise, visions of the night of the murder competing with fantasies of myself as killer.

It might have been then that I began consoling myself with

thoughts of a long silver gun. I saw it clearly, for years after the murder: a shiny barrel at the end of my hands, both weapon and shield. I'd sneak it into the courthouse on the first day of the trial I longed for, somehow using my victim's innocence, my blond harmlessness, to get it past the guards. A few hours of the proceedings would pass before I'd get my moment. The killer would be sitting on a witness stand, ready to defend himself, and I'd stand up from the gallery, stride to the front of the courtroom, and destroy him before anyone knew what I was doing. In the fantasy, my hands and the barrel and the explosion always obscured his face.

Those fantasies, and that rage, eclipsed the grief and love I felt for my mother. My memories of her were becoming dimmer with time, and it was easier to feel fear and anger, because they seemed to have an endpoint: the trial, if it would ever come. Sadness was more dangerous, because I knew it would never end.

32

Near the beginning of senior year, just as I was starting to research colleges, the cops returned. I met the new primary investigator on the case, Walter Grzyb (pronounced "Gribb"), who would consult with Dick Pickett for some time. They'd had a few small leads here and there, but they hadn't made any real progress. Despite the fact that Dennis's DNA had twice failed to match the samples from the crime scene, Dick still thought Dennis was the killer, and still thought that I had repressed some memory that would solve the case. When I met Walt, he seemed more reasonable, more personable and empathetic than Dick, but by then I was angry at all cops. They were incompetent and lazy. They should have solved the case long ago. But still, I agreed to be interviewed again.

After a few weeks of research, Walt found Dr. Daniel Brown, a psychiatrist who specialized in memory recovery using a combination of therapy and hypnotherapy. He had a professorship at Harvard and an international reputation; if we were going to uncover repressed memory, this was our guy. Walt asked if I'd be willing to see Dr. Brown down in Boston, for four to six two-hour visits. If Dr. Brown concluded that I had no repressed memory, the police would never again try to retrieve it. They would take my word that I'd told them everything I could. I agreed. I was sure we wouldn't uncover anything.

I hoped I'd be proven right. And I hoped I'd be proven wrong.

Walt drove me down to Boston himself: four hours of awkward attempts at conversation. He insisted I select the radio station, but it was hard to enjoy the music when I thought he was just humoring me, suffering through the monotony of "Bittersweet Symphony" for my benefit. I was relieved when we finally pulled up and parked next to a long brick office building, when we were finally sitting with Dr. Brown, getting started.

I liked Dr. Brown right away, because he was a bit strange. I liked that this Ivy League memory expert had wild gray hair and a shirt unbuttoned to mid-chest, with a gold chain showing. That he was matter-of-fact and didn't spend a lot of time cozying up to me. Here was a man who drew his own conclusions, I thought, who wouldn't listen to a bunch of easy bullshit. He seemed like a truly neutral party, not a tool the cops were wielding against me.

Walt was excused from the sessions, which were videotaped for Dr. Brown's later analysis. I quickly forgot about the presence of the camcorder, because I spent the sessions with my eyes closed, following Dr. Brown's quiet prompts. The goal was to immerse me in the night of the murder and the weeks preceding it, so I could take another look around and try to report more than I had before. I entered an altered state — just a little more conscious than hypnosis — where I could perceive details but felt little emotion in connection with them. This was meant to make details less threatening, and therefore easier to retrieve. At the end of the session, it always felt like only a few minutes had passed.

The visits were on Tuesdays, and when Carol explained the situation to my school principal, he readily agreed to excuse my absence. The days afterwards, though, always felt a little unreal. I told my closest friends why I was going out of town, and word must have spread — in such a small class, absences were always commented on the next day — but I can't remember anyone asking me anything. Carol and Carroll and I didn't even talk about it, just as we rarely talked about Mom.

The final session came in the last week of school before Christmas. Afterwards, Walt and I sat waiting on one side of a narrow conference table: wood laminate, edges wrapped in black rubber that I pressed my fingernail into, making satisfying hatch marks. Dr. Brown came in and settled into a chair across from us. Winter light flowed in through a tall window, and the hum of traffic below threaded between the panes. I could see the white hulls of boats lined up along the Charles.

"I think we've pretty well determined that Sarah doesn't have any significant repressed memories," Dr. Brown began, and then I stopped listening. I settled back into my chair. The corners of my mouth twitched: a tiny smile. I'd won, finally. After all this time, here was an official who believed me, who could stand up for me, who could get them to stop asking the same goddamn questions over and over and over. I felt relief, and I felt smug, like any teenager proven right in the face of adult conviction.

But still, I would gladly have been proven wrong, to have found out who the killer was. If we had recovered something important in the first session, we could have had him in jail by Christmas. The theory was that memories are repressed for a reason — usually to minimize psychological damage. I had been willing to risk some damage to find this person.

Walt's face remained serious as he listened to Dr. Brown. He nodded, asked a couple of questions. As we walked back to the car he said, "Well, I guess that's it."

"I guess so," I said. "Sorry there wasn't more."

We drove to a deli and got Italian sandwiches, made small talk as we ate. Walt wasn't a bad guy, I thought. But the cops had failed me, and I was sure they would keep on failing. They were so prim in their pressed blue uniforms, so professional in their manner, and yet they weren't actually in control of anything. It had been six years, and still they were helpless.

When we got back into the car, Walt sat there a moment before putting the key in the ignition.

"Sarah . . ." he said. "I'm really sorry that we haven't found this guy yet. I know it's been hard for you to do all this. We're going to keep working. I promise you, we're going to do everything we can to find this guy." He bowed his head a moment while he ran a hand across his forehead. Then he put the car in reverse and twisted around to peer past me, to see the way out.

There had been tears in Walt's eyes; he'd had such hope. I felt uncomfortable, seeing this man cry. I finally had to admit that he and the other cops had been trying as hard as they could. That maybe we just weren't going to find him.

33

Carol and Carroll and I got along pretty well in those final high school years, until suddenly, shortly after my eighteenth birthday, we didn't. Carol and I got into a huge fight — our first, really. I was going to a movie with Jason that night, and she asked who was paying for the tickets. I told her I was, surprised that she knew that when he and I went out, I sometimes — but not always — paid. It made sense to me: I received an allowance out of the remainder of Mom's Shoe Shop money, and his family wasn't able to give him extra cash. He was very kind, always did something nice for me in return. Carol immediately got angry when I told her I was paying, and I was so surprised that I responded with something snotty, like, "It's my money — what does it matter? It's only like ten dollars."

But it didn't really matter what I said; I could see that Carol had been ready to be angry before I'd even answered the question. Everything I said made her angrier, in a way I'd never seen before, an out-of-control escalation. She was particularly irate over the fact that I was letting my boyfriend "take advantage," which I took as an insult, as though I would be blind to manipulation.

Carol's reaction was surprising, all out of proportion. The fight didn't last long; moments after she asked who was paying, she was leaning sharply toward me, yelling. Soon she was chasing me up the stairs. It didn't occur to me to stand my ground. I slammed my bedroom door against her, slid down to the floor, and braced my sneakered feet while she continued to yell. The next day, when I asked her to serve as a reference for potential landlords, she agreed, and that was the only discussion we ever had about my moving out. I was angry at her, but I was more angry at myself, for scurrying away into my bedroom, for taking it.

Later, I found out that Carol and Carroll's son had landed in some serious legal trouble shortly before our fight. And I remembered that Tootsie was going through a divorce when she threw me out. They'd both been raised in a family where people screamed at one another, where if you felt vulnerable you came out swinging. I wasn't perfect, but I think that I was probably the recipient of frustrations that had little to do with me, or, at least, that made dealing with an extra family member much more difficult.

I'd used some of the Shoe Shop money to get my license and a car on my eighteenth birthday. And I was already paying a small rent to Carol and Carroll, out of the Social Security benefits that would continue to be paid out until I started college, money that would have gone to Mom had she lived to retirement. I figured I might as well pay a landlord instead, and lose the ten o'clock curfew.

The only available apartments were in Rumford, home to the smoke-pumping paper mill that was the area's stuttering economic heart. The mill's golden era was forty years past, and now the town was all uneven clapboard and acid-crumbled bricks, the bars of better times long boarded over. Most mill employees preferred to live in one of the clean, leafy towns nearby and commute to work, as Carol and my uncle Wendall did. But those places were too small to have many apartment buildings, and I would have been too nervous to rent a house surrounded by trees.

I met with a handful of landlords I found via classified ads in the newspaper, older men who often seemed a bit threatening. One asked if I had a boyfriend, and as I answered him I told myself that he just wanted to know if I had a backup if I ran out of cash. The apartments were usually moldy, with stained carpets and long-buried cooking smells. I told a girl at school the address of one, and she said that the place next door was where people went to buy meth. I got a little more depressed with each showing, until I found a miraculously perfect apartment: the top floor of a cute wooden house, a clean place with a washer and dryer and a screened-in deck. The bedroom was huge, and from it I could crawl out onto the roof to sunbathe. A previous tenant had stenciled a border of flowers and ducks up near the ceiling; when I saw them I remembered Mom on the ladder in the sunshine, painting hearts and pineapples in the kitchen. The landlord, Rob, was a respected foreman at the mill, a youngish man who knew my friend Danielle's mom. The rent was eighty dollars a week, cash I left in an alcove in the back stairway, where Rob sometimes left me maple syrup he tapped from his own trees.

Two weeks after that fight with Carol, I left. It was one of those rare, beautiful circumstances where I didn't consider a decision at length; I knew just what I had to do. I told my friends my moving date, and eighteen of them showed up to whisk my belongings from my cramped bedroom to the new place. I didn't even have to pack. I felt loved, but I also knew that my move was exciting for them: I was the first person we knew to go out on her own.

Rumford was out of my school district, but my guidance counselor said that if I didn't change my mailing address, I could quietly finish out my senior year without changing schools. I had just enough money to live on my own; to my Social Security income I added paychecks from a part-time job at Viewer's Choice Video, the micro-chain that Mom and I had rented from in Bridgton. A guy from school soon came in and told me I was known as the "hot movie store girl" among the skater boys in Rumford. I felt proud when he told me this, and powerful, but when he left, I suddenly felt more exposed, standing with my back to the plate glass window that separated me from the parking lot.

—

As soon as I moved out, Carol and Carroll appeared more regularly at school events, offering easy smiles and congratulations after plays and award ceremonies. Their hugs had the clutch of apology. When I came by to pick up my mail, I drank coffee with Carol in the kitchen, and she asked after Danielle and my other friends. My uncle, formerly taciturn and cranky, now gave me a kiss on the cheek each time I walked out the door. I was as happy for the kindness as I was for the ability to leave.

My apartment was cute, but it was on Pine Street, which sat just a couple of blocks from the mill. The sky was never fully dark at night, instead glowing orange with floodlights and smoke. When people discovered I lived on Pine, they invariably asked, "Which end?" The section near the hospital was respectable, but as you moved west, the buildings fell progressively further into disrepair, until you reached the welfare apartments closer to the river. My place was right in the middle, a tough call between "good" and "bad" Pine. My life, too, seemed to straddle that border.

There was a man who lived on the bad end of Pine whom I seemed to see too often. He'd be walking down the street or shopping at the grocery store and I'd think, *There's that guy again.* Days would pass, and he'd cross my mind for no real reason; I'd tell myself I was just being paranoid, but then I'd see him later that day. He came to the movie store often and was always too friendly, and he rented videos only from the porn room in the back. My coworkers teased me, said this washed-up older man was my "boyfriend." My "secret admirer." I didn't tell them that he looked a bit like my father.

One morning I woke up and walked out to my car, and there was an unrolled condom hanging from my antenna. Two days later, my friend Jessie confessed, laughing at her prank. "Good one," I said. "Yeah, good one."

I never had any trouble from that man, but his resemblance to Tom disturbed my sense of security. I had been so fully severed from the girl I was the last time I saw Tom — from a distance, that day at the courthouse six years before — that even the thought of seeing him again confounded me. I'd see this echo of my father around town and idle fantasies would run through my head: that he really was Tom, and was just waiting for me to recognize him and say hello. And only that girl I'd been when I was twelve, the girl who had lived through all that fear and sadness, a person who now seemed so distant and abstract, would know if it was him. It wasn't really Tom I was looking for; it was me. If someone from my former life could recognize me as that same girl from long ago, I'd know she hadn't died along with Mom.

—

As I finished up the school year and kept working my video store job, I waited for college admission decisions to roll in. I'd applied to six colleges that fall and was admitted to all but one, Harvard, where I was wait-listed. I didn't want to wait for them to make up their mind about me, so I called and told them to remove me from the list. The woman on the phone was confused, and then surprised — she had never gotten such a call. But if they weren't sure they wanted me, I no longer wanted them. I'd walked through that beautiful brick-and-ivy campus a few times with Glenice, longing burning in me even when I was only ten years old. But I knew I'd never enjoy it as the poor kid who'd barely gotten in. I still wanted to be wanted, and this time I wasn't going to settle for just being tolerated.

I wanted to be bold and adventurous and attend school in a big city, but I ended up choosing Davidson, a tiny liberal arts college in small-town North Carolina. For years afterwards, I regretted my failure of nerve, but now the choice makes perfect sense. When I visited the campus, the weather was warm and lush, and the buildings were stately and impeccably maintained, from the neoclassical library to the small brick hut where students brought their laundry to be done for free. The admissions office could offer me generous financial aid, because most of the students' families could pay the full tuition. The curriculum would be challenging, but nothing else about the place would be. Ultimately, I wanted to be safe.

At Dirigo graduation, I stood for a moment alone, in a momentary break between hugs from friends and hectic photographs taken by Carol and Carroll and Gwen and Glenice. I looked out over a shining green lawn, and suddenly and painfully couldn't comprehend that Mom wouldn't come rushing up a moment later, to wrap her arms around my neck, imprint my cheek with her sticky strawberry lip gloss.

34

I left Maine, closed that chapter of my life. I cordoned off both the hope and the hopelessness, left them up there in the cold and went down south. I read. I partied. I pretended the reading had nothing to do with a deeply buried impulse to write, and I pretended the partying was no different from any other college kid's. I sat in dorm rooms on dusty futons, gossiping and laughing, and danced in frat houses hazy with sweat, pushed up against khaki-clad young men I had no intention of bringing home. I could drink half a bottle of vodka in a night, taking bloated shots straight off the bottle's narrow lip. I felt pain only in that upturned second, when I looked at the convex glass bottom and thought about draining the burning liquid down to it, tipping it all into my throat and seeing what would happen. I imagined the relief I would feel at the end, the sweet, collapsing surrender. I had gained weight but was still small-framed like my mother, would not have survived drinking an entire glassy fifth. I'd stumble home in the gunmetal early morning, the nightmare corpses of cicadas crunching under my heels.

I spent many nights throwing up, my body fighting my impulse to poison, lying on cool linoleum between sessions over the toilet and feeling my heart flutter erratically in my chest. At the end of the night, alone again at three, four, later, I could not give up; I always struggled against the slow suicide I'd begun. Sometimes I got it together enough to run cool water over a washcloth and lay it across my forehead, as my mother had done when I was little. I fought to keep my eyes open, whispering encouragement to my heart, that small, sick animal within me. *It's okay,* I thought. *Just keep going.* One misstep and I would fall, I knew that much, and in the end I did not want to fall.

Eventually my heartbeat would even out, and the nausea would let go a little, and I'd climb off the floor and shuffle to bed. As gray light edged into my room, I'd close my eyes, hoping that I'd wake up again, that I'd learn to stop doing this.

On some of those blurry nights, I'd think of Tom, or of Howard. I'd think about how alcoholism can travel through the family tree like poison up from the roots. But I was okay; I drank only on weekends. Until I drank on Wednesdays. Until I drank most days, could polish off an entire case of beer if I started in the morning. But I was fine; I felt fine. Couldn't feel a thing.

I didn't have a lot in common with most of the girls and boys I drank with. The girls wore neatly pressed shirts and tiny pastel shorts, and their legs were always perfectly shaved. The boys wore polos and khakis and exuded the sort of self-possessed assurance I associated with middle-aged businessmen. Their bodies and faces were capable and unmarred, their smiles too easy; they were already too used to getting what they wanted. When the fringe student newspaper ran an editorial describing an epidemic of unreported sexual assault on campus, the only thing that surprised me was how surprised other people were to read it.

For a time, I joined a women's social club, wore pearls to our weekly meetings, cultivated a well-behaved, sexless prettiness. But I could never get the details right. My nails were dirty or my bra straps showed or my Army surplus jacket covered up my whole outfit anyway. I didn't have the energy for all the powdering and lotioning required to erase the traces of my body, the smell of uncontrolled emotion. When I got drunk, I could be angry and mean, sharp remarks shooting from my mouth before I thought to restrain them. It was rare for the other girls to show anger, drunk or sober.

I loved that Army jacket, and wore it constantly; it had been given to me by a family friend who could find no one else small enough to wear it. But when a lacrosse player, a friend of a friend, sneered at me for wearing it all the time, telling me I should take it off and show my body more, I was overcome with embarrassment. As though the harmlessly pretty girls around me were the real women and I was just some tomboy kid. I charged around in boots while everyone else wore the boat shoes that my mother had deformed her hands to make.

—

My feeling of alienation at Davidson actually made it pretty easy to make friends with others who felt the same way, once I gave up on entering the wealthy mainstream of the place. My close friends were mostly broke northerners, queer kids, international students, and, paradoxically, nerdy students who didn't drink much. We stood out to one another, and clung together.

Two of my closest friends were Christina, the sort of cheery, easy-going athlete who is friends with all sorts of people, and Brent, who was gay but not yet fully out. One night we went to see *In the Bedroom*, a movie that I hadn't realized was set in Maine. As the lights fell, I was transported to a town that could have been a neighbor of Bridgton and Naples and Casco. There was the white Congregational church steeple, the turning drawbridge, the steep hill lined with clapboard buildings. Marisa Tomei played a young, beautiful single mother, around thirty years old, who dates a much younger man. As I watched the first half hour of the movie, I knew something terrible was coming; I knew it was a crime drama. But I was so happy watching her. She had a beautiful, spontaneous smile, and she loved with an easy, optimistic freedom. She was devoted to her two sons, and although she wasn't highly educated, she was smart and perceptive. She endured the judgment of her boyfriend's mother, and of others, with composure and grace. I'd always loved Marisa Tomei, who had been one of Mom's and my favorites ever since we'd watched her in *My Cousin Vinny*.

But in this movie, Marisa is plagued by a violent ex-husband who, halfway through, shoots and kills her young boyfriend. The ex gets out of jail for a while, on bail, and she and the boyfriend's parents have to suffer seeing him around town. I sat in the darkness of that theater, watching this killer buy coffee at the convenience store and drive slowly down Main Street, and I imagined Mom's killer doing the same in Bridgton. Except he would be blending right in; no one would know what twisted his face into a smug grin.

By the end of the movie, the boyfriend's mother convinces her husband, a pliable Macbeth, to kill the killer and bury him deep in the woods. I was thrilled, watching this unfold, but also terrified. I had long fantasized about killing Mom's murderer, or sending someone else to. But would I, if given the chance? Sitting in that theater, immersed in the deep woods on-screen, I felt that I was capable, but that I would ultimately choose not to. It was too ugly, ugliness on ugliness. I had long known this, but now could see it up close.

Realizing that I would never kill, even in the most forgivable of circumstances, should have made me feel good, secure in my humanity. But instead I felt bleak. Because what I realized was that there would be no recompense, there would be no satisfaction. I wanted Mom's killer off the streets, sure. I didn't want him walking around town as though nothing had happened, a violent man who could threaten the safety of others. But I knew then that jail wouldn't be enough, and death would be too much. There was no hope of a satisfying ending. I would have to find my own peace, without one.

When the lights came up, I felt exposed, like a mask had been pulled from my face. As we walked across the dark parking lot, I looked down at the pavement, away from my friends. We were all quiet at first. Then Brent started laughing. "Oh my God!" he said. "She was *soo* white trash! Marisa Tomei is *the best!*" I felt a rush in my chest, like hot water poured across my heart. I didn't say a thing.

—

Despite other moments of disappointment, I still felt more connected to my new friends than I did to the other Davidson students, although I told only a few of them about Mom. I still had an impulse to pretend as though this life and the one that came before were disconnected, unrelated. I kept binge drinking, unable to resist the numb comfort that came with it, and somewhere along the way I started blacking

SARAH PERRY

out. The first time, sophomore year, shocked me. I pieced it together the next morning, my memories skittery and disconnected, representing only a fraction of what my friends told me about the night. I thought about my body walking around, my consciousness switching to autopilot. Talking to people I knew or didn't, words escaping me and traveling out into the void, my memory for the last moment, the last hour, shut off. Memory not repressed, but never written.

That first blackout shook me, but when it happened again, it lost some of its force. I was a college kid; college kids blacked out. I'd spent so much time insisting to the cops that my memory was intact, it was a delicious relief to throw some of the hours of my existence to the oblivion they'd been so convinced lurked within me.

—

I didn't go to Maine for the shorter holiday breaks — Thanksgiving, Easter, the long Presidents' Day weekend. It wasn't worth the quick trip, I thought, and anyway I was proud of the fact that I didn't need to run home every chance I got, like the other students, who sometimes seemed like children to me. I went back north just once or twice a year. I'd stay in Peru and try not to think of that other town. But one day during a summer visit, I left the house and started driving, only half aware that I was headed toward Bridgton. I went the back way, slowly steering along bumpy camp roads that held tight to the lakeshores, before coming out on a long, straight road that led past the turnoff to Grammy's house and the cemetery, then shot down a hill into the center of town.

As I turned at the light downtown, I felt strangely out of place as an adult driving a car. I could almost see my shadow self in the passenger seat where I belonged — chubby kid belly, long blond hair — looking over at me expectantly. We were headed back toward that house. I felt curiosity mixed with some sort of bravado, some need to stare things down. The times I would drive slowly past that house would come to outnumber the times I drove up to the cemetery where Mom's pink-heart headstone sits.

As I drove down Route 93, I almost expected to see that police tape still cutting across my view, fluttering in the slight summer breeze. What I found was almost as sad: chain-link fence around the yard, dark fly screens falling off the windows, cheap children's toys scattered on the lawn. The remaining spruce tree next to the door did nothing to block my view.

There were two cars in the driveway, so I rolled slowly by. I didn't want to get caught, yet another curious stranger. I thought briefly about pulling over some distance away, maybe on the little connecting road across the street from the house, the one I'd given the 911 dispatcher as a landmark. But I knew that if I stopped, I wouldn't be able to step out of the car. The moment my foot hit the road, darkness would snap down like a shade. A mist would envelop me, and 1994 would come roaring into my living present.

Safe behind the wheel, I turned around and went back up Route 93. The distance from my house to the intersection seemed pathetically short. As I turned left onto Route 302, I was careful not to look at the Venezia.

I passed Linda's house, and just as I was wondering if she still lived there, I saw her walk out her front door in a bikini, holding a towel around her waist. I remembered how she used to tan on her lawn and even on her black-shingled roof.

Seeing Linda sent a shock through my body, a strange, bright thrill that made sweat break out in the crooks of my elbows. I kept driving, dimly registering more old landmarks: the big white house where my friend Vicki used to live. The cabins of Highland Lake Resort strung out along a break in the woods, with the water sparkling behind them. The town hall where I used to play basketball in the summer, the shack where I ice-skated in the winter visible just behind it. I turned left at the War Memorial and wound down the hill to the Big Apple, the gas station and convenience store that was the center of town gossip, where, a few hours after Mom died, dozens of people received news of the murder.

When I came to the Big Apple, I pulled into the parking lot to think;

the electric feeling of seeing Linda was still running through me, and I had to figure out what it meant. I wanted to see her, to talk to her. Mom would want us to be in touch, I thought.

I took a deep breath, squeezed my fists around the wheel to force the shakiness from them. I dug some quarters out of the console. When I stepped out of the car and walked to the pay phone, I had to hold myself back from running. A phone book hung there from a steel chain; the pages were feathery under my fingers, and her number was easy to find. That sequence of digits was immediately familiar, lined up neatly with memory I didn't realize was still within me. I pushed the coins in, but my heart started pounding; the blood was rushing through my head faster than I could think. What to say? What if seeing me would be too painful? The dial tone hummed in my skull. Finally I punched a button, and a clean, breathless silence began. I punched two or three more. I paused and held the heavy receiver to my ear. My shaking got worse, and I felt nauseated. I put the receiver back on its cradle. I kept my hand wrapped around it for a moment, holding on.

I didn't call. It was the first time in my life that I'd been physically unable to go through with something for reasons I couldn't explain.

I gave up, got back in the car. I drove over to the parking lot of the Highland Lake beach. The water shimmered in the late-afternoon light, sending up white explosions as skinny kids cannonballed off the docks. A few families sat on the sand, and some teenage boys perched in a cluster on a brick-red picnic table under the trees. I stayed in the car. I thought these people might recognize me, or they might not, and I wasn't sure which would be worse. I lit a cigarette and smoked through my open window, watching those kids jump off the dock, over and over.

35

My final year at Davidson, 2003–2004, was the smoothest one. I enjoyed my academic work and had a supportive group of friends. When I declared myself an English major, I hadn't understood that the degree wouldn't include much creative writing, but I did manage to take one writing class before graduating, and was encouraged by my professor, which gave me tentative hope. I'd fallen in love while studying abroad in Australia the previous year and was planning to move back, as charmed by him as I was by that country's abundant sunshine, its culture of laid-back happiness. But then I lost my courage right before graduation—we broke up, and I threw out the immigration paperwork. I could not commit, could not pull off such a big transition. The happiness that I imagined seemed ludicrous, totally unlikely, so I sabotaged it before I could be disappointed. This left me with no specific passion or profession or love I could follow, no idea where to go.

So the summer after I graduated from college found me stranded at Carol and Carroll's, broke and panicked about the future. Having dedicated so many years to academic success, I didn't know what to do with it. For weeks, I slept too late and shuffled aimlessly around the house, occasionally going out to my packed car to extricate something from the floor-to-ceiling mounds of my belongings. I avoided the television when my aunt and uncle were watching marathon sessions of *Law & Order: Special Victims Unit* or *Cold Case*, shows they seemed to find cathartic and I couldn't stand. Carol and Carroll tactfully avoided asking me what my plan was, but I knew they were wondering. I looked up rent prices in cities from coast to coast and tried on various futures in my head, but I couldn't gain any traction.

My friend and classmate Alex, who had moved to Raleigh for graduate school, saved me. After many sad summer nights of online chatting, countless tears shed in the white-blue light of the computer screen, I read his lifeline: "Just put your shit in your car and come back down. We'll figure it out."

My car was still packed, so I easily surrendered to Alex, a steadfast, responsible person who would never judge me for not being one myself. A couple of days later I said my goodbyes and got on the road. I stayed on Alex's couch for weeks, then rented a room in a filthy apartment in Chapel Hill, near the university. My roommates were expelled stoner undergraduates who cooked so much bacon that the kitchen walls were slick with it. The three years separating me from them suddenly felt like a decade. I didn't have a cell phone or internet connection or landline, and the feeling I remember most clearly from that time is the anticipation of walking through the clinging heat to the huge bank of steel mailboxes outside, hoping someone — who? — had sent me a letter.

Soon I got a job as an administrative assistant at the University of North Carolina, a huge blessing that at the time felt like a failure. I was ashamed to be a secretary while so many of my college classmates were moving on to bigger things, getting their MDs or going to art school or working with high-minded nonprofits in Washington. But then I'd look at my soft hands and think about Mom's swollen, twisted knuckles, and berate myself for wanting more. *You got this great education, and what are you doing with it? What people don't know is that you're actually stupid,* a vicious, ruthless part of me would hiss. *And you can't even fucking appreciate that you don't have to do any real work.*

Sometimes that voice got worse. Sometimes things got out of hand. The generalized fury I'd felt during college, unleashed on those long vodka nights, I now turned inward, I now felt all the time. I'd come home from work and sit alone in my bedroom, on my mattress on the floor, drinking beer from a warming six-pack I'd keep on the old carpet next to me. I could be out walking around town in the nice weather, I'd think, or I could go to a coffee shop, maybe make a new friend. But the idea of actually going out in public when I didn't have to was unfathomable, no matter how much Carolina sunshine sifted through my blinds. There was no hectic social life to throw myself into, to use as distraction, so it became hard to leave the house at all.

I'd try to read or to listen to CDs on my laptop, but I had trouble focusing on the books, and the music sounded tinny and emotionless, like it was coming from an open door at the end of a long hallway. I was full of rage at myself. Why wasn't I doing more, why was I wasting all of Mom's hard work? Why wasn't I at least happy? Finally, the frustrated energy within me had to go somewhere. I'd stand up quickly, as though I could run from that voice, and finally I'd pull my hand back and slap my face, hard, over and over. There was no one to keep me in line, no one to motivate me. No one seemed to care what I did, except me. I could be ruthless, and my ruthlessness paralyzed me.

I recognized this inner voice, but I didn't want to admit it. It was the second self, born into the rain on the night of the murder, the older sister who had helped me move forward under that great weight. She had taken me this far, but now she'd gone rancid within me, bitter and trapped and scornful of my flagging strength.

I fought back against her, though, as my life gradually improved. Courtney, the receptionist in our office, was around my age, and she kept inviting me to spend time with her tightly knit group of friends; eventually I said yes, and my life expanded from there as I met more and more people. I was terribly self-conscious at first, unused to talking to new people, but each time someone smiled upon seeing me again, each time I told a joke and someone laughed, I remembered for a moment that I could be nice to spend time with, that I wasn't as stupid and dull as I felt.

Courtney was a writer, at work on a book. She had talent and hope — she knew what she was doing. She'd polish up scenes between copies and incoming calls. She knew publishing was a long shot, but, unlike me, she wasn't ashamed to be seen trying. When I finally told her that I wanted to write, too, it felt like a huge confession. Part of the reason I'd taken a low-responsibility job was that I wanted time to write in my off-hours — a fact I hardly admitted to myself — but I rarely had the courage to sit down and do so. When I did, all I could think about was Mom. I would be overpowered by a clear memory of her, then sit down at my computer and pour out five or so pages in a fever, desperate to keep that moment forever. But then the fever would pass and I would be left with the screen's infinite blank page, the cursor blinking at me expectantly, and I'd go pour myself a drink. I did this every month or so, until my desktop was littered with disconnected stops and starts. As a child, I had left writing in a moment of terror, and every time I tried to return as an adult, that terror came back, hardwired and physical.

I'd thought slinking back down to North Carolina was some kind of failure, but it turned out to be exactly the right move. Free from the suffocating, conservative atmosphere at Davidson, its academic pressure, I could slowly relax in this land of large houses and mild winters. Eventually I moved to nearby Durham and became the caretaker of a beautiful, comfortably decaying historic house, living rent-free and steadily paying down credit card debt I'd accrued during college. My neighbor Liz exuberantly befriended me, dragging me out of the house and introducing me to her friends. She took me to parties, and we went out dancing at least once a month, when a friend of ours spun soul records in a crumbling four-story building that used to house a boxing ring, all dark corners and red lights.

I dated a little, falling into the comfort of touch and immediacy. Often, a relationship would begin before the previous one had ended; I tried to make myself feel better by joking that I had a "little problem with overlap." I was barely aware that I chained my loves together just as my mother had; I never would have admitted how deeply I needed someone.

I ended up befriending many other people who had crash-landed in the area, artists and writers looking to re-center, people who had been thrown off-balance by turmoil they would not or could not discuss. Six or eight of us started taking turns hosting weekly dinners, the meals becoming more elaborate and competitive each week. After we ate, we'd sit out on the porch and continue drinking the wine and beer we'd begun over salad, our chairs wobble-thudding on the wide, warped planks. Heavy vintage ashtrays from Goodwill lined up next to dirty tea saucers on the railings, and other friends would sometimes amble by and come sit with us. Porch sitting was best in the middle of the summer, when it was still eighty-five degrees at ten o'clock, the evening stretching unnoticed into the still-sweaty early hours of the morning. For me, porch sitting gave me back the night I'd loved as a young child, made it safe and beautiful again. And sitting and talking with these kind, smart friends, music on low, took the hard, speedy edge off my drinks, made me happy with fewer of them.

Looking back, it seems like we were all trying to catch our breath during those after-dinner, red-wine nights on the front porch, all those smoky evenings at the bar. Life was pleasant despite the feeling that if anything important was happening, it was happening elsewhere. Rent was low in Durham and wages were okay; we could put everything on hold for a while. Occasionally, someone would move to New York or Portland, Oregon. We'd have a big going-away party, only to welcome them back a few months later.

We laughed and drank and shared confidences and made love in a musical-chairs kind of way. When parents came up, I made it clear that my father was absent, my mother dead. Everyone assumed cancer and I didn't correct them. I made of these friends a new family that didn't need the facts concerning my first one. I faded away from my aunts and uncles; I called only every six months or so, and for the most part they didn't call me. I was no specific person's responsibility, and they all had their own lives to worry about. I had one friend, Mindy, with whom I had deeper, more open conversations. She knew what had happened to my mother, but we didn't talk about it much. There was no reason to. It all belonged to another era, for a while.

36

Then, one afternoon at the office, time collapsed again. It was a Monday, late March 2006. A quiet day. Polite, mumbled conversations, gurgle of the coffeemaker, the shirring sound of paper piling up in the copy machine exit tray. The occasional warbly, digital ring of a telephone.

The central reception line sang out at about two o'clock, *blurr-blurr-bl'blur* breaking the post-lunch spell.

"Dean's office — this is Courtney . . . Hold on — just a moment."

She nodded at me, hit the HOLD button. I stretched my face into a smile, one that would bend my words so that it sounded, on the other end, like I was chipper and energetic, eager to help. I raised my eyebrows at Courtney while she giggled. I snatched up the receiver, punched the lit button to release the line.

"Hello, this is Sarah!"

"Sarah, this is Walter Grzyb. How you doin' down there?"

The long, rounded vowels of that Maine accent rushed suddenly into my unprepared ears. It had been months since I'd spoken to anyone up north.

"Oh . . . I'm, I'm good. Just, y'know, Monday, working. Just at the office here . . . It's been a while —"

Walt cut me off, abrupt in a way I'd never heard before. "Good, good. Listen, Sarah, I've got some news for you. In fact, are you alone right now? Or can you get somewhere where you have some privacy?"

"Sure, sure," I said, starting to shake, just a little, surprising myself. "We have an extra office; I'll just transfer over. Just give me a minute." I couldn't tell if I sounded normal. I focused on all those old failed leads, tried to use them to hold down my newly pounding pulse. There had been a tightness in Walt's voice, a slightly higher pitch, something different from the even, professional tone I remembered. It almost sounded like excitement.

But surely Walt would read me the name of a town that, no, we'd never visited, a man that, no, I'd never heard of, a supposed lead that would prove to be the product of rumor. Many people called the police because they craved the shadowy fame of being connected to the case, thought it would throw them into relief against the gray background of other people's calm, uneventful lives. They tried to imbue incidental connections with meaning, their imaginations fast-forwarding to headlines about a heroic tipster. They claimed to have overheard confessions, to have found a knife in the woods, to have seen a vehicle that night, eight or ten or now twelve years ago, and the police would cautiously and thoroughly investigate and come up with nothing. As I got up from my desk, I prepared myself for the familiar whoosh of disappointment, the quick loss of hope, followed by the shame of ever having felt that hope, even if just for a moment. My life would not change, I told myself, and that would be fine. Just fine.

I shut myself into the dim spare office. White light from the overcast sky came in through the big window, angling down between our building and the next. I sat down at the large desk, armed with a white legal pad and a blue pen. I uncapped the pen, just in case. I picked up the receiver and pushed the button for Walt's call.

"Okay, I'm ready. What's going on?" I asked smoothly, calmly, in my work voice.

Walt took a breath. "Well, Sarah. We think we know who killed your mother. In fact, we're sure we know."

I can't remember what I said first; my heartbeat hammered in my ears, erasing the words as I spoke them. I do know that the surface of the desk suddenly seemed very far away. *If I faint,* I thought, *will anyone hear it?*

Walt first asked if the man's name was familiar to me: "Have you ever heard of a Michael — Mike — Hutchinson?" I hadn't. But as Walt explained, this was most certainly not another false lead. The sickening feeling of disappointment did not come. My pulse gradually slowed to normal.

Walt was sure. And the evidence sounded good. I lowered the pen's fine point and wrote: "Michael Hutchinson." I still have those notes. The handwriting is tight and cramped, unlike my usual scrawl, as though tentative or disbelieving. But the period after "Hutchinson" is large and sure, his name a sentence unto itself, a complete idea. I'd let the pen tip sit there for a second or two, flooding the paper with ink.

Walt told me that Hutchinson had matched the DNA samples taken from the murder scene. He had been convicted of a felony — kidnapping, plus criminal threatening with a firearm — in late 2003, and so he'd had to submit to a cheek swab for entry into the FBI's criminal database. The typing of each sample can take years, Walt said, because of a long backlog. Violence outpaced lab funding everywhere. Maine's delay at the time was two years; in some states it was up to ten. But Maine had recently received some federal funding, to catch up. Well, the lab had finally gotten to Hutchinson's sample just a week before, two and a half years after his kidnapping conviction, and as soon as they entered it into the database, there was a match to the blood samples that had been waiting twelve years, that had failed to match with nearly thirty other men. A solid match; no doubt about it. Hutchinson was now thirty-one years old. On that day, I was twenty-four, had lived without Mom for half my life.

The typing would be repeated, as was standard, but Walt had already spoken with Hutchinson — twice — in the county jail, where he'd been incarcerated after violating his probation. I listened closely, made a few more carefully inscribed notes, trying to retain each detail. I seized the most surreal one and asked, "You talked to him?" Someone I knew had sat down with this man, just the day before. He was no longer an abstract concept, a blank space behind the explosion of the long silver gun in my mind. He was real, a person upon the earth.

"Yeah," Walt said, and here his excitement broke through; he was thrilled to tell me the story. He sped up, and his sentences were scattered with little laughs: the happiness of victory. "I sat him down and I said, 'Do you know Crystal Perry? Were you ever in Crystal Perry's house?' And he up-and-down denied it, absolutely denied it. I came back the next day, I gave him another chance! And he denied it again. And that's going to be really good when it's time for the trial, because he won't be able to make up some story about knowing your mother — he'll be out of a lot of alibis for why we found his DNA all over the place."

Trial, I thought. *Trial, oh my God. It's going to happen.*

"And, y'know, too: we knew all along this guy had cut his hand. That he must have had a wicked gash across his palm, from the knife — that was the reason his blood was all over. Happens all the time in cases like this: they slip. And as soon as I saw him, Hutchinson, I asked to see his hand, and he has this big scar, right across his palm. He claims it's from a car wreck, but I just knew it — I always knew this guy would have this old injury."

Walt told me that if we got a conviction, the attorney general's office was considering pursuing a life sentence — as Maine does not have the death penalty. He explained that Maine was one of the few states where a life sentence carries no possibility of parole, and because judges can be hesitant to apply such an absolute punishment, the AG's office rarely suggested it. But in this case, it seemed more than warranted.

It turned out Hutchinson had been living right there in Bridgton all along; I hadn't been unreasonable when I'd imagined him walking down Main Street. He had a wife, two kids. Worked as a mason for his father's company, sometimes. Sold drugs, often.

I stopped writing and took a deep breath. "The thing is . . . I have to admit that at some point, I just thought I was never going to get this call."

Now Walt's tone got more serious. "You know, Sarah. I never wanted to say this, but sometimes, especially when there'd be months with just nothing, sometimes I thought I'd never be making this call."

Walt said that he and his colleagues were rushing to collect the facts they needed for the upcoming indictment, when charges would officially be brought and Hutchinson's identity would be made public. Walt had been promoted to a supervisory position but had stayed on the case, assisting the new primary investigator, Chris Harriman, and now they were tying up a twelve-year investigation, making sure that all the evidence was solid. They had to talk to a few more people, Walt said, to check up on some things. It would take a couple more days. I was the only person they'd told — they hadn't yet called the rest of my family.

"Should I tell them?" I said. "I mean . . . when should I call?"

"Well," Walt said, "it's totally up to you. You absolutely can do whatever feels best. If you want to tell them, that makes sense, and of course you can. But you should know that we really do need to keep things quiet — just for a few more days. We are going to do these interviews as quickly as possible, before word spreads — you know how it gets there in Bridgton. We need to surprise certain people. So you guys need to not tell anyone outside the family. We're expecting the indictment to be next Thursday; I'll call again on Monday or Tuesday to update you. And you can call me anytime."

I thought about my nine aunts and uncles. Their children and friends and neighbors. Groups of women sitting around kitchen tables, smoking and drinking coffee and talking for hours on long Sunday afternoons. I thought about how this news would alter reality for all of us, how impossible it would be to know this and then talk to a friend and not mention it. How quickly news flew from Oxford County, where most of them lived, to Cumberland County, where Bridgton was, to the south. My grandmother was desperate to know who the killer was; she would never be able to keep quiet once she knew. Word would leak as soon as she went to her hairdresser's, as soon as the Avon lady came. The Avon lady, incidentally, was my old babysitter, Peggy.

I decided to wait on word from Walt. I just had to lay low for one week.

I didn't want to risk damaging the investigation. I worried that someone would get information they weren't supposed to have, that some key piece of evidence would turn into gossip that would turn into hearsay, and in the process become inadmissible in court. I felt like my silence meant loyalty to Mom, putting her before those who had lost her.

But I also wanted to put things on hold. I'd done my best to move forward without this call. There had been life with her, and now there was life without her—a stark before and after, twelve years of each, splitting me in two. I needed time to adjust. I needed time to think. I wanted to keep it small, controlled. Walt advised me to have my office number removed from the university's website, in anticipation of press coverage, or worse. I was glad to hide.

Finding the man who'd killed her would mean once again imagining life if he hadn't. And I'd gotten so used to ignoring her absence. To pretending that I wasn't supposed to have a mother. That mothers were just something other people had.

I had a good excuse for hiding the news from the family, but in the coming days I would feel like a traitor. Word leaked out, but not through me. Carol called me suddenly, for the first time in months. We talked about everyday things, the usual catch-up basics—my roommate, work, improvements she was making on the house—but the end of the call was ragged, extended, her usual brisk sign-off was forever in coming. Finally she said, "Gloria called that police hotline. They said something about talking to people in Bridgton. It's so strange; she just called randomly, and then they acted like something was going on, but they wouldn't say what."

I wouldn't say what, either. I hedged. I acted surprised but not terribly interested. I got off the phone as smoothly as I could. We all just had to hold on for a little while longer. Walt would call soon.

But two days later, before I was able to call my family, they called me: my grandmother, Grace, had passed away. The next week, the indictment was made public, and I called them back. Walt had spoken to them earlier that day; he was the one to bring them the news, not me. If he'd known my grandmother was nearing the end, he would have called them earlier. But no one had told him. No one had told me, either.

In many ways, my grandmother had stopped living many years before. Her life had more or less halted when Mom died. She was obsessed with the murder, thought and talked about it constantly, could not stop wondering who had killed her daughter. She called the police incessantly, demanding information, detailing her theories about this man or that man. She rarely left the house; she had no hobbies. She told a friend that she couldn't leave, didn't want to: "This is where my memories of Crystal and Sarah are." Isolation and fear accelerated her decline into dementia. It's hard to know for sure what she understood in the end; she was often lost in time, sometimes didn't recognize people. But if we could have told her Michael Hutchinson's name, there's a chance she would have had some peace before dying.

37

Here's how he got caught.

In 2002, Michael Hutchinson heard that a few of his friend Rob Desjardins's pot plants had been taken from a power-line forest clearing. They knew who was responsible — a guy named Ian, a sort-of friend of theirs who would know where the weed was kept. Rob and Michael rounded up another friend, Derek. The three piled into Michael's dump truck, picked up some beers, and drove to the construction site where Ian worked. Just before they got there, Michael dropped Rob off, to wait in the woods a short distance away.

Michael and Derek found Ian, said they had weed and some beers. "Come for a ride," they said.

Ian, just nineteen years old, was dumb enough to get in the truck. Michael drove fifty or so yards down the road and slowed to a stop as Rob walked out from between the trees. Derek stepped out so Rob could climb in and wedge himself next to Ian. It was only after Derek got back in and the truck started to move that Ian noticed that the guys had a gun on the dashboard — an actual Glock. Rob grabbed hold of Ian's fingers and started pressing them back, hard, demanding to know where his plants were. Then they drove him to the woods and showed him the empty spot, like rubbing a bad dog's face into a ruined rug. Derek carried the gun as they walked through the trees. "Where are the plants, Ian?" they asked. "Where are the fucking plants?"

Ian walked around aimlessly, looking for the plants that he knew were actually back at his house. Finally the guys gave up. When the others stopped to smoke a cigarette, Ian bolted. Then he heard the gun fire, and knew things were serious. He ran and ran. By the time he reached the police station, he was so scared, he didn't even lie. Said he'd stolen the plants and he was in danger.

But Ian was just a kid. The next day, he and his girlfriend, Alyssa, were driving down Maine Hill when they saw Michael and Derek coming up in their rearview mirror. Ian leaned out the window and gave them the finger, and when he and Alyssa pulled into the Big Apple parking lot, Michael and Derek pulled in behind them. Derek grabbed Michael's gun, got out, and pointed it in Ian's face. The two exchanged words, and moments later Derek got back into the truck and Michael drove off. They didn't get far before the police pulled them over, dispatched to respond to the 911 call Ian had made from the Big Apple.

Both kidnapping and criminal threatening with a firearm are felonies in Maine; Derek was charged and convicted, and so was Michael, most likely because it was his firearm and because he drove the truck. Eventually Michael had to submit to a cheek swab for entry into CODIS, the FBI's Combined DNA Index System, which contains DNA profiles of thousands of forensic samples from suspects, convicted criminals, and crime scenes nationwide. There's no way to know what this meant to him, if he understood that opening his mouth for this brief moment could end up revealing that he was a killer. Still, two more years would pass before the match. Maybe by then he thought he'd gotten away with it. Or maybe not. A friend of his later told the police about a party where Michael, wasted beyond comprehension, had held his hands in a campfire, fingertips out. Looked like he was trying to burn his prints off.

In those two years between the swab and the match, Michael Hutchinson served six months in prison, got out on probation, and returned to Bridgton. Then he violated his probation when he failed to show up in court to answer a driving-to-endanger charge, one that involved driving high with his children in the car. He had also tested positive, on separate occasions, for weed and cocaine. His probation officer recommended that a warrant be issued for his arrest, and the Bridgton Police were eager to comply, happy to haul in a guy who had always given them trouble — driving under the influence, domestic violence calls, drug possession, the usual. But first they had to find him.

The Bridgton cops knew Hutchinson would soon be getting married to his second wife. "Let's get him then!" they said, laughing, having no idea they would be arresting the killer who had evaded them for almost a decade. They pulled him over as he was driving from the ceremony to the reception and transferred him back into state custody immediately, leaving the confused wedding guests waiting who knows how long at the VFW hall. It was Bernie King, who had been one of the first on the scene of Mom's murder, who made the arrest. A mere twenty-one days later, the state crime lab caught up on their backlog and discovered that Michael Hutchinson's DNA matched the samples from the Crystal Perry case. After all those years, the timing aligned perfectly. He would remain in jail until the murder trial began.

Upon hearing about the match, Hutchinson's new wife, Christy, called her cousin, Dennis Lorrain. Christy knew, of course, that Dennis had once been engaged to Mom.

"They charged Michael again!" she said. "They're saying he killed Crystal Perry." She was distraught. "Do *you* know anything about this?"

He didn't. But as they talked, Dennis rewound the tape in his mind. He remembered a day back in 1998. He and his friend Tammy had been standing in her driveway, talking about the murder, and she said, "I thought Michael Hutchinson did it." But Dennis didn't take her very seriously. At the time he thought, *Nah, I'd fucking know that.* He and Michael weren't friends, but they'd been in the same high school class. *I know him,* he thought. *I'd know that.* But when it came down to it, Dennis knew anything was possible. And despite all the trouble he'd been through as a suspect, all of the polygraphs and blood draws and the aggressive interviews with Pickett, he had continued to cooperate with the police over the years, even calling them up and bringing them leads when he found them. He respected Walt, and he understood the science of DNA testing. As Christy spoke, he could feel himself getting twitchy, warming up. He started to get angry, thinking he had missed this guy. He had been *right fucking there.*

Dennis interrupted Christy's tears. "Just so you know," he said, his voice level, a man giving a reasonable warning, "he's safe as long as the cops have got him. But if he gets out for any reason, I'm sorry, but I'm going to have to kill him."

38

The day Walt called me, the Durham County district attorney went public about an investigation into an accusation of gang rape by several members of the lacrosse team at nearby Duke University. The house where the attack was alleged to have happened was less than a mile from mine. Suddenly I wished my house had more secure windows. Suddenly the drafts and the chill that seeped in through the warped floorboards made it seem like anyone could come in. I asked my roommates to please remember to lock the doors at night.

The case went national; the woman was black, the boys were white. The press was far more interested in the effect these accusations would have on the lives of these promising young men than in the effect of the possible rape on this girl. The district attorney had asked news outlets not to use the alleged victim's name, but MSNBC let it slip: Crystal. This was when I learned that many people considered Crystal to be a low-class name. To me, "Crystal" meant beautiful. To others, it meant disposable.

Regardless of their guilt or innocence, I'd always feared young men like these, high on their own privilege and secure in their image of boys-will-be-boys innocence. I had long known that evil could hide in plain sight, that this must have been the case in Bridgton. And now I had proof that it had been, that Michael Hutchinson, at nineteen, had a baby face, that he had a soft voice, that he worked hard at his job.

That you'd never know, just by looking, that he was a murderer. And I was learning that some people still weren't convinced he'd done it. *That's impossible,* they said. *He's such a normal guy.*

A normal guy who had been the subject of numerous domestic violence calls. Who had beaten his ex-wife, Melanie, in front of their children. She had an active restraining order against him at the time of the DNA match, and still she went on television, polished and calm, and said, "I don't believe Michael's a murderer. I don't believe he's capable of it, and I support him fully."

Lisa Ackley, the *Bridgton News* reporter who had insisted that the paper run the body bag photo at the time of the murder, immediately wrote an article contrasting Melanie's statement with what she had written in her application for the restraining order, which she had filed just one month earlier. Melanie had described a night when Michael assaulted her while their young children were at home. "When I attempted to go to my daughter," she said, he locked her in the bedroom with him, refusing to let her out. She eventually managed to call the police, who took Michael to a motel. "He immediately called me and threatened to kill me if I didn't go bring him cigarettes to the motel," she said. He told her that he'd walk to their house, and "the longer it took the angrier he'd be and the worse I'd suffer."

—

The indictment was handed down on April 6, 2006, around two o'clock, in a hearing where the DNA analyst, the state prosecutor, and Detective Chris Harriman presented affidavits to a grand jury, who agreed that there was enough evidence to charge Michael Hutchinson with murder.

Early that April afternoon, I sat at my desk, ears tuned to the shrill fax-machine clatter that would mean Walt had sent me Chris's affidavit, which would contain a clear summary of the facts of the case and the evidence that had been presented. Once I read that statement, I would finally know many of the details the police had been unable to tell me before. I sat at my desk tensely, waiting. My coworkers now knew what had happened—I'd had to tell them so that they would be prepared if reporters or others tried to reach me. But I didn't want any of them pulling those pages off the machine and reading them. It would be unseemly, too personal. At the end of that day, the charges would be made public, media coverage would heat up again in Maine, and thousands of people would know what I was about to discover. But I didn't want anyone around me to know. I wanted to stay within the safety of distance.

As I waited for that fax, I tried to focus on light work, filling in a spreadsheet or answering e-mails. Courtney had been closely following the news of the rape allegations at Duke, and that day the police had released e-mails a player had written his teammates on the night of the alleged event. It was all so fascinating, so wild—everyone wanted to hear. I sat nearby, listening and trying not to listen.

"Oh my God," she said, eyes glued to her computer. "Listen to this! He said he was going to hire more strippers, and wrote, 'I plan on killing the bitches as soon as they walk in and proceeding to cut their skin off—'"

White lights flashed within me, alarms blared. *Run. Make it stop.* "Wait!" I said. "You have got to stop reading that right now. I can't take that right now."

I watched all of Courtney's excited, curious energy evaporate in an instant, only to be replaced with scrambling remorse. "I'm so sorry," she said. "I—I wasn't thinking . . ."

"It's fine," I said, wrestling my voice back down. "Just stop, though."

I felt cruel for having shamed her. She hadn't thought ahead, hadn't made the connection; she'd forgotten that there were people behind these news stories, that I was one of them. This was the first time I had asked someone not to talk about violence in front of me, and I was immediately embarrassed. I felt like I had done something wrong by imposing my messy feelings, and my uncommon experience, into a supposedly "normal" discussion of a news story.

The Duke rape allegations would prove to be untrue, but that wouldn't change how the country had talked about them, which parts were found to be interesting, who was considered credible. It wouldn't change how alone I'd felt, hearing and reading most of that coverage.

—

The affidavit finally came through on the fax machine around three o'clock, and I drove home early. I couldn't really pretend to care about anything else that day, and no one expected me to.

That Saturday morning was perfectly beautiful, the kind of fragrant, bird-filled spring morning that had pleasantly shocked me my first year in North Carolina. I made coffee and brought it outside to my friend Evangeline, who'd flown into town the night before. We'd been best friends since meeting as roommates in a high school summer education program. She was one of the few people I could speak frankly with about Mom's death.

She was settled into a whitewashed porch swing, her strong, compact body curled up because her feet didn't reach the floor.

"I'm sorry," I said, "but . . . will you read something for me?"

"Yes," she said. "Of course."

"It's the statement from the police," I said. "I mean, I've read it. But I need someone else to read it, someone who isn't a damn reporter."

She nodded. I went inside and retrieved the three sheets of paper. When I came out, she put down her coffee and took them from me briskly before I could grab them back. As soon as they left my hand, I felt embarrassed, melodramatic, exposed, like it would have been more polite to keep those terrible things to myself.

Her serious face became more drawn. When she pulled the first sheet off the second, it stayed there, hovering in the air, the fingers of her right hand gripping it just hard enough to bend the paper.

Finally she looked at me, and I could see that we were thinking the same thing: it was actually worse than we had thought. Worse. She said, "Fifty times?" and I could tell it was anger that kept her voice from cracking. I nodded.

Although I must always have assumed there was more than one knife wound, the coroner's count of "approximately fifty" was so much larger than I ever could have predicted. The sturgeon sound that night, which I'd always thought to be some sort of seizure — some last, heroic impulse of the body — was made of one blow after another. I heard every one.

But that wasn't the information that I most needed Evangeline to read. There was another thing, the one thing I had never thought to expect, the one thing that weighed so heavily upon me that I knew I could not carry it myself. Not only had Crystal Perry been raped, but she had been raped anally. I could not quantify the additional pain and humiliation caused by this, but I could sense it. I could feel it threatening to push all the air from my body. Neither Evangeline nor I even mentioned it aloud. We couldn't. Not then.

Violence is violence; it shouldn't matter exactly what form a rape takes; there isn't a way to compare the effects of one rape to another. But it felt so much worse to know that she had been raped in this particular way. It feels so much worse, even now. And the autopsy report shows that she was on her period. Of course, it is impossible to inhabit Michael Hutchinson's mind, but I can't help but think that he noticed this, found it dirty, and decided to outdo her, out-dirty her, to hurt her even more, punish her both physically and mentally. Everything about his crime indicates a man full of elemental hate, whose every action is meant to convey that he is bigger, meaner, harsher, more powerful than his victim.

I hate that I am compelled to think all of this, that I can imagine his impulses for even a moment. I hate that he's made all of us think any of this, that's he's given us this one last entirely unspeakable thing to share in silence.

—

After the indictment, I agreed to do an interview with a reporter named David, from the *Portland Press Herald*. He seemed kind, and it was a good paper. He arranged to come to my house in Durham to interview me, and this meant I finally had to tell my roommates that my mother had been murdered. I had been friends with them for two years.

David wrote a good story — courteous, with little sensationalizing.

Still, when I read it, I was embarrassed. I'd talked about volunteering to feed the homeless. I'd talked about what a great success I was, how I'd done well in college, how I'd done it all to respect my mother's memory. I'd been reaching during the interview, trying to put together some kind of story for David, and now I saw my words broadcast for all to read and was repelled by them. In the aftermath of Mom's death, I'd worked so hard to avoid the cliché of failure, and now I'd fallen into a self-congratulatory narrative of success, the same old story of bootstraps and determination. I had done well considering my circumstances, sure. But I was too eager to let people know, to perform the good-girl routine. But I didn't know what else to do. Back then, I didn't know how else to make sense of any of it.

I didn't actually believe there was a way to "make her proud," and I never really had. I didn't believe that her spirit was hovering out there somewhere on a cloud, that she was enjoying an afterlife. Any faith I'd had in such things was destroyed on the night she died.

But over the years, I have sometimes wondered what my mother's last thoughts were. I know she loved me very much; there is no doubt of that. And I'm positive that even in the midst of the pain and humiliation and terror that was inflicted on her, she thought about me. But when I try to imagine exactly what she thought, it's a lot darker and more complicated than well-wishers must think when they smile and tell me, "I'm sure her last thoughts were of you."

There was never any sign of forced entry into our house, so Mom must have let Michael Hutchinson in. He was either an acquaintance who said he wanted to talk to her, whom she wasn't expecting but wasn't afraid of, or a harmless-looking guy with a convincing story — broken-down truck, perhaps. In this case, it might've been the rain that killed her. I can imagine her barring entry to someone in the middle of a clear night, but it's harder to imagine her leaving someone out in bad weather.

As far as anyone has been able to determine, Mom and Hutchinson were not friends; he was not supposed to be there that night. If they knew each other at all, they didn't know each other well. Maybe they had seen each other in a bar once or twice — he, nineteen, in there thanks to a fake ID or a bartender's goodwill, Mom laughing and leaning into Linda's shoulder at a little table in the corner. He would have known enough about her to figure out where she lived, once he wanted to. His parents were recently divorced: he lived with his father on High Street, almost within sight of Linda's house, and his mother lived about a half mile from us, farther down Route 93. He would have driven past our house about once a week to visit her, on that same trucker route that Gwen had worried about. In warm months, our walks would take us past his father's house, out to the War Memorial and back. As Walt had told me, Hutchinson had plenty of opportunities to see Mom — her brilliantly red hair marking her like a target — and become fascinated with her. Obsessed.

I had always suspected that she had been raped, but until Chris's affidavit confirmed it in harrowing, bleak legal language, there was a small, willful part of my brain that hoped she hadn't been. Looking back at the records, I now see that in Texas, Dale Keegan had told me, "We also know that your . . . your mother had sex, just before she died. Did you — when you looked down the hall, did you see her having sex? Did you know that? We know that she had sex, that night. That's another reason we think the person must have been someone she knew." Being raped is not "having sex." I doubt Keegan thought the act was consensual; I can only think that he chose those words to convince me that the police knew for sure that Mom's killer was someone she knew, so that if I was protecting someone, I would get scared and give them up. But his choice of words also may have let me believe that Mom wasn't raped that night.

I had never asked the police for clarification on this point; I assumed that the answer was one of those details that had to be kept secret so as to remain incriminating. This assumption was also a form of self-protection: if I didn't ask them, I didn't really have to know. But when I'd allowed myself to think about it, I figured she had been raped, simply because that fit the murder story I was most familiar with from movies and TV: intruder rapes and kills beautiful young woman. No objects had been removed from the house; we owned few things worth stealing. But he must have left with something.

Whatever Mom and Hutchinson said to each other that night, there would have been a moment when he started getting rough, when he kissed her against her will or grabbed her breast or pressed her against the wall, when he made it clear that he was going to get what he wanted. Mom would have seen the violence in him, would have known that he was going to try to rape her; she might even have worried that more abuse would come after that. She would have realized that she had made a terrible mistake letting him in. That she had miscalculated.

I didn't fully wake up that night until I heard her final screams. Earlier, when I had briefly awoken to the beginnings of an argument, I hadn't so much heard a disturbance as sensed it, and then drifted back down to unconsciousness. But this was different. When she woke me screaming — really screaming — she was emitting all the sound her body could produce.

So before that, she must have been much quieter. She was raped on the living room floor, I now know, just a few feet and a thin sheetrock wall away from my bed. Our house was very small, barely more than nine hundred square feet. It was almost impossible to do anything in one room without being heard throughout the entire place — I knew because Mom was very sensitive to noise. And so all those years later, as I lay in bed the night the indictment was handed down, I realized: she must have tried to be quiet. Surely she struggled, but she must have struggled quietly, taken her rape quietly, so I wouldn't wake up, so I wouldn't be put in danger.

If he had left her alive, if he had only raped her, would she have called the police? Gone to the hospital? Or would she have locked the doors once more, taken a shower, and lain down, shaking and sleepless in her bed, vowing never to tell me about the horrible thing that had happened in our home, a home she could not afford to leave for another? Would she have thought the police would dismiss a story about a random Wednesday night rapist, one she let into the house herself, no less? Would she have known how frequently rape victims are cast as having brought the crime upon themselves?

But Hutchinson did not leave her alive. For some reason, the rape wasn't enough, and he killed her. I cannot know when she started screaming — after he pulled the knife? After he punctured her chest? But at some point her nervous system overrode her determination to keep quiet. At some point she became a body singing fear.

To the deep wound just above her heart, Hutchinson added knife blows to the head, utterly destroying her beautiful red hair. The medical examiner would find a sliver of the steel tip in the muscle of her temple. At that point, I'm certain thought was drummed out of her. Under a certain amount of terror, the mind bends. More, and it breaks completely.

I have repeatedly relived that moment when the screaming first woke me and I yelled "Mom?!" It is the moment that still brings retroactive fear: he could have heard me and come down the hall to extinguish the witness. Those boot prints that Dale Keegan showed me, which I forgot about for years after that interview, indicate that he might have started to.

But as much as it scares me, that moment also fills me with a terrible, terrible sadness. For if she heard me, she did not answer. Her child called out to her, and she was unable to go down the hall and help her, to smooth the hair back from her forehead, to tell her it was all just a bad dream. All she could do was scream more, and louder, to conceal from this man the sound of another girl in the house. All she could do was scream "No!" — a sound loud enough to contain another message: *Sarah, get out — get out now.* And then her screams quieted, and then they stopped, and then she died, not knowing if I would make it out of there alive.

39

As a child, I had always been sad that I didn't look more like my mother. When I was very small, this was about my love for her, about wanting to be even more closely connected. In first grade, I begged her to let me dye my hair red, and didn't understand why she said no. Anytime someone told me I looked like her, I figured they were just being nice, and I've never been able to shake that feeling. Later, my desire to look more like her took on a tinge of jealousy. I imagined bringing future boyfriends home to meet her, and seeing in their eyes that they thought she was more beautiful. I didn't want to compete with her, but I wanted to share that power and attention. I felt it was terribly unfair that I hadn't inherited her unique looks. But I liked that we both had blue eyes, even though mine are more gray.

When I'm heavier, I look like my father; when thinner, more like my mother. In the pictures accompanying that *Portland Press Herald* article, I am blatantly Tom's daughter. The wait between the DNA match and the trial was projected to be a year, and I decided then that I'd use the time to remake myself in Mom's image. I had been dyeing my hair red for years by then, but at that time it was much shorter and darker than hers had been. I had just enough time to grow it out to my shoulders and lighten it gradually until it looked naturally bright auburn.

I was the heaviest I'd ever been, and weak and unhealthy from too many late nights and too little exercise. I planned to pare myself down to essentials, muscle and bone, until I was almost as thin as she was. I knew I couldn't expect to hit her 117, not only because she was an inch shorter than me but also because I had my father's thicker frame. I told a close friend that I was aiming at 130, down from 150, but the real number was 125. That number was like a talisman I carried. I kept it secret; I didn't want to seem crazy. But I wanted to scare Hutchinson. I wanted him to walk into that courtroom and see Crystal sitting in the front row, staring him down.

I ran a lot that year, sometimes outside, but mostly on the treadmill at the gym. A row of televisions faced the cardio machines, and when they weren't taunting everyone with cooking shows, they were playing *Law & Order: Special Victims Unit*. Every episode featured a woman's splayed corpse, lengthy discussion of her rape and murder. I tried not to look, but I always caught a pale limb extending from under a tarp, or tangled hair cast over a face. It seemed it was always raining.

I resented having these bodies paraded before me while I was trying to gather the strength to face down a real murder; it felt like an absurdity that no one else could see, like O.J. all over again. My fellow runners, lined up next to me and going nowhere, seemed to watch with impassive eyes. They couldn't know how my breath caught in my throat, how I wanted to take the remote and hurl it through the nearest screen.

But maybe some of them did feel the same choking anger. I looked to the left, to the right, taking in girls with long strides and bouncing ponytails, and other women marching along, faces tense with what looked like desire. Twenty percent of American women are victims of rape. In Bridgton, that would make about five hundred women, twice the high school's population of girls. I was then living in a town four times the size of Bridgton, and so I wondered which of the women around me might also be struggling to breathe, keeping their faces neutral and stoic. But we were an invisible club, estranged by the need to cope. To pretend all day, every day, that everything was fine. To imagine that society and law enforcement and the courts would behave exactly the same way if something so terrible happened to one in five men, that conviction rates would be the same, that the world would find those crimes just as entertaining as it found these, that we weren't being further subjugated by having to be still and take it, pretend outward calm and enjoy the show.

So I did nothing — even to change the channel would have been to admit weakness. Instead I tried to enjoy the plot lines, the well-written dialogue. Be a normal person. I thought about what I would eat when I got home, whether it was time for that week's weigh-in. Time to see how close I was to scaring him.

When I ran, I also thought about the night of the murder, the journey from my house to the Venezia. The distance was just under a mile, but I didn't run the whole way. I ran from house to house at first, but then in that final long stretch, weakness crept upon me like strong arms wrapping around my chest, pulling me back. I would run a few steps, but then the air would slice my lungs, my heart would threaten to leap out, and I'd stumble down into a thump-heeled walk. I'd try to catch my breath, try to run again. Then I'd break down and walk again. I felt like a failure every single time. I felt like crying every single time. I should have run the whole way, but the truth was that I didn't have the strength.

Running continuously would not have made a difference. If I'd arrived at the Venezia thirty seconds or one minute or five or ten minutes earlier, I do not think Mom could have been saved. If I'd popped out my window screen and run the second I heard her screaming, I do not think Mom could have been saved. But I still felt shame; I still wished that little girl had been able to sprint heroically.

This time, I would do everything I could. I would run several hundred miles, gather my strength and whittle myself down until I resembled Mom as much as possible. As I slimmed down, I couldn't help but be pleased with my appearance, a happy bonus. When I ate, I limited my portions, thinking of Hutchinson at every meal: a strangely intimate connection. If it was true, as Walt guessed, that Hutchinson had targeted Mom because he had seen her walking along our road and around town, then it was Mom's beauty, ultimately, that had gotten her killed. I refused to hide mine. Instead, I polished it like armor.

—

It was important not only to resemble Mom, to be thin and strong and able to run, but to be mentally strong, psychologically prepared, so that when I took the stand, there wouldn't be another 991 slip, some moment when I thought I was saying or doing one thing but was really doing another.

I wanted to be a good witness — the best. It didn't matter how I felt about any of it; I had to be powerful, persuasive, correct. I continued to take notes during Walt's calls, and occasionally I would pull out those notes to fix the details in my mind. As with all important stories, I first had to tell this one to myself.

The attorney general's office sent me tapes of my Texas interviews so I could study them and make sure I wouldn't contradict anything the defense had on record. I arranged them in a neat stack of ten cassettes, at perfect right angles to the edges of my unused writing desk, then spent weeks looking at them sidelong. When I finally got the courage to sit down and listen, they were full of unintelligible murmurs and white noise. I sat and listened as the scribble filled my head and felt like a fool for having asked my roommate to make himself scarce.

The next day, I called and asked for new tapes, but I never received them. The tapes would magically work years later, but in that time when I felt I truly needed them, they were a sonic mess I could not untangle. So instead I rehearsed my testimony, staring into the video camera on my laptop, trying to feel something in advance of the real event. I've never watched that recording. It was more a test than a rehearsal. I needed to know which parts of the story made me the most nervous, the most upset, to figure out where the weak spots were so they wouldn't take me by surprise. It was very important that I not break down on the stand. I wanted the jury to see me as strong and therefore eminently credible, and I wanted Michael to see that he hadn't broken me, that it was impossible, that I would be the one to break him.

When I thought about Michael Hutchinson or wrote about him in my journal or took notes during phone calls with Walt, I had a lot of trouble with his name. Most of the time, it seemed best — safest — to refer to him as "Hutchinson" only. I could thus hold him at an icy distance; "Hutchinson" is more of a legal entity than a person, and this underlined the fact that I had never known him, was sure Mom hadn't. Our family had never even heard of Hutchinsons living in the area.

But at other times, this distance seemed like a cop-out, for him and for me. A way to avoid reality. People in Bridgton didn't call him "Hutchinson," they called him "Michael" or "Mike." A specific person, known to many, had committed this crime. He wasn't some abstraction; he was a human who had made the decision to rape and kill my mother. If anyone had the right to refer to him informally, personally, it was me. There is power in naming, as there is power in knowing.

I received more material to review, and I was glad, because each additional item pulled me away from daily concerns, allowed me to settle further into the state of mind I needed to be in to think about the murder and the upcoming trial. I watched videotapes from the Dr. Brown sessions in Boston, and I felt disoriented. I could see myself there on the couch; it was my round face, framed by hair that flowed down past my elbows. But I had no memory of sitting there; I couldn't see or feel anything outside the frame.

At times the girl on the tape was almost too quiet to hear; at others her voice had a harsh, loud, stripped-down quality that I didn't like at all. When she sounded like that, her eyes were unfocused, looking inward. She said some things that scared me, things that I didn't think were true — like when she said that after running to Mom's room, she thought a man might be "hiding in the closet, looking at me" through the louvered doors. Dr. Brown had determined that these apparently recovered thoughts and details probably weren't true, were just collateral of the process, but it was surreal to look back on all those afternoons meant to recover my memory and not remember the afternoons themselves. Still, it makes some sense. I don't remember those afternoons on the couch because I didn't spend them there. I spent them in my old house, walking through that night, over and over. Now I would have to do so again, in front of a much larger audience.

—

That November, it was announced that O.J. Simpson had written a book and that he would soon appear in an interview on Fox News to promote it. The book was called *If I Did It,* and it was touted as a "hypothetical confession": if he *had* killed Nicole, here's how he would have done it. The timing felt personal; it underlined that mystic sense I'd always had that O.J. and I were connected, that I would never get away from him. Again people were excited to talk about the case, about the murder, about O.J.'s arrogance. And each time O.J. came up, I was reminded that it was possible to have all the evidence in the world and still not get a criminal conviction. That I couldn't count on it.

But in the end, the book did provide some unexpected hope. As its release date and the date of O.J.'s television appearance approached, public outcry grew louder and louder. No matter how fascinating the book might be, it was simply too much, too distasteful. Denise Brown, Nicole's sister, loudly demanded that Fox pull the project. I was surprised and relieved and gratified to see so many people agree with her. By the end of the month, both the book and the TV special had been canceled. So O.J. had not won this time, and maybe Hutchinson wouldn't win, either.

—

Finally, I flew to Portland for the trial, arriving on a sunny Sunday in April. That day I met Susie, from the attorney general's office, the victim witness advocate who would be in my life from that point on. Our first task was to sit down together and look at all of the crime scene and autopsy photos, so that when they were projected onto a huge white screen at the front of the courtroom, I would be prepared.

My college friend Ashley, who now lived in DC, had insisted on flying to Portland to be with me during the trial, even though I said I'd be fine on my own. She sat with me as Susie showed us the pictures one by one, describing the content of each before handing us the glossy three-by-five. Susie would say, "This is of her body, on the floor in the kitchen. You can see her leg, but not her head . . ." She knew from experience that having the words first made the images easier to handle: imagination will often surpass even the worst reality. We handed the pictures around, and as Ashley looked closely at each one, I was deeply grateful and deeply sad. Like my mother, we were pretty young women. I felt like I was showing her what could really be done to us, if a man decided to.

40

The first morning of the trial was shrouded in a thin gray mist, a perfect echo of the morning after the murder. Ashley woke first, bringing in the wooden tray of coffee things from the hall; the hotel the attorney general's office usually used was under construction, so we were staying at the Regency, a historic inn in downtown Portland. It was uncannily pleasant — each night we had mints on our pillows, along with letterpress cards predicting the next day's weather. Small, merciful extravagances.

For that first day, I made sure to wear a suit. It had been made clear to me that having a "classy" appearance could enhance the credibility of my testimony. I tried to look my best but didn't wear too much makeup, and I buttoned my shirt one button higher than I normally would. I wanted to wear a tie, as I sometimes did at work, but left it at home — I didn't want the jury to find me unfamiliar or strange. I knew I should look feminine but not aware of my own attractiveness. I was my mother's representative, and if I was seen as good, as normal, I could help keep the defense from slandering her. I hated all of this and did all of this.

Ashley and I walked the few short blocks to the courthouse, a classic building with columns on its upper stories and large bricks on its lower, made of several shades of limestone — a gray-on-gray fortress in the clinging rain. I had no memory of having visited when my father gave Carol temporary custody, didn't give it a thought. I hadn't heard from Tom since that day, and I knew he wouldn't dare attend the trial. As we approached, we saw a crowd of reporters and cameramen. For years I'd thought of reporters as scavengers, but now I found their presence gratifying. The public would bear witness along with me.

As we climbed the steps to go inside, Ashley held a large umbrella over us, though she mostly used it to cover me; she would be the mysterious woman with the cascade of blond hair, shielding me from the cameras. As the days went on, observers took her to be a cousin; she fit right in.

Susie found us as we stepped off the elevator and ushered us to a conference room for last-minute preparations. She handed me a notebook with photocopies of interviews I had done with the police, and I read through it quickly to make sure my story had no major discrepancies. Everything I'd ever said to a police officer had been given to Hutchinson and his lawyer for review, which was standard procedure. I tried not to think too hard about Hutchinson reading my words, tried not to hope that it destroyed him to read them.

The notebook also contained xeroxes of several pages of my diary from the year following Mom's death. I didn't mind the invasion of privacy as much as the fact that people had read my feverish and flowery adolescent prose. Seeing those pages, I realized that while I was being polygraphed by Dale Keegan, Tootsie must have sifted through my room to hand my diaries and journals over to the police, then slid them back onto my shelves so carefully that I hadn't even noticed. I shook my head and laughed. It was so like her. She could have just asked me.

When Ashley and I emerged from the conference room, Gwen and Dave were already waiting in the third-floor hallway with Carol and Carroll and a few others. Carroll gave me a tight hug; he seemed happy to see me, regardless of the circumstances. We were all friendly, as though meeting up for a holiday, but quieter than usual. There was no precedent for how to behave. Several people pointed out how thin I was, but no one told me I looked like Mom. Our resemblance has remained impossible for me to evaluate — it's like trying to see the back of my own head. Still, throughout that week, people would sometimes slip and call me Crystal.

After a round of hellos, Susie took me and Ashley into a small, white room just off the main hallway—a refuge where the family would huddle during breaks, a place to be while the bailiff marched Hutchinson down the hall at the beginning and end of each day. It was strange to think of him using the same hallways we did, walking in the open under those fluorescent lights. Somehow I'd expected him to be smuggled in through a subterranean tunnel, like a minotaur.

I was sequestered until I gave my testimony, unable to enter the courtroom until after I had taken the stand. The defense attorney, Robert Andrews, had agreed to let me be the first witness so that I would miss only the opening statements. It was important to me to see everything I could, to bear witness in all ways possible. Our prosecutor, Assistant Attorney General Lisa Marchese, reviewed the content of her opening statement with me. She agreed with Walt's interpretation of the likely sequence of events that had led Hutchinson to our door. She would tell the jury that Hutchinson's parents' respective houses bracketed ours, and that Crystal Perry, this gorgeous redhead, had often walked along that corridor with her young daughter, had played and sunbathed in her exposed front yard. Hutchinson had plenty of opportunity to see her, either when she walked past his house or when he drove past hers. He'd had plenty of opportunity to become obsessed. Then finally he'd come to our house late one night, determined. Years later, Lisa would tell me, "I still believe your mother was targeted because of her beauty."

No one else in the family would be called to testify, so they went into the courtroom while Ashley and I waited. We had an hour or two before it was time for me to go on. The waiting was difficult; I was ready to take the stand, and each passing moment made me feel more tense. Stronger than this feeling, though, was the desire to get in that room and take a good look at Michael Hutchinson. I had seen a photocopy of his mug shot from the kidnapping arrest five years earlier, and there had been more recent pictures of him in the paper, side views taken as he walked into his arraignment. I knew he was stocky, had brown hair. He wore ill-fitting sport coats, clearly purchased for court. But I wanted to know what it was like to be in a room with him, to see how his body displaced air, to watch what he did with his hands, at what angle he tilted his head. I wanted to see who this person was. And I could feel him waiting for me, too.

Susie kept dipping into our room to keep us updated, and at one point she came to tell us she had a surprise for me.

"Oh?" I said, anxious.

Susie kept smiling as she went into the hallway for a moment, then came back and pulled the door open with a flourish to let in, of all people, Dennis Lorrain.

Dennis stepped in with a huge smile on his face, filling the room with muscles I didn't remember. I'd known him as a lanky nineteen-year-old boy with a tiny gold hoop in his ear, and here he was, broad, buzz-cut, with fine lines around his eyes. But he had the same snaggly eyeteeth, the same dimples.

Somehow, our natural response was to hug hello. He pulled back and said, "You're all grown up!" I let out a short laugh and said, "So are you!" I had this strange sensation of being older than him, of being my mother's age. He still emanated that unmistakable current of twitchy energy; I was relatively composed. Really, the procession of years had shrunk our effective age difference; I was twenty-five, he was thirty-three.

I turned to Ashley: "This is Dennis . . ." I could see her face go still, an attempt to hide surprise. She knew who Dennis was, and what he meant. She knew how long it had been since I'd spoken to him, that I'd last seen him that night, in the hospital.

Dennis plopped down into one of the little plastic chairs, long legs spread wide, and started talking. He spoke with the rapid excitement of someone who has been waiting a long time to be heard. He told us he'd gone into the military as soon as Walt took over the case in 1998 and he was cleared through a second round of DNA testing. His job skills training was in installing and maintaining security systems, which reinforced my sense that the universe has a twisted sense of humor — while I was sitting in my bedroom in Texas, eyeing my shut blinds and thinking of him with fear, the Army was flying him to DC to help repair the White House security system.

But Dennis had also focused on special combat training, learning as many ways as possible to kill a man. When he returned to Maine a few years later, he spent most of his free time and energy trying to figure out who had killed his fiancée so he could put to use all that he had learned. He was a man obsessed — he wanted revenge, and he wanted exoneration in the court of public opinion.

"To this day," he said, "I mean, it happened just this week — people will move out of my line in the grocery store. I'd like to leave Maine for good, to where people don't know me, but I couldn't leave until this was solved."

Ashley and I mostly nodded during that hour. Everything Dennis said was so dramatic, I thought, like in a movie. He was still freshly torn and heartbroken and unable to move on. He'd forgotten, perhaps, that he had often been mean and controlling. Watching him, I could see the wide space of this omission, but strangely it didn't reduce my sympathy for him. The character traits that made him both an unhappy person and a target of suspicion had only been amplified by the stress and rage and sadness he felt in the wake of the murder. His impulsive, reactive personality had made him both the perfect suspect and the worst survivor.

But he was a good storyteller, and thoughtful. I was struck by his evident intelligence. I'd spent years thinking my mother dated this man mostly because he was there: he was convenient, he was insistent, and he was cute. But now I could see what she saw: an interesting, smart, passionate man. She hadn't simply been under his power. She had also been a victim of her own kindness, her desire for his better nature to prevail.

Dennis told me that he now shows up early to everything — eternally haunted by the consequences of his running late on the night of Mom's murder, forever sprinting in a race he's already lost. He always tries very hard to do exactly what he says he's going to do. He said, "I don't wish what happened to us on anyone . . . I'm living proof of what

can happen — and so are you — when you say you're going to do something and you don't do it." By "us" he meant me and him.

He also said that he still had the brown paper bag Mom gave him
the last time she made him lunch for work. She had drawn a little
character on it, a bubbly smiley face surrounded by long curls like
hers. I can picture it perfectly; it's the same face she drew on the notes
she put in my lunchbox every day. I wish I'd saved mine, too. He has
another present from her; he describes it as "a little stuffed sheep. And
I won't let anyone touch it." I remember the sheep. His name is Sher-
man. Denny has pictures, too — some of her, some of me — all in a big
wooden chest. He said, "I haven't opened it in a few years — every now
and then I do. Either on her birthday or, y'know, May twelfth. Every
now and then, I'll sit down with a bottle of bourbon and go through
it . . . Remember: You never drink to forget. You drink to remember,
'cause that's what ends up happening."

Seeing Dennis, and having Susie casually hand us back to each
other, seemed to restore a bit of order to the world. I'd been right to
hold out against the cops' implications about him. But I had always
had to guard against the chance that the police were right, that his
feral temper had snapped. He had long been the face of fear, and now
we could sit and talk with each other, trading stories like we were old
friends. This gave me a feeling of freedom that I never would have
known I was missing.

But at some point, I realized I needed to use the restroom. I missed
one break in the conversation, and then another, and another. I just
couldn't leave. I absolutely could not leave that room, couldn't leave
my friend — beautiful, desirable Ashley — in there with him.

It wasn't a fair thought, I knew. But I also knew that survival isn't
about fairness.

—

I became so immersed in seeing Dennis again that for a while I forgot
what I was waiting for. Susie had been smart to bring him to me. By
the time he'd finished speaking, the opening statements were over in
the courtroom, and after a short break, it was finally time to go in.

Susie ushered me into the courtroom, a large, high-ceilinged space filled with winter light streaming through tall windows. The walls were plaster, heavily edged in polished wood paneling, rising to a high ceiling covered in ornate molding. Long oak pews faced the bench and witness box. I sat in the front row, and found Michael Hutchinson immediately, sitting with his lawyer behind a wooden table.

He had gotten hepatitis in prison, was jaundiced. He was wearing a tan sport coat. He didn't much resemble the person I'd seen in the mug shot, a shirtless young man with tousled hair and a smile, head thrust forward from his rounded shoulders: a sarcastic young punk. It was in prison, apparently, that he had picked up the aura of slow brute strength that one might expect from a killer. His hair was buzzed, neck and forearms thick. He was barrel-chested. His blue eyes were unnervingly pale, but otherwise he was thin-lipped, round in the face, forgettable. His gaze was so blank it was hard to ascribe anything to it at all. He wasn't even that tall — officially, five foot nine. He could have been nearly anyone on the street, or in the woods, of Bridgton. Or anywhere.

Over the course of the next few days, as I watched the proceedings from the front row, Michael kept his eyes forward, and I could see him only in profile. But when he was led in and out of the courtroom, he always took the opportunity to turn and look at me. His eyes went right to me; he didn't have to search. He knew exactly where I was. His look remained unreadable — not menacing, not sorry, not ashamed. If I had to pinpoint it, I'd say it was the look of a man who has something to say.

Lisa, the prosecutor, was a short, blond, direct woman — kind to the family, satisfyingly sharp and bullheaded in the courtroom. With her fair coloring, tough attitude, and dark humor, she fit right in with us. The lawyer assisting her was Lara Nomani, a quieter woman with sleek, dark hair. I loved that they were both women; it was an unexpected bit of poetic justice.

I was sworn in at two thirty on the afternoon of Monday, April 2, 2007. Lisa began her questioning by asking me simple things, verifying my identity and current residence, that I was from Bridgton, that I was

Crystal Perry's daughter. Nothing was true until entered into the court record, and anything not entered did not officially exist, so what the jury knew and what everyone else knew were sometimes miles apart. The jurors were instructed to listen to the facts only and do their best not to draw inferences. But emotions lay under the facts like shadows. The pain of loss. The cold grip of fear.

The jury sat across from me, in two elevated rows perhaps fifteen feet away. I addressed my answers to them, but my eyes often wandered to Hutchinson, who sat just to their left, next to Andrews, angled toward me. Every time I looked at him, his eyes were already on mine, as though waiting for my glance. Over the next two hours, I sometimes held his gaze for a few moments, and he never backed down or looked away. His face did not move or change. His expression was unreadable, and I hoped mine was, too.

I'd been advised to keep my answers short so Lisa could direct the conversation according to the argument she was building. But I did occasionally stray from simple facts. When called upon to describe Mom, I couldn't resist adding, "I have all my life wanted to be as pretty as she was."

At some point, I was speaking too quietly, and Lisa had to move the microphone a little closer to me. I briefly had an opportunity, then, to speak directly to the jury: "Can you hear me? Is this all right?" It was a moment of sudden intimacy, watching them nod back at me. For those few seconds, I saw them as twelve individuals, people with lawns and apartments and spouses and friends. People I could have met under a hundred different circumstances.

From there, Lisa and I continued our call-and-response until just after Mom's screaming stopped, when I prepared to walk out of my room. At this point, she yielded the floor to me, and I told the story of the rest of that night, minute by minute, my voice going on and on in the perfectly silent courtroom.

Looking at the trial transcript now, I am most drawn to the part where I say that while I listened to the murder happening, I could do nothing but sit on my bed, "entirely still, absolutely frozen, hearing all of this so loud in my head." I read this from a distance of years — many from that night, a few from the trial — and suddenly I pan out and up, free from that loud place within my mind. I see my house, so small, like a cardboard model. The place vibrates with the sound of terror. Dark figures struggle near the kitchen; they are hard to see, because what's happening between them is so awful. But just as scary is the girl there, on the other side of that wall. She sits immobile, not reacting, like a doll, a body the soul has left. It amazes me that she was ever reanimated.

—

Hutchinson's lawyer, Robert Andrews, was smart enough not to bully me too much in his cross-examination; it would win him no favor with the jury. But we were still opposed, lightly sparring. At one point, I corrected a date for him and felt a rush of petty satisfaction. At another, he was unsatisfied with an answer I gave, and he slapped an interview transcript down in front of me and asked, "Does this refresh your memory?"

A pervasive difficulty during the cross-examination was distinguishing between my memory of that night at that moment, in 2007, and the way I remembered having described it in interviews at earlier dates. It was difficult to hew closely to what I actually remembered on that first day of the trial — the only way, as I saw it, to avoid perjury — without looking evasive about slightly different things I'd said previously, small inconsistencies that Andrews tried to exploit. So many years had passed, and I'd been interviewed so many times, that these layers had become interwoven. The whole afternoon was a complicated dance between delivering information from my live memory and perspective — re-inhabiting long-ago events in real time — and trying to understand and interpret several earlier versions of myself: at twelve, at fourteen, at eighteen.

At one point, Andrews mentioned the interviews in Texas and asked, "Were you aware that you were being treated as a suspect?" At that moment, all my earlier suspicions were confirmed. But if Andrews had wanted me to get angry or upset on my own behalf while on the stand, he failed; I just felt sad for that skinny, polygraphed thirteen-year-old from so long ago.

—

When Andrews and Lisa had finished their questioning, I was dismissed, and court recessed for the day. Gwen and Glenice went back to their hotel in town, everyone else went home, and Ashley and I went to the Regency. Before the trial, when she had announced that she was coming with me, I had protested: I didn't need hand-holding, I said; it was ridiculous for her to take time off. But after that first day, I was glad that she hadn't listened to me. For the rest of that week, she was at my side: she would run out to get me coffee or sandwiches during breaks in the proceedings, when I needed energy but couldn't risk leaving the building because we might be resuming any minute. She held my hand at the most intense moments. My family was there, too, and I could have leaned on them more than I did. But Ashley was someone from my new life, from the previously murderless present. She was a bridge.

In the evenings, we would briefly talk through the day, then try to unwind. That first night, we went out for a nice meal, drank a glass of wine in our room, and watched some TV. The day was important, but it had been difficult, and, left alone, I would have run through every detail until I was exhausted. With Ashley there encouraging me to take a break, I could admit that I needed one. And in the night, I had the comfort of her quietly breathing in the second bed, between me and the window to the cold outside.

—

On the morning of the second day, I settled into the courtroom with everyone else, and had some time to get oriented. Members of the press sat strung along the back row, scribbling in notepads: no cameras allowed. Our family and some friends of the family, about twenty people in all, sat in three or four rows on the right side of the large room. Gwen was on my left, Ashley on my right. On Gwen's other side sat Chief Bell of the Bridgton Police, whom I'd last seen in Texas. He had retired two years before but had continued to work the case from home. Every time a document was read or quoted, his lips moved along with the words.

On the left side of the room sat Hutchinson's father, Brad, his stepmother, and his friend Justin, with some officials and other observers behind them. His mother did not appear. We were split on two sides of an aisle, like a horrible parody of a wedding. We didn't look at them; they didn't look at us. Or, rather, each side stole flickering glances at the other. And we kept running into the stepmother in the restroom. I washed my hands next to her once; we met each other's eyes in the mirror, but neither of us said a word.

One evening, as Ashley and I were sitting on our beds at the Regency, we were talking over the day — there was so little opportunity to react to things and think about them as they happened. After a moment's visible hesitation, Ashley told me that Justin, Hutchinson's best friend, his only apparent supporter other than his father and stepmother, had approached her in the hallway during a short break. "I was leaning over the water fountain," she said, "and I heard this voice in my ear."

Justin said, in his way, that he found her very attractive and wanted to see if he had a chance to sleep with her. I stared at her in momentary disbelief. But I wasn't really that surprised. *There's no limit to these guys,* I thought. *They think we're always here just for them.* By all other outward appearances, Justin seemed sane, even if deluded and possibly malicious. The next day, he asked Susie if Lara, the assistant prosecutor with the beautiful dark hair, was single.

—

Justice Thomas Warren presided over the courtroom. He was a thin man with short, dark gray hair and a long face. He wore wire-rimmed glasses, like a nerdy college professor, and his ears stuck out from the sides of his head, but he could be stern. He was particularly impatient with any sort of procedural delay or illogical questioning. He was just a little sarcastic, sometimes, but was notably kind and respectful when speaking to the members of the jury. I liked him right away, in part because he reminded me of Alan Alda in *M*A*S*H*. And as the days went on, I gained more and more respect for him.

The first person to take the stand on the second day was Bernie King, one of the first policemen on the scene that night, who had taken such pleasure in arresting Hutchinson on his wedding day. Officer King described the general chronology of that night and very early morning, and the basic layout of the crime scene. As he spoke, I tried to remember how he had looked thirteen years earlier, when I had met him in the living room of the Venezia apartment. I could not. I wasn't even sure I would have recognized him on the street.

Next was Craig Handley, a state forensic expert, who went over the scene in the kind of careful, precise detail I'd been unable and unwilling to see in the dark. Despite his dispassionate thoroughness, Handley had the unexpected habit of referring to my mother not as "the body," as others might have, but as Crystal, as though he had come to know her by closely studying her home. He took every opportunity to say her name, constantly reminding the jury that we were talking about a real person — not just a body, but someone who had lived.

When I had reviewed the crime scene photos with Susie, she had told me that the police had also taken a video camera and walked through our house. I had been glad to look over the pictures, despite how gruesome they were — facing them was better than remaining in the dark. But to watch that tape would have been to walk through that house again, much more viscerally than in memory. I've still never seen it, but I've since read a description. The police began filming at 7:15 a.m., when the world was still gray and dark, shrouded in misty rain. They had not yet removed Mom's body and would not do so for another three hours. They slowly recorded every inch of our house. The bloody kitchen and living room. The pictures on the walls, greeting cards on the dining table. The angle of her leg. The narrow hallway, the bed I left, my desk and all my stuffed animals. Our spare bedroom, crowded with a pink pullout couch and my bookshelf. Mom's bedroom — her dresser and perfume bottles and her neatly folded-back bedcovers.

That day at the trial, when the bailiff wheeled in the television and turned it away from us, toward the jury, a deep quiet descended on the courtroom. The judge asked for the thick window shades to be pulled down, darkening the room so the jurors could more easily see the screen.

The bailiff pressed PLAY, the button making a loud plastic thunk. The jurors shifted, settled in. A couple of them leaned forward, just slightly.

The room was still, only tiny gray coughs occasionally breaking the dry air. The video was not muted, but all we could hear was the whispery pickup of ambient sound from the house, the cop or cops behind the camera just as quiet as we were. I watched the faces of the jury and was very glad I had chosen not to see this video. They mostly maintained their serious expressions, but I could see revulsion break through — a widening of the eyes, a distracted, open-palm stroke of the chin. They didn't look at one another or out at us. Their eyes remained fixed on the screen. We watched them watching. It went on and on and on, much longer than I had anticipated. Sixteen minutes of feathered silence that I wanted to break with a scream.

The VHS stopped with a heavy clack. The bailiff bent and pulled the tape from the machine, and the jurors settled back into their seats. Murmurs and sighs spread around the room under the quiet thunder of the bailiff rolling out the TV.

Craig Handley resumed his testimony, explaining, "The reason we process a scene is the theory that when you come to a place, you leave something of yourself there. And when you leave, you take something with you."

I've recently learned that in the ambulance that night, I kept asking to return to my house. I don't remember this desire, and the idea terrifies me. But now I see: I thought that if I could just get back there, I could regain what I had lost. Like walking back into a room to retrieve something you've forgotten.

Handley had "turned the kitchen black" with fingerprint powder, and all he had found was one palm print and five fingertip prints on the glass of the kitchen door — my last mark upon the place, the mark that had matched my inked hands in Texas. This was one of the many moments during the trial when an expert witness stressed how clean our house was — nearly every house carries countless fingerprints of those who live there. Handley said the dearth of prints in our house was "extremely rare" and admitted that Mom's cleanliness was "very frustrating" for an investigator — she may have been so thorough that cleaning solution lingered on the countertops, dissolving marks as they were made. "The house from one end to the other was in impeccable order," Handley said. "It was extremely clean, cleaned from one end to the other." Cleanliness being next to godliness, this was an excellent way to imply that Mom would have had nothing to do with Hutchinson.

Handley also pointed out that sometimes people who work with abrasive materials and chemicals wear their fingers so smooth that they leave no prints upon what they touch, their hands turned ghostly by work. Examples of such people, he said, include dishwashers, bricklayers, and masons. Although he was not technically able to say it, it was easy to hear the rest of his sentence in our heads: "masons, like Michael Hutchinson."

Now, years after the trial, I pull out Handley's original typewritten catalog of items in the house. It is heartbreaking in its precision. I know that it's his job to be detailed and thorough, but still I feel a strange affection for him: without his careful attention, I would have lost these details forever. On the coffee table, next to a couple of round drops of blood, was a stack of magazines. The top one was *Better Homes and Gardens*. He notes that there were two stuffed animals on the floor next to the couch: a cat and a mouse. On the accompanying diagram, about an inch from the outline of Mom's body, they are represented by two irregular circles, one slightly larger than the other. Handley took the time to add tails: a long line for the cat, a squiggle for the mouse.

—

The trial lasted a total of six days: the rest of that week and the following Monday, dozens of hours of intimate facts interspersed with forensic details. Most were distressing, but some offered unexpected comfort. There was a solace in the mortal wound: a major vein and artery had been cut, very near her heart. There was nothing I could have done, no door I could have reached fast enough to save her.

As the days passed, the invisible was made visible. One expert described the use of orthotolidine, a spray that reveals traces of blood that the naked eye can't see. Normally, we see only red blood cells; orthotolidine reveals hemoglobin. I had seen the substance in the photos of the crime scene, particularly in the kitchen: a dirty blue-black in the shape of additional smears and splatters, and, most important, boot prints. Because orthotolidine is so reactive, it's usually the last thing done in crime scene processing — in order to see the hidden, you risk destroying all that can be seen.

This idea of undetectable blood haunted me. Before the trial, I would never have thought that blood could hide — that it could sit on an otherwise harmless-looking surface, a tiny web of stray molecules. Although I'd tried to step on only clean floor that night, the investigators found my small, faint barefoot prints. And treading on her blood seemed like a desecration.

But orthotolidine was interesting to me — blood as invisible ink. That evening, I called a friend down south and told her about it. I was in a good mood, sharing something I'd learned — a small, weird benefit of the trial.

My friend said, "Oh, yeah. I know about orthotolidine."

"Um, what?" I couldn't imagine why she would have heard of it.

"Y'know. From *CSI*."

"Oh," I said, and felt absurdly silly. It was an uncool, last-to-know kind of feeling. I didn't say anything more about it, because I didn't want to have to explain. I knew about orthotolidine because I had to, but I wanted my friends to be safe harbors. And I felt nauseated, knowing that my friend sought out this kind of information for casual weeknight entertainment, and that it hadn't occurred to her that I'd be disturbed by that. After all this time, I still felt so distant from other people, and the distance was increasingly exhausting.

In the coming days, I would also learn about bloodstain pattern analysis: the difference between passive and active blood spatter, droplets and directional castoff, a whole system of codifying the intersection between physics and common sense, illustrated by abundant blood that was perfectly visible without the help of special chemicals. There were some droplets in the house that especially bothered me. They went beyond scientific interest, were scary in a way that was different from the horror-movie splash of directional castoff. Droplets are round, undistorted by lateral movement: they indicate blood that fell from directly above, dripping from a stationary or slow-moving source. The crime scene processors had noticed droplets in the scene, and found that they belonged not to Crystal but to her attacker, the same person who left the semen found by investigators and the medical examiner. The droplets went from the body to the kitchen counter, where it seemed the person had pulled off a paper towel from the roll mounted under the cabinet. They also dotted Crystal's legs, and there were orthotolidine boot prints straddling one of her calves, indicating a person standing still and bleeding on her. Just standing there. Minutes before — or minutes after — I'd stood in just the same place.

As opposed to a droplet, a swipe is blood transferred onto an object by a combination of contact and motion. There was a swipe on the dimmer switch in the kitchen that I became fixated on. It suggested that after killing my mother, Michael had turned off the light. If he hadn't, I would have seen every gory detail, fully lit, rather than the softer outlines afforded by the lenient darkness. I can't help but feel an isolated, bizarre gratitude toward him for that one act.

—

My year of preparing paid off. As I sat there, hour after hour, I learned a lot, but not much of it was surprising. As the trial progressed, we fell into a rhythm, and much of it began to feel normal. One day was truncated by foot-deep snow — a reminder that Maine was unstoppably itself, no matter what — and when I got to the courthouse, I felt a bit like I'd been running late for work.

By day three of the trial, we were deep into detailed evidence, and my mind was starting to wander. The droning exchange between Lisa and the first forensic chemist to take the stand, combined with the dry heat of the room, had soothed me into a state of near relaxation. I was almost bored. I thought briefly of my office down south, wondered how my boss was getting on without me. Whether Mindy was enjoying her trip to England. If Evangeline had started her new job.

And then Chris Harriman stepped back behind the witness stand and went through a door to retrieve something for Lisa. He came out with a big sheet of plastic. It hung stiffly between his outstretched arms, and there was something pressed flat between two layers of the transparent material. He walked up to Lisa, coming much closer to us, and showed the object to the court, making an arcing semicircle so the judge, the jury, and those of us watching could see it.

It was Mom's blue bathrobe. Less than twenty feet away from me.

The terry cloth robe that she'd owned for years, that she always wore in the soft early mornings, the cozy late evenings, the times when the world seemed far outside, harmless, unable to reach us. The robe she'd made me breakfast in so many times, that she wore in one of my favorite pictures of her, holding our cat Max and smiling. The robe I found her in.

It felt like a little hole had opened up in the universe, just big enough to show us this object. It was here in the room with us, but surely it came from another planet, another reality.

Seeing that bathrobe was so different from seeing pictures of her body, from sitting across from Michael Hutchinson and looking into his eyes. It was flat, the shape of her absence. The body that should have filled it no longer existed, was long ago ashes. I knew the robe was still bloody because it had been preserved in that stiff plastic just as they had found it, but suddenly I wished that someone had cleaned it all those years ago. Blood comes out if cleaned right away — Mom always got it out of my knee-skinned jeans. I imagined putting it in the washer, water on cold, plenty of soap, no other items to share that load. I'd put it in the dryer and it would come out clean and warm and fluffy. I could fold it up and put it on her bed.

—

That evening, I got in the shower and was gripped again by that feeling of physical disgust from long ago, the corpse feeling. I could not escape how closely my legs resembled hers, those legs that figured prominently in so many of the crime scene photos. How the curves above my ankles exactly matched that thrown-out left calf, the last place I'd touched her. I stood motionless and staring in the steaming water until Ashley knocked on the door and asked if I was all right. "I'm fine!" I called, and snapped awake, finished soaping and rinsing. She said nothing of the length of my shower, and I did not acknowledge it. But that night she lay next to me, holding my hand until I fell asleep. It was this, and only this, that saved me from becoming an island, that allowed me to let anyone touch me upon my eventual return to North Carolina.

41

When it was Walt's turn to take the stand, Andrews gave him the tough cross-examination that he had resisted giving me. Walt was a stand-up guy, a strong and gentle person. It was his job to investigate the case, of course. But investigators have to set priorities, and he always prioritized us. When asked why this case was especially important to him, he would always say that it was because of me: the tragedy of an only child losing her single mother, the horror of my being home for it. It was difficult to see Andrews lay into him.

Andrews's major point of argument was that Walt and others had been erroneous in assuming that whoever "had sex" with Crystal had killed her, and that they had no reason to conclude that a rape had occurred. The line he took while questioning Walt either revealed his ignorance or was meant to manipulate ignorance in the jurors.

"Just so we're clear: she wasn't tied down anywhere, was she?" Andrews raised his eyebrows benignly.

"No, she was not," Walt answered.

Andrews continued. "Okay. And there weren't any obvious signs that she had her wrists or ankles restrained?"

"No, there weren't signs of that."

"And there was no blunt force trauma visible to the face?"

I thought I could see Walt's face flinch, just slightly: a small crack in his professional demeanor. "Well, she had a lot of injuries to her face. I don't know about blunt force trauma, but I mean her face was covered in blood and stab wounds."

"Okay. But that wouldn't necessarily mean that there was a sexual assault, right?

"No."

Andrews continued: "Now, it's true that what really formed your opinion was the picture of her anus, right? When you saw the picture, you didn't think to yourself, 'I should talk to a doctor about this, because maybe this is evidence of consensual sex'?"

Walt paused. I could see him take a deep breath, an effort at gathering his patience. "I'll be honest with you." He leaned slightly forward, toward Andrews. "When I saw that picture, I didn't believe it was consensual. The photo, in my mind, when I looked at it—I mean, it took my breath away. I mean, it was . . ." He leaned back, lifted an open palm and swept it to the side, searching. "It looked—the visual, what I saw there, I said, 'Oh my God.' That was awful, the damage."

Others apparently agreed. Justice Warren himself had said he didn't want to look at that picture if he didn't have to. Our prosecutor, Lisa, would eventually decide not to show it, deeming it unnecessary. I had seen it with Susie the day before the trial and was glad to be spared seeing it again. Unfortunately, this was the photo that I would accidentally turn over while sifting through the records in the Gray police barracks years later.

Andrews barreled past Walt's evocative stutters and focused instead on timing. How could Walt know that the sex was related to the killing, when the medical examiner, Dr. Kristen Sweeney, had said that the injuries in the photo—officially, fifteen lacerations, and bruising —could have been incurred at least an hour before the time of death? To me, Sweeney's testimony meant that there could have been up to an hour of torture, not that Mom and Hutchinson were having some sort of affair. I hoped the jury would see that, too. To debate whether the sex had been consensual seemed, to me, like a complete waste of time.

But then Andrews pulled out what he thought was a trump card.

"Now, when you were also reviewing the case file, you knew that Crystal didn't necessarily mind that kind of sexual activity?"

I took a sharp, deep breath. I was so glad to hear Lara Nomani object before I could even exhale. It was like being pushed off a cliff and then caught in midair.

Everything ground to a halt. Justice Warren sent the jury out. I could see him making an effort to speak to them calmly and neutrally.

As we knew from earlier motions out of the jury's presence, Andrews was referring, obliquely, to a letter in the case file from Tim to Mom, one of those letters that kept coming in the months of her engagement to Dennis. They were ardent letters, in which they relived nights they'd spent together and shared their fantasies. In this one, Tim had referred to a discussion they'd once had about trying anal sex. Essentially, they had considered it; Crystal was interested in trying it, but they never had. I felt so sad for her. What a travesty, to have your love letters used against you, to have them leveraged as part of the defense of your killer.

Andrews wanted this letter to imply that the act that caused those terrible injuries was consensual. Once again, he was either betting on sexual ignorance or was ignorant himself. But Justice Warren did everything right. The Tim letters, he reminded Andrews, had already been discussed — out of the jury's hearing — and he had ruled that they were off-limits, inadmissible as hearsay. Andrews apologized, said he'd misunderstood, that he thought he could ask the question if he didn't mention the letters explicitly. But without them, he couldn't offer any basis for asking the question. I sat and fumed while I heard him say, several times, "I apologize. I understand that." He was too calm. He'd already gotten what he wanted by throwing the question out there. It had already escaped from his mouth, like a plume of dark smoke, and could not be retrieved.

Justice Warren was perfectly intelligent; he said everything I could not. "The witness did not say he reached the conclusion of rape just because of anal sex," he told Andrews. "He said he reached that conclusion after looking at a picture with a lot of — which he thought was just horrendous — a lot of trauma . . . The fact that someone may have discussed some certain kind of sex at some point in their life does not mean that they engaged in it consensually on May 11 or May 12 of 1994."

This would have been enough, but it was even better to hear Justice Warren make it personal: "I'm pretty annoyed that we went to that place. I will not conceal my annoyment."

"I understand that."

"Annoyance," he added, firmly.

Andrews pursed his lips. "I understand that, Your Honor." But I remain convinced that he was never confused about procedure, that he was purposely pushing, trying to see what he could get away with.

Warren brought the jury back in. "Ladies and gentlemen, I am sustaining the objection. The question was inappropriate. You should entirely disregard the question in this case; it's not part of this case at all."

I hoped that it was possible for a person to unhear something. To cast such a salacious detail entirely out of mind. Unfortunately, the prosecution had only one more witness to call, so we didn't have a lot of material in which to bury this one moment before the defense began.

42

I had no way of knowing if my attempt to look like my mother bothered Hutchinson, or surprised him. If I'd ever hoped it would shake him up enough to confess, that was not to be. But it turned out that Hutchinson was looking to unbalance me, too.

On the fourth day of the trial, after many hours of testimony from police officers and forensic experts, it was finally the defense's turn. Their first witness was Michael Hutchinson.

Andrews treated Michael like a lost little brother. I sat and stared at the lawyer, ungenerously focused on the fat rolls at the back of his neck, the straining seams of his suit jacket, his childishly pursed lips. It was almost easier to hate Andrews than Michael — he operated in the known world. Over that long week, I had seen him speak to many people, had seen him defer to some, condescend to others. I had watched him struggle with an overhead projector. I had seen him nervously button and unbutton his jacket when he didn't think anyone was looking. I knew he shuffled his papers to buy time. He was more real than Michael, who had mostly been still and silent through the long hours. Michael's testimony was the first, and perhaps only, chance for me to figure out who he was.

Andrews slowly walked us through Michael's background — his upbringing, his poor grades in school, his masonry work for his father. He prompted Michael to talk about his parents, who fought constantly, often leaving him "stuck in the middle." His mother was, allegedly, irrationally jealous of other women, and mentally unstable; Michael said she would tear off her clothes in the middle of arguments, even in public. Before the trial and after, people would tell me stories about Michael's father, Brad; the cruelty in that home seemed widely known.

Andrews made it clear that Michael was raised by a violent man who insisted that his mother was crazy and worthless. He didn't clarify, of course, whether she was mentally ill or whether she had been driven crazy by abuse. Or why, if she was sick, Brad's response had been to inflict torment rather than care for her. I wondered how pointing out the misogyny and violent dysfunction in that family could possibly help their defense. I kept waiting for some clever turn to the argument, but none came. It was foolish for the defense to think that from the jury's perspective, sympathy for the boy and condemnation of the man could not coexist.

Michael and Andrews worked together to tell the court a story: that Michael came to our house that night for consensual sex, and then a mysterious other man appeared and did the killing. To me this sounded like a bad eighties thriller, so unoriginal that it was almost funny.

Michael said the mystery man had suddenly rushed into the house and started arguing with Crystal. He told the jury that he hadn't seen the man's face, but he knew that he was tall, that he wore a black motorcycle jacket. When pressed for more details, he said, "It all happened so quick." When the guy pulled a knife out of his sleeve, Michael lunged at him, receiving a deep slash across his palm. Of course, the jury didn't know that he had told Walt a different story, about a car wreck. He said he was knocked unconscious for an undetermined amount of time, and woke up to find the stranger "scooched down" on the floor, stabbing Crystal. Michael "body-slammed" the man, he said, then gazed down at the floor to find Crystal "looking up at me, completely covered in blood." Then he ran out to his truck, drove home, and hid in his bedroom for the rest of the day.

That bedroom was in his father's house, three doors down from Linda's. This part of his story, about his hiding out, I did believe. If no one had come to the door at the Venezia, if I had made it all the way into town that night, I could have knocked on his door.

Andrews paused, seeming to think. "You didn't call the police?" he asked.

"No."

"Why not?"

"I was ashamed of what I had done." I could see Michael flush with emotion. The response seemed genuine, but it could easily have come from something other than shame. Fear of imprisonment. Or rage. I took a deep breath. Something clicked into place: I knew exactly what he was about to do.

"Did you kill her?" Andrews asked gently, as though referring to an unfortunate mistake. His tone implied forthcoming forgiveness.

"No."

"What were you ashamed of, then?"

Michael reached out a thick arm, extended his finger, and pointed at me. I heard the loud whisper of many simultaneous gasps, like fire suddenly eating air.

I held bolt upright, still. My face became very, very hot. I held my neutral expression while desperately hoping I wouldn't faint. I kept my eyes on Michael. I would not give him the satisfaction of a response.

Andrews stepped back. "I don't understand what that means, Michael." Here he indicated the jury with a dramatic sweep of his arm. "You've got to tell us."

"I knew Sarah was there. I did nothing. Am I done? Can I leave?"

He wasn't done. Andrews had a few more questions to wrap things up. He paused, apparently allowing Michael to recover.

"Michael, did you like Crystal Perry?"

"Yes."

"Why were you there that night?"

"She invited me over."

"Did you have sex with her?"

"Yes."

"Did you force her?"

"No."

"Was it consensual?"

"Yes."

"Did she want to?"

"Yes."

"Your Honor, I have nothing further."

43

Lisa destroyed Michael in cross-examination. She handed him a long wooden pointer and made him walk out from behind the witness stand to indicate the position of the three players in his story — him, Mom, and the faceless man — on the diagram of our house. I'd held that pointer, too, indicating to the jury the positions of windows and contents of rooms, and it felt strange to see it in his hand. His choreography was terrible, and Lisa was relentless. He claimed that he had struggled with the other man in the tiny area between the door and the kitchen table. But the police had found only one set of boot prints, and the table had several greeting cards still standing on it, undisturbed. The cards had been from me and Dennis, for Mother's Day.

While Michael was still standing out in the open, Lisa got close to him and pointed her finger in his face, and in that moment, he became real to me, as though color had suddenly flooded into a black-and-white scene. *Oh my God, Lisa,* I thought. *Oh my God, that man is a killer.* Michael is short, but Lisa is even smaller. He had no weapon, and still I thought, *He's a killer. You're the bravest woman alive.*

Our kitchen had consisted of two small areas in an L shape: a longer rectangle containing our dining table, with a wall broken by the external side door, and a narrow aisle with counters on either side. Michael claimed he'd bled droplets on the right side of the kitchen next to the sink, not because he was reaching for a paper towel, but because he was reaching into a drawer for a weapon after he "woke up"

— anything to defend himself against the "real killer," the one with the knife up his sleeve. He must have meant for this to explain the drawer noise I'd heard from my room. Lisa let him finish his story, gave him a big, slow nod, then showed him a photo of that right-side counter: the paper towel holder, the sink, and the cabinets below. She urged him to take a close look. "There's no drawers there, Mr. Hutchinson."

She was right; there were no drawers on that side. The drawers with the utensils and all the knives were on the left side of the kitchen, and there was no blood over there — on the counter or the drawer handles or anywhere else — so yet another part of Michael's story didn't hold. The only record of there ever having been drawers on the right was one of my old police interviews. Just before the trial, Lisa had asked me which side the knife drawer was on. "On the right," I'd said, blithely unaware of the mistake. "Next to the sink." She'd nodded, moved on to her next question, wisely not correcting me. If Andrews had asked me about the drawers during the trial, my answer would have been consistent with the old interviews he'd reviewed with his client. My mistaken memory had helped Lisa lead Hutchinson right into a trap. I nearly laughed out loud. I was so happy to have remembered it wrong.

Lisa continued, detailing more of Hutchinson's lies, painting a picture of a killer who had stayed close by, deceiving everyone around him.

"You lied to people about how you cut your hand, right?"

"Yes," he replied.

"You lied to people about where you were that night?"

"Yes."

"You're the victim of a crime, according to you, but you never came forward. You knew the police were begging for information about Crystal Perry's murder, didn't you? You saw the signs. You live in Bridgton. There were signs all over Bridgton. Did you see them?"

"I believe I saw one, yes."

"Did you see the ten-thousand-dollar reward?"

"Yes."

As Lisa continued to push forward, methodically dismantling everything Hutchinson had said, I thought of him driving around town in the months after the murder, Mom's face following him from telephone pole to telephone pole.

There was only one moment when I felt like Lisa disregarded my feelings and those of my family, when she must have known she'd hurt us and decided it was worth it. When she brought Michael to the point where he ran out of the house, when he claimed the last thing he saw was Mom gazing up at him, covered in blood, she countered, "Are you sure you don't remember her eyes as you were stabbing her in the head, Mr. Hutchinson?" I felt revolted and heartbroken and exhilarated, and I knew then that we were going to win.

—

On day six, the jury went in to deliberate the case. After less than two hours, they came out with a verdict: guilty. Three months later, Michael Hutchinson was sentenced to a term of life with no parole. It was August 2, 2007: thirteen years, two months, and twenty-two days after my mother, Crystal Perry, was killed.

44

After the trial, my family members and I returned to our respective homes. I flew south, and they went back to the houses they'd lived in for decades, resumed work once again. Friends and neighbors who hadn't attended the trial or sentencing went on as they had before. Bridgton was still a beautiful little town where a bad thing once happened. My friends in North Carolina talked to me about closure, about relief, but I didn't feel either of those things. I didn't even feel safer.

Of course, I was relieved that Michael Hutchinson was finally in jail. I was glad he'd been punished, and more glad that he couldn't hurt any more women. But each time I heard about another rape, another murder, each time I read another "shocking" news article about the prevalence of these crimes, I felt a kind of paralysis in my limbs, a coldness in my chest. One violent man in jail, out of the thousands, seemed to make hardly any difference at all. I'd stopped fearing Mom's killer hunting me down long ago; but there were a lot of other dangerous men in the world.

The latter years of my twenties passed. I moved into a nice apartment just a twenty-minute walk from work. I started to buy real furniture—a bed frame, a brand-new couch—and learned to cook a little. Every few months I received an update from Susie, the victim witness advocate: Hutchinson kept appealing both the conviction and the sentencing. He would appeal for a few years, she said, until he was out of options. Standard procedure; no reason to worry.

I wasn't worried, partially because Susie's dispatches had a feeling of unreality. They seemed to come from a distant place, one that had little to do with my life of friends and nights out and petty work concerns. Every time I heard from Susie, I was reminded that my mother had become abstract to me. I still sometimes tried to write about Mom, to remember her with clarity, but after an hour or two I would run out of the compulsive energy that had gotten me started. It seemed impossible to do her justice. And I still hadn't written any stories since I lost her.

Sometimes I conducted cursory research to learn more about new things I'd discovered during the trial. After a few minutes of reading or searching, I would sigh and snap my laptop shut. I would scribble notes — "Call Walt," "Ask Susie" — but I wasn't ready to involve anyone else in my search. I was afraid they would ask me why I wanted to know more, and I didn't have a clear answer.

In the couple of years after the trial, Court TV aired two docudramas about our case — one for a series called *Suburban Secrets,* one for *Forensic Files.* I refused to participate in *Suburban Secrets.* I did watch it when it aired, though. It had been written in a tone of breathy excitement, and the main point was how very shocking it was that this crime had happened in a small town of beautiful lakes and summer camps. It was just another story designed to hold violence at arm's length, another hollow way for the audience to reassure themselves that this sort of horror could never happen to them.

I was glad I had turned down the *Suburban Secrets* producers. But a few months later, when the *Forensic Files* people called, I felt a little different. They insisted that their show wasn't sensational, that they would focus more on the triumphs of DNA evidence and other technology than on the lurid details of the crime itself. They said the episode would be a testament to the hard work that so many people had put into the case over the years. With some hesitation, I agreed to the interview. I think, when it came down to it, the story felt unfinished. I had a sense of the inadequacy of the trial, of wanting to say more. But when it was time to send me a copy, the producer asked if I wanted the version that would air on television or the "family edit" — the softer, less bloody cut. I opted for neither. I felt like a traitor.

—

A few years later, I moved north, closer to the source. I started making a new home in New York City, on the edge of the winter zone. I was angry about those television dramas. Although I had not yet gotten the nerve to do so, strangers had called Walt, strangers had talked to Susie. They had filmed my old town and spoken to my aunts. Two new stories had been added to a long list of newspaper articles and six o'clock news update reels. Two stories that didn't talk much about Crystal Perry, that just recounted, again and again, the grisly details of her murder. I wanted to do better. Even after the trial, there was so much I still didn't know. Then I turned thirty, a milestone that felt like a miracle: it looked like I might outlive Mom after all.

Shortly after that resonant birthday, I picked up the phone and called Susie, feeling like a teenager asking permission for something strange and forbidden. Maybe if I read through the police records, I thought, I could make something more meaningful of them. Five years had passed since the trial, but I discovered that I was still welcome to go to the police barracks and see whatever I liked. Susie was perfectly natural on the phone, unsurprised. She had expected me to call someday; she knew the trial hadn't been enough. "Whenever you're ready, we can have everything accessible for you in Gray," she said. "Just let us know when you're home."

—

During that first record-gathering trip, Susie warned me about more than the pictures that might be hiding in the files. "I know you can handle it," she said. "But you're going to learn some things about your mother. Some things you didn't know before. People have a lot of secrets; you'd be amazed how many secrets people have. There's some stuff about her friend Linda in there ... Well. I'm just sayin'.

Try hard not to judge your mother. She was a good person, you know that."

I was reminded then of something that had happened during the trial, a moment that had caused me to question the nature of Mom's friendship with Linda. Lisa and Walt had told me that they might call Linda as a witness, both to testify to Mom's character — namely, her devotion to me — and to verify that we had taken all those walks past her house and Hutchinson's father's. But later, when they called Linda into the attorney general's office to ask some preliminary questions, they said, she collapsed. She was extremely upset, shaking and crying and yelling. She was not sober when she arrived.

As soon as I heard this, a strange, clear thought popped into my head. *They were lovers,* I thought. *That's it. Of course.*

And then I immediately pushed this thought away. I had no real reason to think it — no evidence that my mother had been physically intimate with any woman. And anyway, my sudden, illogical conviction was unnecessary, superfluous to more important facts. Linda's best friend had been violently murdered. She had lived in the same community as the killer for years. It wasn't so surprising that her sanity had slipped, that stress and fear had addled her mind. Why did I need to make things even more dramatic, make everything about myself? Why had this thought come at me out of nowhere?

That day in the courthouse, I told Walt that I'd considered seeing Linda in the past but that something had stopped me.

"Well, that's probably good," Walt said. "She's . . . she's not doing well. She's kinda lost it, honestly."

"What do you mean, 'lost it'?" I thought, *She must still be so sad. She must be drinking too much or something.* I could understand how the trial might be too much for her.

"Just like . . ." Walt looked embarrassed. "Behavior that's not good. Bizarre. Like . . . here's one: Somebody called and Bridgton Police had to go over there, 'cause she was sunbathing totally nude on her front lawn. Right there, just ten, fifteen feet from the road. Uh, faceup. And, y'know. Just not bein' in her right mind, exactly. I mean, she'll be okay for a while and then do something strange, out of the blue."

"Oh," I said. "I see." As though I were saying, *Oh, that sort of thing, now I understand.* I didn't understand, but I didn't want to embarrass Walt by pressing him with more questions. And I didn't want my voice to shake as I thought about how horrifying it was, picturing Linda's aging body lying naked and vulnerable on the upward slope of her lawn, right there on High Street.

Susie had mentioned Linda at the trial, too. "She just hasn't been the same since your mother died," she said, shaking her head. "The murder really scared a lot of people . . . but it was worse, her losing her best friend, and living alone, too. And then within a year, she dated Hutchinson's best friend, there, that Ray King. That guy who shot himself in the head a few years later. Everybody was pretty sure he knew something. And then Linda's other boyfriend, Mike Douglas, was Hutchinson's cousin, I'm pretty sure. But who knows what Linda knows. Who can even tell now."

Ray King has been a whisper in the back of my mind ever since that day. I have this scene in my head: Linda and a wiry, bearded man sitting on a summery, pine-plank deck drinking beers, loosely holding hands from one plastic lawn chair to another. Hutchinson stands over them, leaning on the railing, and next to him is a blurry, indistinct woman; there's a sort of camera lens flare over her. I don't want to think about her, what could have happened to her. Michael is excitedly telling a funny story, thick hands gesticulating, and Linda laughs, her eyes locked on his while she tips the cool, dewy bottle to her mouth. She has no idea. The friendlier the scene in my imagination, the more terrifying I find it.

But then I think: Maybe Linda wasn't friendly to Michael Hutchinson when she met him — and it seems she surely would have met him, whether it was on that porch I imagined or in a sunken, carpeted living room or at a bar or at the lake. Maybe she was terrified and silent, because she knew that he had killed her best friend — either because Ray King told her or because there was something else to the story, something only she knew. Maybe sadness wasn't the only thing that had damaged her sanity.

Within a few hours of arriving in Gray, I found a suggestion that, on at least one night, Mom and Linda's relationship might have been more than platonic. Pickett interviewed a man named Donald, who claimed that after drinking with Linda and Crystal at Tommy's, he brought them back to his house. At some point when he returned from the bathroom, he said he found the two women in bed together, and then joined them for a threesome. Even in Pickett's notes, you can tell how eager this man was to share the details of this story, and he goes on to say that afterwards, he got in a lot of trouble with Crystal for running his mouth. He told Pickett that "one-third of people could see the girls doing that type of thing, one-third knew they did those things, and one-third didn't believe it of them." I wasn't sure what to believe. It was clear that Donald was, to some degree, a bullshitter. But still, I thought about Linda, alone in the back row at the funeral, and it made me terribly sad.

It took me months to get back to Maine, then work up the nerve to call her. I looked her up in Carol's well-worn phone book, the dense yellow pages spilling fluidly over my lap. Linda's number was still the same, and I dialed it quickly, breathing light and fast. It was her voice on the answering machine, sounding just as friendly as ever, but she didn't call me back. I was disappointed, mostly because I was sure she knew things about Mom that no one else did. But I also felt hurt, and strangely abandoned. What if she didn't want to talk because she thought I knew how close they'd been and I judged her? If I couldn't reach her, there was no way to explain that their possible intimacy, far from upsetting me, made me happy. I was glad they felt free to express themselves however they saw fit in the moment, even if it might have been only that one moment, that one night. But I think I also sensed that their close connection made Linda the best chance I had for a kind of second mother, though I don't think I ever could have explained that to her. I didn't want to face that desire myself.

45

I struggled through the following May, shouldering the weight of the anniversary of Mom's death on the twelfth. That night, I lit a single white candle. Drank a glass of the strawberry wine she loved. Felt I should start doing something more. I found my balance again in June, then used the bright months to begin sifting through the stories in the police box. I read interviews with her friends, with members of our family, with acquaintances in town. With people who didn't know her at all, with former loves and other suspects. I encountered, once more, the theory, voiced by a couple of townspeople, that I'd killed her. In competition over a man. A lot of people who thought they were providing information about us ended up revealing more about themselves.

I got glimpses not just of the crime but of her, the real person my mother was, and I started making long lists of questions. I was most interested in learning more about her: Why did she go to California with Tom? Who in the family knew her best? Who did she call when she was sad? But lurking under all these questions were others, ones I suspected were unanswerable: What, exactly, happened on the night of her death? Why did Michael Hutchinson come to our door? And why did she let him in? Was Walt's theory right, or was there another story, waiting to be found?

I returned to Maine at the end of the summer and brought my list of questions with me, along with a list of people who might have answers. If there was more to know about the night of her death, I wanted to know it. But more important, I wanted to plunder the collective memory of everyone who knew Mom, gather what artifacts I could, set them on an altar and cast a spell that would bring her back to me, fully formed, if only in my mind. My own memories of her had degraded with time, had been warped and shadowed by the killing. I'd think about a time we had played with our cat in the afternoon sunshine, watching him dart after toys we threw into the soft grass of our backyard, and I'd immediately think about how Max's scratching post had been found in two pieces, broken in Mom's struggle against her attacker. I wanted to know her again, separate from what had happened to her.

I started with friends of Mom's whom I knew but hadn't been very close to. The stakes were lower with these people; I felt less nervous. Richard — "Hairball" — was happy to hear from me, received me like an affectionate uncle. We sat on his wide deck under the trees while he talked, mostly unprompted. He remembered Mom dancing — how much fun she had, how good she was at it, the best. He remembered everything, really. Still kept a picture of her on his refrigerator. He'd had to leave the Shoe Shop a few months after her death, because he could no longer stand to see her empty bench. His wife had competed with his memory of Crystal until finally they divorced, for a host of reasons.

Next I visited Darryl, another coworker. He told me about a sewing test he'd had to complete at the Shoe Shop: he was a slacker, so his bosses wanted to see how much he could actually produce, to determine how much he'd been messing around. Although hand-sewers were paid by the case, management had to ensure that they sewed enough to be worth employing. Darryl had taken speed pills that day, and Mom kept kicking his bench and whispering, "Slow down! Slow down!" half-joking and half-coaching, so he wouldn't make himself look too bad by suddenly producing far more than usual. The Shop kept him on, but gave him a daily quota. Darryl also had an ex-wife who didn't measure up to Mom. I thought about the pockets of loneliness in Bridgton, an epidemic of isolation.

As I sit with these men who still love my mother in some capacity — and there are a few of them — sometimes I feel uncertain about them. Most of them are friendly and kind, and keep repeating that they still think of me as a twelve-year-old girl. I can see them struggling to be candid with me, to tell me things you might tell a grown daughter but you would not tell a child. I don't want to judge any of them for missing their friend, for remembering her beauty. But some of them seem fixated on her in a way that makes me uncomfortable. Mostly because their fixation is one thing that they don't hesitate to share with me.

—

A year later, when I was back in Maine, I tried Linda again. When her answering machine picked up, I told her that I just wanted to know, one way or the other, if she was able to talk. I said I wasn't sure if she had gotten my earlier message but that I'd love to see her again. "I have your number in my phone," I said, "and when I see it, I won't pick up. That way you can just leave me a message, just so I know either way and know you are getting these calls." I gave my phone number, slowly, twice. I kept my voice cheery and casual.

This time, she did call back. I was sitting with Carol and Carroll, watching television, when her name came up on the screen of my silenced phone. I stared at it, willing her to leave a message saying yes.

When I saw that she had left a voice mail, I went upstairs to listen. I stood just inside the bedroom door and bent toward the phone, hunching my shoulders as though holding in a secret.

"Hi, Sarah . . . this is Linda. I'm calling you back . . . I . . . I can't talk to you right now. Um, maybe? Sometime, in the future? I could. But I can't right now, Sarah. Um, there's one thing, I certainly can tell you, is . . . your mother loved you more than anything. You were her world. I know that for a fact. Um, good luck? And we'll stay in touch. Take care, Sarah."

I put the phone facedown on my dresser and sat on the bed. I suddenly felt very heavy. I had not expected to feel so sad.

I longed to see Linda, and my inability to reach her was nerve-racking; I felt guilty for contacting her, but knew I would have to try again, even though I was afraid of what she might know. But the conversations I was most nervous about having were with family. I was worried about violating the silent circle we'd drawn around Mom and her death. They have said that I never wanted to talk about her, or about "what happened," but I can't remember them ever really trying, either. They've said I would get angry when they brought up the murder. Of course I did. I was furious. We all were.

Gwen was closest to Mom, so she was the first aunt I spoke with. I drove to her house in New Hampshire, making sure to pass through Bridgton on the way. It seemed important to do so, like part of a ritual that I was instinctively feeling my way through.

Gwen and Dave had lunch waiting for me; for an hour or so, we pretended this was a normal visit. After we all settled in, I started to ask questions, mostly of Gwen, though Dave stayed close in the background, speaking up now and then. I put a recorder on the table; I didn't want to forget anything about a conversation we might never repeat.

We began with Gwen and Mom's childhood, and I was happy to give her an excuse to reminisce about the fun they had managed to have. She also mentioned Ray — his temper, the "incidents" that Mom had with him that caused her to leave the house, run away on her bike. About an hour into our conversation, we started talking about Tom.

"I came across a story about Tom cheating on Mom with one of their high school classmates," I said. "This person who told it — I can't remember who — said it really broke Mom's heart. Said that's where the trouble started between them."

"Oh yeah?" Gwen said. "I don't know anything about that. I guess it wouldn't be surprising, though."

"So you don't have any idea who that could be?"

"Would it be Linda? That'd be my only guess," she said. Then her tone hardened. "But good luck with talking to *her*."

I didn't think that Tom could have cheated with Linda, or that Mom and Linda's friendship would have survived that. But I wanted to talk about her more. I told Gwen that Linda actually had been the only person to refuse to talk to me so far. I did not say that I half-feared that

Linda knew something she would not tell, that I was actually afraid of talking to her, if the day ever came.

Gwen's voice rose just a little. "That girl makes me very upset. That girl makes me upset as all hell. Because they were extremely close, they went out to bars together. They did . . . a lot . . . of stuff together."

Dave, half-listening from the living room, said, "Ya think?"

Gwen went on: "And that girl probably knows a lot more than anybody else."

"They were *really* close," Dave said, and let out a little scoffing laugh.

I sat there, my cheeks warming, desperately wanting to know what Gwen meant by "extremely close," what Dave's laugh meant. But I could tell that wasn't the path Gwen wanted to go down, so I let her steer us toward whatever else she wanted to share.

She continued, "I'm very upset that Linda is acting like she's too emotionally . . . It's almost like she feels *responsible,* sometimes, when I think about it. Linda knew this Hutchinson guy, and knew what type of guy he was, to be introducing him to Crystal . . ."

"Wait," I said. "You think Linda introduced Mom to him?"

"Potentially, yeah," Gwen said, her lips tightened in thought. "'Cause he was a cousin of Linda's boyfriend Mike Douglas, wasn't he? So Hutchinson and your mother probably met through Linda."

I took a slow breath, tried to stay open to what she was saying. I wanted to know what she thought, and why she thought it. "So you think Mom and Hutchinson met? Or dated? 'Cause there's no proof . . ."

"Yeah. I mean," Gwen hesitated. "I thought, I thought that they . . . *it was said* that he did know her." I could see her reviewing the facts in her head.

I jumped in. "*He* said that."

"True," she conceded.

"That's *his* story," I said, a little more harshly. I wanted her to tell me something else, some other reason that she thought that Mom and Hutchinson had met, or been somehow involved. But it was clear that even though Hutchinson's defense hadn't convinced anyone of his innocence, it had still managed to wend its way into the story of Mom's life.

"That's from *his side*—it was part of his defense," I said. To this day, there is no evidence that the two knew each other at all. But this is something that's impossible to prove definitively, and I wanted to keep Gwen talking. I wanted to admit a wide range of possibilities that might lead to insights. So I made myself add, "Not that I actually do know for sure whether they knew each other . . ."

Gwen sat back a little. "Well. Now I have to think, y'know. I have to think about it. 'Cause I don't know, either."

We paused for a moment. A chickadee's call rattled against the silence. Gwen lowered her head a little and looked at me closely. "I . . . I have this question that I want to ask you. And I don't want to make you mad." She cleared her throat, folded her hands.

Dave had been walking around the living room, straightening things up, half-watching the quiet TV. He turned to us. "Huhm," he said. A muted laugh of tense anticipation.

"Okay . . ." I said, a ragged giggle coming out of me, too. Our sudden awkwardness filled me with fear. My skin flooded with the electricity of impending sweat.

"So there's this thing I've been meaning to ask you. And you can turn that recorder off if you want."

Dave rushed over and jokingly wrapped an arm around my shoulders, as though to hold me back from attacking someone. "Go ahead!" he said to Gwen. We all emitted big, desperate laughs. *Ha. Ha. Ha.* I suddenly understood that I had stumbled into a moment they had imagined many times. I definitely did not want to turn off the recorder, was glad when they agreed to leave it on.

"So, I don't even know if you remember," Gwen began. "There was this day, and we never knew if you remembered it, but maybe it would tell us something if you did."

In that moment, all the things I had been telling myself—that I was having these conversations, collecting the evidence, to get to know my mother again, that I wasn't playing detective in my own mystery—fell away. Suddenly I found myself looking into the dark heart of our un-knowing, and all I wanted was for Gwen's long-withheld question to lead us to all the answers, solve all the old mysteries.

Gwen told me about a Sunday in April, about a month before Mom died, when she and Dave had spent several hours with Grammy, drink-ing coffee and talking, mostly listening to her go on and on. After a while, they gathered their things, stepped backwards down the porch steps. *Goodbye, goodbye,* they said. *We'll come again next week, give us a call.*

Gwen got into the car and Dave slammed his door, started the en-gine. If you didn't interrupt Mumma, it could be dark by the time you got out of there. It had been three hours of visiting and they were tired. They hated driving home in the dark — the roads were narrow and winding, and there were quite a few densely wooded stretches be-tween Bridgton and their house, a thirty-five-minute trip. The danger of hitting a deer was real. And they never wanted to come home late on a Sunday, before the workweek. But on that day, it was still early, really — about four o'clock — and as they pulled out of the driveway, Gwen said, "Dave, let's stop at Crystal's house on the way home." She often said this.

"Nah, it's too late. By the time we leave . . ."

"No, Dave, let's go. We'll just stop in for a minute."

They drove through town, took the inviting Y-shaped turn down Route 93, coasted the one mile from the Venezia to our house. Gravel popped and rolled beneath their tires as they pulled into the driveway behind Mom's black car. They stepped up onto the side porch, a little slab of cement. As they knocked, they peered through the wide glass pane of the door and saw me sitting on the couch, alone, reading. Upon hearing their knock, I jumped up from the chair, opened the door.

"Hey!" I said. Weirdly drawn out, a little bit louder than usual.

"He-ey!!" Gwen said, echoing me, gently teasing. "What're you doo-ing?"

I swung the door open slowly. I glanced back through the living room, toward the bedrooms. It was very quiet in the house. "Mo-om!" I yelled. "Um, Mom?"

Something felt off to Gwen. She said, "What's your mother doing?"

I walked quickly down the hall, tapped on her door. "Mom, uh, Gwen and Dave are here."

Her reply came muffled through the door. "Ohh-kay."

I sat back down on the couch with Gwen and Dave; we turned on the TV, volume low. We talked for a couple of minutes. My attention was divided between them and my book, as usual. It was a big book. They'd ask me a question and I'd answer, then look back down and read a sentence or two. Occasionally I asked them something back. I was acting weird, but I was often weird. A few minutes passed, not more than five, but those minutes felt long. Gwen and Dave wondered if Crystal had been napping? Was pulling on clothes and fixing her hair a little?

And then she walked out of her room, followed by a very young man they had never seen before.

It wasn't Dennis. It wasn't Tim.

Gwen and Dave froze on the couch. Desperately wished they'd called before coming, or left in a hurry before Mom had come out, made excuses to me about the late hour or something. Awkward tension crowded the oxygen out of the room. Muscles strained in the effort to pretend that nothing out of the ordinary was happening.

"Hiiiii!" Mom said, clearly embarrassed. The man behind her was fit, with a baby face. Looked no more than twenty. He plodded along behind her. She turned toward him, looked at Gwen and Dave, and told them his name. "This is _____," she said. He mumbled something. They nodded hello. He made a quick exit through the kitchen, out the side door.

After the young man left, everyone pretended nothing had happened.

—

"So we don't know who that was," Dave said. "We just don't know. We can't remember the *name*."

Gwen said, "It was a one-syllable name, and I swear to God, the more I think about this and dream about this, over and over and over, I almost swear she said 'Mike.' And it scares me to death that it could've been him right there. I saw a picture of him when he was like eighteen, and he had a babyish face then. The problem is, we could never go to the police and say, *'That was him!'* We can't do it."

"We can't. We can't picture the face from that day." Dave shook his head.

"But it was a *moment*," Gwen said. "We always remembered, we were so embarrassed. She was supposed to be engaged to Dennis at the time."

"And so then, after the trial, we were thinking, 'Does Sarah remember that day?'" Dave looked at me.

"No," I said. "I don't remember that at all." I shook my head. "Not at all."

Gwen sighed. "I didn't want to make you upset. 'Cause I can't bring this any clearer to myself. So I was hoping that, if you might have remembered, even if you were pissed at me, or embarrassed that I said it, that you might then recall something about that day. I was going to be like, 'Oh my God. Maybe we just figured it out.'"

And I sat there and thought about what it would be like in that very moment if I suddenly had a memory of Michael Hutchinson in our house. It would have told a story, sure. But would that story bring any satisfaction? It wouldn't change anything, ultimately — not her death, not his guilt.

But I also think this: If Gwen's story *had* knocked my memory loose, maybe we could have "figured it out" years earlier, maybe long before the DNA match, if not for her worry that I'd be embarrassed about my mother sleeping with one man when she was engaged to another. As though I would value fidelity to a controlling and obsessive fiancé over my mother's right to pursue joy where she could find it.

I was frustrated that I didn't remember that afternoon, and I was a little angry that Gwen and Dave hadn't ever asked me about it before. I'd spent all that time with the police, being interrogated about everything from major facts to tiny details, while they had failed to mention this to anyone at all. Maybe if they'd said something in 1994, they would have still remembered the name. But they didn't want to embarrass anyone. How dangerous shame is.

But I know that they were more disappointed than I was. They had been thinking about this for years.

And I did realize, sitting there with Gwen and Dave, that if there's more to know — however ultimately unsatisfying it might end up being — I do want to know it. I try to whisper to the shrouded part of my brain that holds old memories, willing it to pass that long-ago afternoon forward into the light of consciousness. Later today. Later this week. Later this year. I can wait.

Nothing has come. The idea of interviewing Hutchinson has started to press on me. Maybe he'd tell me something, whatever it was that was in his eyes when he looked at me in court. Why not.

Every kind soul I know tells me not to do this, that to sit and talk with Hutchinson is to risk my heart, my mental health. That it's not worth it. But the thing is, I still feel connected to him. I still feel like there's something that only we know. Something I just can't remember.

46

I keep going back to Bridgton, talking to more and more people, casting a wider net that I fear I'm becoming tangled in. I'm collecting facts, certainly, and theories about "what really happened": alternatives or supplements to Walt's educated guesses, to Lisa Marchese's logical courtroom arguments. And I'm learning more about other people's experiences of Mom's death, what her loss has meant to them, what it means that the world no longer includes her. But I have a selfish motivation, too: I want to exist up there, really and fully. I want to be present, no longer an abstract concept — the girl who left, the girl who went down south. There is still a small part of me that misses my original home, that never wanted to leave Bridgton. But I can never live there again. New York is close enough. And just far enough.

My search turns up new information all the time, some of which produces more questions than answers. Miranda White, for instance — the woman who told the police about my father's explosion at Ray Perry's party — actually appears in the investigation file a few times. The first is long before that party. It's May 14, 1994 — two days after the murder.

That first time Miranda spoke with the police, she was the one who called them; they weren't seeking her out. She told Pickett a story about the night Mom was killed. She was working late that night, making sandwiches at Subway. Closed up the shop around one in the morning. While sharing a cigarette in the parking lot after taking out the trash, Miranda and her coworker saw an ambulance leave the municipal garage across the way. She immediately thought of her boyfriend, she said. He was a troublemaker; maybe he had gotten himself into trouble. She jumped into her car and followed the ambulance. But then, she said, she turned around near the Venezia, did not follow all the way to our house. She never said what made her turn around, why she didn't follow the ambulance until it stopped, but she had already passed her boyfriend's house by then. When she pulled up to the stop sign at the end of Route 93 to turn back into town, a vehicle came up behind her, fast, blinding her with its lights. She was emphatic that the bright headlights made identifying the vehicle impossible. She turned onto High Street, passing her boyfriend's house on the way back into town, and, seeing nothing out of the ordinary, continued home to her parents' house. The vehicle tailing her turned off on a side street, she said. When she got home, she heard on the police scanner that the ambulance was on its way to the Venezia. Her dad told her to go to the police with her story, that since she'd been in the area, she needed to talk to them.

In that interview, Miranda didn't give her boyfriend's name, or if she did, Pickett didn't write it down. When he interviewed her over a year later about Donnie Martin and the night of Ray Perry's party, he noted that she also repeated "pretty much" the same story about the night of the murder. Pickett ended his summary: "She was dating Michael Hutchinson who lived up on Route 302 at the time."

More than a decade later, when Hutchinson was finally identified, the police brought Miranda in to the Gray barracks for questioning. When they asked if someone else might have been seen in her car that night, she replied, "I don't know—maybe." We'll never know quite what her answer meant. We'll never know whether there really was a vehicle driving close behind her that night, blinding her, or whether she made up the bright lights to blind the police to something else. When the police officer began the polygraph examination to which Miranda had agreed, she got uncomfortable. She ripped the equipment off and walked out.

Back in 1994, no one followed up on anything contained in that first interview. If they'd gone to Michael's house and spoken with him casually for a moment, perhaps asked if he'd seen anything unusual in the vicinity, as they might have done with any neighbor, they would have seen his injured hand. They could have asked him the same questions they asked other men they found to have injured hands around that time. They could have asked for a DNA sample.

When I try to figure out why Pickett and the others didn't do any of this, I can only think that they must have dismissed Miranda as an emotional young woman. They were so diligent about so many other leads, no matter how flimsy. When a psychic called, claiming to have important details about the killer's identity, Pickett contacted the new owners of the house and arranged a walk-through.

Not long after I read Miranda's first interview, I found a report of a wreck Michael was in. I figured this must have been the accident that he presented to Walt as the reason for the scar across his hand. In the middle of that summer night, Michael sped along the Naples causeway, one town over from Bridgton, in a black pickup. It was June 26, 1994: forty-five days after the murder. I can see it: the black truck in the black night, flashing clean like a strobe as it passes under the streetlights. On one side, quiet clapboard houses and shops, hours silent. On the other, the deep, close waters of Sebago Lake, a light chop reflecting the shore light like stars.

Michael's at the wheel, alone, drunk or more, but I can't see him. Just before the narrow drawbridge, he turns down a smaller road to the right. A few minutes later, he jerks the wheel to the left, pulling a sharp U-turn before careening into a tree.

It's impossible to know who called 911, but the police and ambulance come just before two in the morning. At first, they find no driver. The truck is towed, and the police call its registered owner, Michael's father, Brad. He and his wife arrive shortly after and start scouring the woods. After three and a half hours of searching, they find Michael lying under the trees, having drunkenly wandered or run from the scene. The paramedics are called back; by now it's five thirty. At the hospital, Michael's chief complaints are listed: femur pain, chest pain, head injury. There is no mention of a large cut across his palm.

Michael had sped directly into a tree, causing almost twenty thousand dollars in damage to a two-year-old vehicle. The steering wheel was bent back, the windshield shattered. It's the kind of accident that could easily kill a person. It's the kind of accident that might not be fully accidental. If Michael had died that night, we might never have known who killed Crystal Perry. We would have waited for answers, never knowing they were buried. But also, Michael would not have married and terrorized his first wife, he would never have had children of his own, he would never have had any number of undeserved days of happiness and freedom.

The vehicle he was driving was a black 1992 F-150 pickup. New Hampshire plates, numbered BBX-639. As I finished digesting this report, my brow furrowed and my head moved slowly, mechanically, my ear turned down, as though I'd just heard something very confusing. My fingertips gripped the paper tighter, as though I could force meaning out of it. This number was familiar. A black pickup, license plate BBX-639. New Hampshire.

I flipped back through some other papers, reports I'd read before. Found the one I was thinking of. May 20, 1994, eight days after the murder. In the afternoon, Pickett gets a call from Linda. He scribbles a summary: "She just noticed a newer-model Ford pickup with New Hampshire plates up the street from her. The plate number is BPX-638. Crystal and Sarah use to walk by that residence on occasion when they'd go for walks with Linda or come down to visit Linda."

One number and one letter off. Parked right across the street. Eight days later. And as far as I can tell, Pickett never even checked it out.

—

I can't bear to contact Pickett. I don't think real communication between us has ever been possible. I'd probably act like an angry, difficult teen and hate myself for it, and he'd offer a bunch of excuses for what I, with my 20/20 hindsight, see as avoidable errors. And since, at the time of the trial, Pickett still thought Dennis had something to do with Mom's murder, I really don't think he'd have anything useful to say.

But conversations with other officials have been surprisingly heal-

ing. The two threads of my search — the personal and the forensic —
are not as separate as one might expect. When I visited officer Pete
Madura, who was one of the first on the scene in the early-morning
hours of May 12, at the Bridgton police station, he told me I could
consider him a grandfather, if I wanted, that his home would always
be open to me. The new chief of police, a man I'd never met, quietly
interrupted us, insisting that he had to meet me. It was strange to be
known by someone who hadn't even been on the Bridgton force in the
nineties.

But it was Kate Leonard, the cop who picked me up at the Venezia,
who sat in the back of that ambulance with me, that I most wanted to
see. Still, I was terrified of calling her. I was afraid of casting us both
back there. I could immerse myself in the past as much as I wanted,
but I couldn't assume anyone else wanted to join me. I feared that just
a phone call from me could drag a person down into fear and sadness
once more.

When I finally found myself sitting down with Kate, I realized how
curious I was about her life in the years since we'd last seen each other.
A few months after the murder, she had left the police force and gone
into social work, dealing with at-risk and traumatized kids. It was too
hard for her, she said, to go through that night with me and then never
see me again. There was so little she could do. Kate is single, with
one daughter. When her daughter turned twelve a few years ago, she
thought about me and Mom more than ever. Her best friend is Laurie
Hakkila, the 911 dispatcher I'd talked to from the Venezia.

Kate, who's around Mom's age, was born in a wealthier coastal
community, but she's lived in Bridgton since shortly before the murder. She sees the town from inside and outside, a dual perspective that
is strengthened by her experience as both a police officer and a civil-
ian. On the afternoon we met, she said, "I was surprised, the other day,
to see Michael Hutchinson's father, Brad, sitting with a bunch of gentlemen who were on the fire department, and other really entwined
Bridgton folk, at our local Dunkin' Donuts. I thought, 'That's *interesting.*'" Because after the trial, she said, it had seemed like people in
town were shunning Brad, especially when he publicly defended his

son. You could see people physically avoid him, avert their eyes. Now, it seemed, Brad had been accepted back into the fold.

Kate provides another glimpse of Hutchinson. She talks about his upbringing, about how Brad trained his son to treat women, leading by terrible example. "After it came out that Mike had murdered your mother, I thought back to the interactions I'd had with him. One would assume the murder would be a hugely traumatic event, even for the person who did it. But, y'know, it clearly wasn't. With all the violence he'd been witness to at a very young age, he had a real high capacity to just shove it off, to just shake it through the next day and move forward."

When I think about that ability to move forward seamlessly after violence and fear, I'm reminded of Mom fighting with Dennis, crying and screaming and raging, and then, a day or two later, taking me to the planetarium in Portland and smiling up at the synthetic stars while gently holding my hand. I think about hearing her cry herself to sleep and then seeing her appear in my bedroom the next morning, kissing my forehead and tickling me, darting forward and back and laughing until I finally sat up, cranky but smiling begrudgingly. As a kid, Mom learned how to recover quickly from danger and fear. And when she grew older, she was brave enough to maintain the hope that she could make things better; through all her difficulties, she was determined.

But Michael was a coward who visited danger and fear upon others. I imagine a little boy trying to save his mom from a scary dad. I think about how this boy might have felt as he failed, over and over, too powerless and small to make a difference. Eventually it might be less painful to conclude that, as his father said, she got what she deserved. And then when he got bigger, he'd find other women, decide what they deserved. Be powerful.

Kate tells me how shocked people in Bridgton were when they learned that the killer had been living among them all along: "We had assumed whoever had done it had walked away." Of course, no matter where he'd been, Mike would have been living in some community, somewhere. But it's worse that it was his own town, that it was ours. That so many people he saw each day were connected to Mom and to me. That Linda saw him at parties and dated his good buddy Ray King. That he bought cookies from Adams Bakery, owned by another childhood friend of Mom's, and worked on a house construction crew with my father.

My sixth-grade teacher, Ms. Shane, also knew the Hutchinson family. I met her in a little park behind Renys, a new addition to the town, and waited nervously for her to show up, afraid I wouldn't recognize her. Of course, I did. She had changed so little, was even still teaching in Bridgton, in her thirtieth year. Very early in her career, she'd had Michael Hutchinson as a student. His father was intimidating and demeaning to her in after-school conferences, and Michael was impossible to handle. "Even at that age," she said, "he was always a problem. A huge discipline problem. He had absolutely no respect." I thought about this. I wanted to be intelligent about it. I suggested: "Maybe he was so dominated at home that he had to act out at school?" "No," she replied. "He already had the markings of a sociopath."

But I don't want him to be a sociopath. I don't think sociopaths feel empathy or regret when they harm others. I hope that the emotion he showed on the stand, when he pointed his finger at me and told the court that he hadn't tried to save me, is proof that he spends every day in anguish.

I also don't think Michael is insane. There's no reason to think he wasn't mentally present that night. I think he raped and killed my mother because he believed he could, because he thought he had the right. And I think it's worth examining where he might have gotten that idea.

There is nothing that could lessen Michael Hutchinson's guilt and responsibility: he chose his actions, and they were senseless and vicious. Even in the realm of murder, he stands out: Justice Warren called what he did to my mother "butchery," and the precedent he applied during sentencing concerns a crime so horrible I can barely read about it. It would be easier to think he was just a monster, an aberration; it would make us all feel a lot safer, now that he's locked away. But I think it's a lot more likely that Michael was born with a natural tendency to violence, which worsened in a violent home, and easily found a target in a world where many men are trained to exert power over women. Punishing him should not prevent us from trying to understand how he was made. I'm glad Michael Hutchinson is in jail. But I'll be more glad when there are no more Michael Hutchinsons.

47

In the years after Mom died, so many things made me think of her; every detail in the world seemed to be associated with her. There were so many opportunities for pain. Some days, the colors and sounds and textures of the world still seem to conspire to bring her back to me, but now it is mostly gratitude I feel for the shadow of her presence. These are deep memories, things the cops do not know, the everyday details that make a person's life. I gather them while I can, before they disappear, as so many others have.

She loved summer thunderstorms, and when they hit, she'd turn off the TV, turn down the lights, and open the windows and doors to the cool breezes and mist. She and I would sit and watch the lightning flash, our faces and shins in the spray, our noses full of the metallic scent of the fly screen.

On long drives through the woods, she'd pull the car over to pick tiger lilies from grassy ditches. At the Dump, with Dale, we always had pussy willow branches in a deep, dry, bottle-green vase.

She liked Boston, where her sister Glenice lived. The rest of the family found it too big, too crammed full of people, too hot, too cold. She liked its museums, its interesting food. The view of the Charles along Storrow Drive. The grimy adventure of riding the T.

She whistled poorly. She was right-handed. She had been a majorette in high school, before she dropped out. She got me a silvery baton when I was about eight, and she could still twirl pretty well. She tried to teach me, but my hands were slow.

She licked every finger meticulously clean when she ate something messy.

She loved tiny, waxy Dixie cups, and we always had pullout dispensers of them in the bathroom and the kitchen. They were convenient for little sips of water, for mouthwash at night. And for rinsing paintbrushes.

Once, at our annual extended-family pool party, my aunts and uncles were competing to see who could do the best backflip off the diving board. I wanted to do one, but I was afraid. As I stood at the end of the board, hesitating, she pushed me over into the water. Thought it would be good for me. I scraped my thigh on the rough board, bled into the chlorine and cried.

She was a mediocre swimmer.

Sometimes after I took a shower in the evening, we would sit on the floor in front of the TV while she wound all my long, long hair into tiny braids, dozens of them, about the width of a pinkie, secured with elastics meant for Marie's braces. The next morning, we'd unravel them, and my hair would be soft and crinkled, thousands of tiny waves floating down my back.

Vodka was her drink when she went out. She hated whining. She became furious the one time she thought she heard me swear, and would not be convinced that I'd said "Kitty gas!" instead of "Kitty's ass!" Dennis laughed at this but would not back me up. She sent me straight to my room.

She would not go to bed with dirty dishes in the sink.

She liked solid plans and good surprises equally.

Walking across summer-hot parking lots, she would sometimes stoop to pick up tiny bits of trash — gum wrappers, receipts — that weren't hers. Then put them in the nearest garbage can without comment.

One rainy day when I was in third grade, for no particular reason, she let me stay home from school. The morning was cozy and gray, and she had a rare midweek day off work. We watched some TV, lounged in our pajamas. We drove to Renys and got a box of popsicle sticks and some Elmer's glue, and when we got home she taught me how to make a box by alternating the sticks over and under one another at right angles. She kept my box for years.

—

These are all small pieces, like shards of colored glass in a kaleido-scope; I spin and combine them to make a glowing, shifting picture. But they are finite in number. I cannot know my mother as others know their parents — I will never have an adult conversation with her. But in addition to memory, I do have something else, something that most children would never see: notes from the therapist she started seeing nine months before she died, the records subpoenaed by police two days after her death. The dead cannot give permission; I shouldn't have this access. But it helps me see that time, and my mother, more clearly. This profile of her internal state, her thoughts and feelings, matters more to me than all the official evidence ever could. So the most valuable document from my trip to Gray was created before the investigation even started.

These notes show me that the truly terrible fights with Dennis started happening much earlier than I'd remembered, right at the beginning, really, when I still believed in them, still wanted to brush aside the bad things about their relationship. I can see that she was making a monumental effort to hide most of her pain from me, that we were conspiring in a sort of white-knuckled optimism.

Mom's therapist, Anna Parker, was young, just finishing up her training. Mom may have been one of her very first patients. It is per-haps Anna's common name that keeps her hidden from me; I have been unable to find her and speak to her, have only these notes. Mom's final appointment, before Anna was to leave the state for another in-ternship, was scheduled for May 13, the day after she died.

On her first visit with Anna, Mom said, "If it were not for my daughter, I would probably kill myself." I wonder if this was one of the appointments that I went along to, when I brought homework with me, filling in spelling worksheets in the stuffy, wood-paneled waiting room, bored and impatient. I wonder if I was right there on the other side of the door while she talked so frankly about wanting to end her life. If she would have felt differently had she known that it would soon be ended for her.

And so opens a steady vein of disappointment and self-doubt, anxiety and ambivalence: feelings I knew she was having at the time, but that were far more abundant than I realized. She spent the final nine months of her life trying to understand her feelings for Dennis and for Tim, trying to find a path to happiness through the chaos of anger and sex and love.

Mom seemed, at first, ready to take action: by her second week of therapy, she'd broken up with Dennis. They'd been dating for about six months. She realized — partially because of his many failed, premature proposals — that he was too immature, too impulsive. But she dreaded the unfilled weekend hours. Anna suggested different activities that could help keep her busy, to stave off loneliness and keep her from breaking down and calling Dennis. She offered one idea after another: going to the movies or a new restaurant or driving to the coast and taking a walk on the beach. But Mom was afraid to go to a new place by herself, and she couldn't drive very far because she worried she'd be stranded by a migraine. Nothing sounded fun to her, and she left the appointment merely resolved to suffer through the empty days. When I first read these notes, I was exactly the age Mom was at that appointment — one month past my thirtieth birthday — but I was overwhelmed with sympathy for this young woman. I have never had a physical ailment that restricted my freedom, and I have never been afraid to go to a movie or restaurant on my own. Suddenly she seemed so fragile, so girlish and young, so different from the vivacious woman I knew, cloaked in the willed bravery of motherhood.

There is no way to neatly plot Mom's feelings for Dennis over those last nine months of her life. She accepted Dennis back, broke up with him again, asked him to take her back, and stayed with him — all while sharing with Anna her feelings of ambivalence and dread. Her resolve to leave him waxed and waned, as did her fear of being alone. At some point, Tim came around again and "pressured" Mom into sex, which left her feeling confused and angry. I can't tell who called whom. I also can't determine, from Anna's clinical notes, what "pressure" meant. Soon after, Dennis staged his paper-bag marriage proposal, and Mom accepted.

Two weeks after the engagement, Mom told Anna that she was trying to set some limits with Dennis: "He can't swear at me or break things," she said. This was meant to be a starting point. He needed to understand that this was abusive behavior, even if he didn't touch her. She was scared, but determined. Through shaky tears, she told Anna that she did not want to have "any kind of violence in her life."

The next day was my twelfth birthday—the last we would spend together. Mom gave me an emerald ring I had seen at Kmart, and I was ecstatic to have my own gold band and jewel. I remember opening the gray velour box at our kitchen table, then leaping up to hug her, bumping the table and tipping a glass of soda over onto the cake while she and Denny laughed. She must have worked so hard to make it a happy day for me. About a month later I lost the ring, and I remember her disappointment when I told her, her sadness about the loss mirroring and amplifying my own. She had been so happy to give me this thing I desperately wanted. I found it at school, three weeks after she died. It was a joyous moment marred by the fact that I could not share it with her. One of the first of thousands.

—

Over the next few months, Mom told Anna about the neglect and violence in her family, even pointing out that her parents never hugged or kissed their children. I am surprised that she spoke so frankly, even to a therapist. But I'm glad someone was listening.

At some point, Mom bought a desk for my room, and Grammy insisted that we needed Dennis to put it together for us, even though he and Mom were broken up at the time. It was just a cheap drafting table—a pressboard surface supported by hollow metal tubes, with a little plastic bag stapled to it, filled with sturdy screws and an Allen wrench. Mom and I ended up putting the desk together, but she still felt weak in the face of her mother's criticism, and within days she was back with Dennis. Anna helped her start to see the effects of her upbringing; Mom finally admitted that she wasn't quite sure what a healthy relationship was supposed to look like. Grace had taught her daughters that they couldn't survive without a man. And so, then, how could one ever leave?

By then, I was fighting with her, about Dennis and about Tim. Seeing her shuffle around the house in Tim's absence, so sad and breakable, was as painful for me as sitting in my room hearing her and Dennis scream at each other. I wanted her to let us off the roller coaster, to free us from the shifting moods and whims of unreliable men. When letters came from Tim, I considered throwing them away, although I didn't dare. I thought she would get over it if he would just leave her alone.

Once, when Mom got back together with Dennis days after breaking up with him, Anna wrote that "she is upset that she has not been able to stay single and her daughter is equally upset."

I thought I could step in and save her, but of course Anna knew that she had to save herself. She pointed out that Mom was already more independent and resourceful than Grace had ever been, and told her that she could decide how she would be treated, what she would put up with. They talked about how Mom had quit smoking and significantly cut down her drinking years before. "But this is the hardest one," Mom insisted.

With Anna's help, Mom kept trying to reduce the intensity of her arguments with Dennis, to at least keep him from physically acting out. But the violent outbursts continued. Through winter and early spring of that final year, more and more nights were marred by loud, angry fights that Dennis escalated with fits of rage.

Less than a year after the murder, at age thirteen, I described Dennis's behavior to a Maine State Police officer:

"He'd call Mom all sorts of nasty names when he'd get mad. He had a temper, you know — if he gets mad he just throws a fit," I said, laughing. "Once he hit the screen door so hard he knocked it off the hinges." It seems that I found this hilarious, or at least that I wanted to. Then I said, "Dennis never really did anything violent."

It chills me to think about what that young girl thought was normal — what everyone thought was normal. Couples fought. Men got pissed. Official violence started only when someone got hit in the face. You didn't want to make too much of anything, get labeled hysterical, paranoid. Even after the murder, I wanted to laugh off Dennis's aggressive, intimidating behavior. Later in that same police interview, I described their on-again, off-again, out-of-control romance as a "typical adult relationship." Loons crying out at each other, unable to stay away.

—

Mom's final therapy session, on May 5, 1994, caught her on an upswing. She was wearing Dennis's ring, "but still maintaining some distance from him." Even in the wake of a recent call from Tim, she felt balanced. She and Anna talked about "maintaining this distance from both and not falling into the either/or trap — even holding the door open for a Mr. X who might come along."

Anna Parker would leave Maine without knowing who killed her patient, this beautiful young woman who was trying so hard to cast violence out of her life. She would not know if it was the fiancé or the ex or a Mr. X who came along, knocking on that open door.

I so wish that Mom had lived long enough to recognize her formidable strength, and it saddens me to see that she spent so much of that final year struggling with self-doubt and fear. But there was happiness, too; it shines in my memory, as undeniable as those notes she scribbled on our calendar.

As I read this therapy record over and over, trying to get closer to her, it is Mom's first appointment that I keep going back to, the one where she says that she would kill herself if not for me. I realize that even though we could do nothing for each other on that final dark night, we have, at least sometimes, kept each other alive.

48

This story will never be over. I could make calls and conduct interviews forever, contacting one person and then another and then another in an ever-widening circle, each person suggesting another until I've talked to the whole town, the whole state, the whole country, the whole world. We are connected by violence; we are connected by love.

I will never know exactly how and why we lost her: it is a puzzle I cannot solve, and even Hutchinson probably doesn't know the answer. I've had to find my own ending, decide for myself when to move on.

Before I quit, I knew I had to do one last thing. Almost two years after my last attempt, I decided to try talking to Linda one last time. I could not go forward, could not return to my current life in any state of peace, if I was still afraid of someone I was supposed to love. I was staying in Portland at the time. One morning, I woke up and knew it was time. *Get in the car,* I told myself. Drive to Bridgton. Park in her driveway, and get out. See what happens.

It was a beautiful day, warm gentle wind pushing cotton ball clouds across a blue sky. Route 302 runs all the way to Bridgton from Portland, and I took a sharp interest in all the little towns along the way, to keep my mind off what I was doing, what road I was on, what might lie at the end. Linda could refuse me with a slammed door or a screaming cry. Her mind could be so addled that she made no sense at all. She might seem normal and friendly at first, and let me in, then become angry or scared. I wondered if she might try to hurt me, if she could.

I wondered if my mission was terribly ill-advised. But I had to go. I reminded myself that I was a strong, capable adult. There was also the chance, of course, that she might simply not be home. I knew that even if she had just left for an hour or so to get groceries, I wouldn't be able to return.

I entered Bridgton and everything came into focus. I drove past Otter Pond Road and the empty space where our first house with Dale — long since torn down — once stood. All the familiar buildings advanced upon me, one after another, their edges in high relief. I looked up to a window in the downtown strip where I used to take dance lessons, high up in a nineteenth-century building whose floors creaked with every plié. I passed the café that used to be a barbershop that used to be the liquor store. Turned right at the War Memorial, where the vise around my heart tightened. Passed a few more houses, a strip of lakeshore, and then: Linda's house. Tan siding, brown trim, same as ever. I drove past. It occurred to me that I could just turn around and drive back to Portland without stopping, and I wondered, in a detached way, if I was about to watch myself do just that. I drove to Route 93, turned around at the Venezia, the easiest place to double back. Went back down High Street, and turned, finally, into Linda's driveway. Switched off the ignition. Got out. I was no longer on autopilot; I could do whatever I wanted.

A line of hung laundry wavered in the breeze, strung across the edge of her back porch. The sheets parted and came together like slow wings, and through the gaps I could see her, lying facedown with her top off, sun-tanning. I stood on the porch and peered through. "Hi?" I called out. Her face turned toward me with a smooth robotic motion. She just looked at me. She didn't move to get up. Kept staring. I retreated around the corner so she could come see who was at her door. She could be nearsighted by now. She might need a moment to get herself together, to re-tie her bikini top. I stood there for a minute or two, then said, "Hello?" throwing my voice around the corner. She still didn't approach. The radio was on, quietly, playing a song from those long-ago years. I stepped around the edge of the house again, and again she looked at me through the flapping sheets. I said, "Linda? I'm Sarah."

And then it was like someone hit PLAY on a freeze-framed movie. She got up and wrapped a white towel around herself. Her face crumpled into tears, a sudden release. Her mouth bent into a tight, wide smile, and every muscle of her small face was in motion. She came forward and hugged me tight, her soft curls brushing my face. I could see the top of her head as I looped my arms around her tiny shoulders. I held her and said, quietly, the first thing that came to mind: "Little Linda!"

—

I stayed at Linda's house for ten hours that day. She cried often, she laughed openly, she kept apologizing: "I know you're all grown up right now, but you're still just that little girl to me, I can't help it." She referred to Mom only in the present tense. "For your mom and me, part of us will always think of you as that little girl."

Her face was riveting. At first I thought it was just because I was seeing it again, when I had nearly given up. But over the hours I saw that her face, at fifty, was wildly mercurial. Her profile is like a fine-penciled drawing, like a girl, only shaded here and there with age. She has a delicate nose and lips, and her fine, dark blond curls are cut short around her face. Her hands are tiny and very soft. She began with them in her lap, leaning forward to sip from a bendy straw stuck into a tall boy of Natural Ice beer. Then, finally, she reached for my hand and held it for hours.

In other moments, especially after the sun went down, she looked like an old woman, twenty or even thirty years older than she was, than Mom would be. All her years of tanning had actually touched her quite lightly; it wasn't the lines that aged her. It was a certain sort of tension, a widening of her eyes, a compression at the corners of her mouth. Sadness and fear and resignation. It would happen in a moment, linger, and then vanish.

Occasionally, strong expressions took hold of her face, appearing for only an instant. A grimacing smile, which often came after a self-deprecating remark. A fretful, worried look, where she peered down at her hands, then snapped her gaze back up. And sometimes when she was making a point, she lowered her forehead a bit and looked at me intensely, and I could see the whites at the bottom of her eyes. And in that moment, I could see what Walt had warned me about. I felt dizzy, like I was peering into a ravine. It was a moment of looking into wildness, a moment I fear will start growing and taking over more of her existence. There seemed to be an unleashed quality to it, as though she could tip over into something like madness. But then she would come back, perfectly placid. All this blew over her face like dark clouds and bright light speeding across a summer sky.

—

Linda told me about the days after Mom died, about talking and talking to the police. About her frustration as the years went on with no news of the killer. I asked her about Michael Hutchinson, if she knew him, if she thought he and Mom had dated. She only knew him after, she said, through his friend Ray. She met Mike at a party once, and he went pale. Acted really weird, she now recalls, although at the time she had no idea why. She is confident that Michael and my mother never met, that they were not dating. "We had been wild, in our day!" she said. "We were best friends, we knew *everything* about each other. I would've *known*." She said she had driven herself crazy trying to figure out who had killed Mom. "I just kept thinking I should know. That I should figure it out!"

And I believe her. I believe her fully. When I asked her why she wouldn't speak to me before, her voice got very small and she said, "I'm so sorry. I just didn't know what to say to you. I was just so nervous." I believe this, too. Sometimes the truth is less strange than fiction, and it can be a great relief.

Linda talked about times she and Mom had gone out dancing, how their friendship was more important than anything else. "We'd go out with two guys, y'know. Whoever it was at the time. And they'd sit in the front of the car and we'd sit in the back, and we would hold hands with each other! We would hold hands and just laugh and whisper and ignore them." And, without my even asking, she brought up that one night, when the two of them were with the same man. She said there was a moment when he left the room, a kiss on the neck, and nothing more. They were young.

As evening fell, Linda led me to her back bedroom to show me the clothes she and Mom had gone out in: "We used to wear the most amazing things, you know. It was the eighties and nineties!" She opened a wardrobe and pulled out dress after dress. "I wore this one on New Year's, and this one when we went out for our thirtieth birthday. Our birthdays are just six days apart, you know. We always celebrated together." It was like a dream, where things you've lost return to you, whole and just as you remember them. I stood there, amazed that she still had all these dresses — fantastic ensembles with big shoulder pads and attached jewelry and cutouts in the torso; innocent shifts printed with tiny flowers or trimmed in white eyelet; electric blue suits with huge lapels and short, tight skirts. She had saved them all, although she no longer dressed up, had aged beyond them. But I could see Mom standing there in a slightly different version of so many of those outfits, with Linda right next to her, thinner and younger and happier.

Linda wanted me to sleep over that night rather than drive back to Portland so late. But as good as I felt, as happy as I was to be reunited with her, I knew I could not sleep there in her little house, so close to my own. She had done laundry recently, and against her protests I made up her bed, smoothing an old blanket over her flowered sheets. She'd been drinking all day, delicately sipping from one tall can after another, but was nowhere near drunk, and I wondered how long she could keep it up. How many years. I wanted to buy her a better blanket. I wanted to get her into AA. I wanted to do many things that I knew I would not do. She kept saying, "Now, I know I'm not your mother, but I'm the next best thing." But I knew it was far too late for that; finally seeing her again had brought me to face that fantasy, which I could now let go. I asked if she would be okay for the night, if she would be lonely. She said, "I'll be fine. You know what I'm going to do after you leave? I'm going to just sit here in the living room and talk to your mother." I smiled and hugged her and promised to keep in touch.

I left shortly after midnight, eager to get away before one o'clock, before the death hour. As I drove, listening to all those old radio songs, I felt happy and whole. I felt as though different parts of me had come together. But I was also relieved to go, to head back to the present. I knew that serene feeling of connection would fade, in and out, like a flickering light.

—

Last September, I was in Maine for a few weeks, coasting to the end of my research and also, finally, taking some days to enjoy myself, visit friends, drive aimlessly through the mountains. One weekend, I went over to Bridgton to see my old friend Marie. She and her husband were hosting a barbecue, the last of the season. I was the first to arrive, so we sat and talked for a while. She left the TV on, playing a mesmerizing feature on the custom-designed pools of millionaires, long, hypnotic shots of perfectly bordered, teal water. She had just moved back to Bridgton after seven years away in the city and was glad, she said, that her two girls, and her son on the way, would now grow up swimming in real lakes, that they would feel sand under their toes. Her new house is right near Woods Pond, a place we visited many times when we were small.

Marie sat calm and unperturbed while we chatted, often glancing at the TV. It was like I'd just dropped in on my way to the grocery store, or on a walk from my house nearby, like I'd been there just the day before. It made me feel like I could come back the next day, or the following week. It was a moment from the life we might have had.

She had sent online invitations to the barbecue, so I had an idea of who might be coming. The first to arrive was an old friend of ours, Shauna, one sister in a big family. She wasn't one of the sisters I knew well, so I hadn't seen her since before Mom died. She was kind, and asked the usual catch-up questions, and I felt loved when it became clear that Marie talked about me occasionally, that Shauna had some idea of what I'd been up to in recent years. But the conversation was weighted for us both. When she said she was glad I was doing well, I could hear the unspoken "in spite of . . ."

More people had gathered around the fire by then. I reached the bottom of my second beer and started thinking about what I wanted off the grill. Some people were introduced to me, and others blended into the other side of the small crowd; this was a weekly gathering, and everyone was easy with one another. Little kids started arriving with parents, and Marie's daughters, Brianna and Kayla, ran around with them in the slanting light. I felt welcomed but different, apart. In moments when everyone else was engaged in conversation and I had no clear way in, I played kickball with Brianna. At some point I drifted back to the grown-ups, and Marie introduced me to a redheaded man who had just arrived. "This is Rob," she said.

I knew which Rob this was. This was Rob Desjardins, the man whose missing pot plants had led to Michael Hutchinson's arrest for kidnapping. Rob looked a little serious, a little nervous, maybe. We shook hands. I gave him my most assertive grip, the one that a Republican friend taught me my freshman year of college. He introduced his girlfriend, Alyssa, whose name I also knew: back at the time of the kidnapping, she had been the victim's girlfriend. She was thin and beautiful and had excellent hair, the sort of natural-looking highlights and precise cut that are hard to get in a small town.

Then the three of us stood there, in the semicircle around the firelight. I felt I should ask Rob some questions, learn something about Hutchinson, but couldn't bear to bring up any of that at a neighborhood barbecue. I felt like I had him trapped; it seemed unfair. I could tell he knew who I was, but I could not tell what that meant to him.

An hour or two later, parents started leaving; it was Sunday, a school night. I went home not long after, to a lakeside cabin that some friends had lent me in Casco, less than a mile from Tenney Hill Road. It was the off-season, and all the other places along my narrow dirt road were abandoned until spring. To get to the cabin, I had to walk down a very steep hill, climbing down from a long ridge. There was no cell reception, no internet, no landline. When someone at the party asked me where I was staying, I had been intentionally vague. Just in case.

That night, I sat on the porch as the sky fell from deep blue to black, watching the stars reveal themselves. I didn't turn on a single light. I listened to the loons sending their ghostly calls across the water, my gaze drawing a straight line over the low hills to Highland Lake, to my old house. And I felt at peace, there in the darkness.

CODA

As many times as I've tried to remember, I have never been able to re-call the hours before Mom and I went to bed that final night. They're completely gone, wiped out by the violence of what followed. When the police asked me to think back, I had no sense that anything strange had happened, was quite sure we had watched TV, then gone to bed at the usual time — nine o'clock for me, no later than nine thirty for her. But I couldn't see it — she and I curled up on the couch, laugh-ing. Eating ice cream, or not. The phone ringing, or not. I couldn't re-member what we had talked about, what we had eaten for dinner. I couldn't remember anything at all, and that emptiness made my loss even heavier. She was just so completely gone.

My memory will not bring that evening back to me; imagination must suffice. I close my eyes, slow my breathing. Here she is now, at my door, for the last time. I've brushed my teeth, washed my face, climbed into my high daybed. I'm surrounded by curlicues of white metal and my most special stuffed animals, the ones who get to stay on the bed with me at night. Mom smiles when she peeks her head around the doorframe and says, "All ready?" She's still wearing her eyeliner, but she is wrapped in a bright blue bathrobe. I say, "Yeah!" and she comes to my bed. When she leans over to kiss my forehead, I see her freckled breastbone through a gap in the robe, and her hair makes a bright cave around me. She smells of vanilla perfume. We say I love you. We don't know to say goodbye.

AUTHOR'S NOTE

After the Eclipse is a work of nonfiction featuring real people and real events. While it is a memoir, it is a work not only of memory but of journalism, and involved a substantial research component. I conducted dozens of interviews, gathered hundreds of documents, and read and watched as much news coverage as I could find. I reviewed my own personal archives of photographs, home movies, journals, letters, and notes and consulted those of generous family members and friends of my mother. I also visited many of the story's locations in Maine, returning in all seasons, over a six-year period.

While Part One weaves together different time periods, rather than offering a straight chronology, I have made every effort to verify the sequence of events depicted in this story, cross-referencing my memory and that of others with all available data, placing each event on a master timeline that begins with my mother's birth and leads nearly to the present day. Police officers' field notes have been invaluable, especially for the days immediately following the murder, as have interview subjects' references to contemporary events, such as the eclipse and the ice storm in 1998. Wherever possible, I have confirmed my memories of my own experiences with third parties and with accounts I gave (in writing or while being recorded) in the past, closer to the time of the events depicted. When accounts have deviated significantly, especially in regard to important events, I have tried to present that deviation in the text and discuss what it could mean.

Forensic details come from various documents in the investigation file, including the autopsy report, as well as the testimony of experts at the trial. I reviewed select photographs of the scene for the purposes of this book, but avoided the worst ones. I still have not watched the videotape of the crime scene. The words of the man who called 911 for me from the Venezia — Pasquale Orlandella — are from my transcription of the call recording. The outer world of the book was verified by and built from a variety of sources, including Google Maps, historical weather data online, and contemporary newspapers on microfilm at the Portland Public Library.

Nearly all dialogue uttered by police officers and detectives — with the exception of any names that have been changed to pseudonyms for reasons of privacy — is verbatim from transcripts, either found in the investigation file or from interviews I conducted for the book. Every word of Dick Pickett's and Dale Keegan's speech is verbatim. Each uninterrupted sequence of Keegan's dialogue that appears during my interview in the hotel in Texas is composed of his exact statements, presented in the order in which they appeared, with my responses removed and some of his statements removed for length. The recordings are part of a collection of audiotapes that the Office of the Maine Attorney General sent me prior to the trial, which I transcribed in 2014.

Some of the older police interviews with suspects and witnesses were not tape-recorded, but written up by the officer in a paraphrased report. This is especially true of interviews with individuals more peripheral to the case, and of brief initial conversations the police conducted with key figures while planning to conduct more in-depth interviews later. In these instances, I have worked to represent the tone of the conversation and the personalities of the people involved, combining my prior knowledge with an analysis of the report, keeping an eye out for any deviations from the dry, procedural tone of official documents. The words of Detective Charles Stevens on the morning of the murder are imagined, based on his paraphrasing, as are Linda's words in that scene. Lieutenant Walter Grzyb's words are verbatim from transcripts when he's testifying at the trial. However, in the visit to Dr. Brown, in the DNA match call, in the conversation about Linda's decline, and in my visit to Gray at the beginning of the book, Grzyb's words are reconstructed from my notes and memory. Dialogue with Susie Maynard (previously Miller), the victim witness advocate at the time of the trial, is reconstructed. Every quotation during the trial proceedings is pulled directly from the official trial transcript.

Direct quotations from the social worker who visited my grandmother's house, as well as the psychologist I saw in Portland immediately after the murder, are pulled from a Maine State Police detective's field notes from that time. Tom Perry's quotations in the sections about his meeting Mom and their time in California, and in the short scene where he and his friend see Mom crossing the road in Bridgton, are from my 2012 interview with him. Tom's words during the party scene at my uncle Ray's, and when Mom confronts him at the Sulky Lounge, are reconstructed, based on detailed accounts of other people who were present. Dennis's quotations are all verbatim, from several long conversations we had in 2011, where he repeated much of what he'd told me during our reunion at the trial. The accounts of him and Mom kissing at the drugstore and directly after his divorce are based on his memory. The words of the many men who reported being attracted to Crystal Perry appear as quoted by police officers in their reports.

All of my aunt Gwen's and aunt Glenice's words are verbatim from transcription; most other family members' dialogue is from memory — either mine or a trusted source's. Linda's words during our long-awaited reunion are verbatim, as are those of Kate Leonard and my former teacher Ms. Shane. For personal and logistical reasons, I was unable to interview either Peggy or Tootsie. I did my best to corroborate my experiences with both women with the memories of others. Diary entries I wrote at the time were also useful in this regard.

Family history is tricky for a researcher, perhaps even trickier for one who is part of the family in question. Memory is both created and distorted by emotion and personality, and I have worked to identify and omit those distortions, especially in scenes that re-create my family's past. I collected as many perspectives as possible on Grace, Howard, Ray, and the experience of being their children, but there will undoubtedly be disagreements about what I have written here. I confirmed Howard's rape conviction and his sentence at the Maine State Archives office in Augusta, and calculated his release date using my mother's date of birth and the memories of family members. His victim was not available for an interview, and I hope she will forgive my inclusion of this sad tale. This book would not be complete without Howard's crime, Grace's tacit acceptance of it, and the messages both sent to my young mother and others in their family.

Some people gave me their secrets, and I hope that where I have included them, I have done them justice. Other people's secrets were revealed to me indirectly, via their interviews with police years ago. I have included only those that I have deemed absolutely necessary, and have done my best to independently verify each story that appears, or make it clear to the reader that what's presented is a rumor or in doubt. In certain instances where embarrassing or incriminating information appears, I have employed pseudonyms. This is especially true of people whom, for various reasons, I did not have the opportunity to interview. However, each pseudonym represents a real person, either living or deceased — there are no composite or made-up characters in this book.

The line between personal quest and journalistic project can sometimes be difficult to draw. There was a lot of research I did for due diligence, to make sure I thoroughly canvassed all the available information, but some that I did not. Michael Hutchinson is not a pseudonym, and for several years I considered approaching him for an interview. Ultimately, I decided that hearing whatever he might tell me wasn't worth the psychological danger of being near him. To be in conversation with someone, you must cooperate with them, however briefly, and I have no wish to cooperate with him. I also decided not to interview Hutchinson's friends, associates, or family members. This book isn't about him. It's about Mom.

ACKNOWLEDGMENTS

This book is a sad one, with a great loss at its center. But writing it has brought me more love and support than I ever could have imagined. It is impossible to list everyone who contributed, and as I write this, I am thinking of many others not named here.

Thanks to my mentors, who encouraged me artistically, professionally, and personally. Alan Michael Parker: this would not exist without you. You caught me just in time. Margo Jefferson, your gentle yet incisive guidance was invaluable in those very early days. Lis Harris, Richard Locke, Amy Benson, Michelle Orange, Benjamin Taylor: your feedback and advice made this much better. Most especially, thanks and love to Patricia O'Toole, whose kindness and wisdom have helped make this and uncountable other books possible. So proud to be part of your crew.

Thanks to Jin Auh for your patience, from the very start, and for strengthening my resolve in challenging moments. Jessica Friedman, your sweetness and attentiveness have been so reassuring. Huge thanks to Andrea Schulz, who took a chance on a first-timer, and even bigger thanks to Naomi Gibbs, the most intelligent, tactful, caring editor I could have asked for. I do not know how I could have pulled this off without you.

Endless gratitude to Will Palmer, the best copyeditor on earth, and a dear friend.

To Hannah Harlow, Lori Glazer, Alexandra Primiani, Savannah

Jones, and Rachel Fershleiser, whose enthusiasm for and dedication to this book continue to move me: thank you for helping this story find readers.

I wrote this book in many places of refuge. Thanks to the Eastern Frontier Educational Foundation, the Edward F. Albee Foundation, PLAYA, Joan Leitzer and Kenneth Spirer, Cerese Vaden, Val and Mark Jacobs, and Bridget Potter for solitude and space in which to work. Thanks to Andriana Iudice and Jesse Crowder for digitizing many, many hours of tapes and videos so I could work on the road.

Marina Blitshteyn, words fail me. Logistically and personally, you've contributed so much to this book, and you've picked me up more times than you know.

Thanks and undying respect to just some of the badass ladies of the Columbia MFA, circa '10–'13: Tara FitzGerald, Raina Lipsitz, Rebecca Worby, Ashley Patrick, Melissa Rhodes, Dale Megan Healey, Elizabeth Greenwood, Austen Rosenfeld, Athena Thiessen, and Meghan Maguire. Honored to count myself among you. Special thanks to Valerie Seiling Jacobs for her legal expertise and for her help cutting through bullshit. Love to Karen "Dred" Williams for patiently listening and helping me get back to sanity, so many times. Thanks to Jyll Hubbard-Salk for the space you've made for all of us.

Derby love to my friends and teammates from Red Stick Roller Derby, Gotham Rec. League, and Suburbia Roller Derby for keeping me sane and getting me away from my desk occasionally, and to Maine Roller Derby, for being so welcoming that I actually felt at home again, against all odds.

Thanks to Ashley Wilson for lying and saying she had time off school the week of the trial, thereby making an incredibly hard week much more manageable.

Evangeline White: you weren't the first person I told this story to, but you were the first who really listened, and I thank you for listening still. I can never be too cynical about a world that has brought me your friendship. Marin Sardy: your love and editorial guidance alone were enough to make Columbia worth it.

To all the people featured in this book who not only provided thoughtful answers to my questions, but who made a point of giving me permission to portray them as truthfully as I could, character flaws and all: thank you. May all memoirists be blessed with such generous subjects.

The cooperation of the Maine State Police and the Maine Office of the Attorney General made an incredibly difficult task much easier than it might have been. Thanks especially to Deputy Attorney General Lisa Marchese, former victim witness advocate Susie Maynard, and, of course, Lieutenant Walter Grzyb. Thanks also to the Bridgton Police, particularly Lieutenant Peter Madura.

To Dennis Lorrain: thank you for your generosity, and for understanding that it is impossible to tell all sides of this story.

Thanks to Linda Arris for being brave enough to let me in, and for keeping Mom's memory so very much alive.

This is also in memory of Grace Bartlett, Gloria LeBlond, and Elizabeth Brinson.

Finally, to my family, particularly Glenice Russo, Gwendolyn Fontenault, Carol Noyes, Webster Farnum, and Wendall Farnum: thank you for being so willing to help with this, and for being so honest and thoughtful in telling me your stories, about Mom and about yourselves. I hope I've done them justice.